LIBRARY ORGANISATION

By

Deepak Kumar

BLISc, MLISc

Librarian

Sardar Patel Subharti Institute of Law

&

Subharti Institute of

Fine Art & Fashion Design

Subharti University, Meerut (U.P.)

(India)

DPH

DISCOVERY PUBLISHING HOUSE PVT. LTD.

NEW DELHI-110 002

Published by:
Tilak Wasan
DISCOVERY PUBLISHING HOUSE PVT. LTD.
4383/4B, Ansari Road, Darya Ganj
New Delhi-110 002 (India)
Phone : +91-11-23279245, 43596064-65
Fax : +91-11-23253475
E-mail : discoverypublishinghouse@gmail.com
sales@discoverypublishinggroup.com
parul.wasan@gmail.com
web : www.discoverypublishinggroup.com

***First Edition:* 2014**

ISBN: 978-93-5056-393-9

Library Organisation

Printed at:
Dynamic Printers
Delhi

Preface

Most libraries have materials arranged in a specified order according to a library classification system, so that items may be located quickly and collections may be browsed efficiently. Some libraries have additional galleries beyond the public ones, where reference materials are stored. These reference stacks may be open to selected members of the public. Others require patrons to submit a 'stack request,' which is a request for an assistant to retrieve the material from the closed stacks.

Basic tasks in library management include the planning of acquisitions, library classification of acquired materials, preservation of materials, the deaccessioning of materials, patron borrowing of materials, and developing systems. More long-term issues include the planning of the construction of new libraries or extensions to existing ones, and the development and implementation of outreach services and reading-enhancement services.

—Author

Contents

1

Managing a Library

INTRODUCTION

One of the most important aspects of adult learning. It explains that libraries in adult education set-ups have an important role to play in facilitating access to information for learning, education and training. They also play important role in supporting research programmes of adult education set-ups as well as their outreach programmes designed to educate and inform adult user groups on social, economic and educational issues, and problems. Another role of libraries is to raise awareness about economic opportunities available in the marketplace.

Like any other library in academic set-up or research institutions, adult education libraries have also to be planned, organised and managed using standard management principles and standard library procedures and techniques for access and retrieval. These issues and provides PALDIN learners with very useful skills to perform their tasks better. Besides enabling physical access to collections, libraries have to be organised for rendering information services such as instructions in the use of library catalogue and reading materials, reference service, information dissemination, etc.

LIBRARY OBJECTIVES

Strategic planning and development of a library is guided mainly by the goals and objectives of the parent institution of which the library is a part.

In any given adult education set-up, you could frame library objectives along the following lines:

- Facilitate access to information for knowledge,

education, and learning;
- Support research activities and programmes of the set-up by offering proactive information services;
- Support outreach programmes of the adult education set-up, designed to educate and inform adult user groups on social, economic and educational issues, problems, and opportunities of interest them;
- Offer proactive services for effective use of all types of library materials;
- Store and preserve information of archival nature such as local traditions, customs, and locally generated process documentation reports, etc; and
- Use library as the platform for social, economic, and cultural development of the target communities.

HOW TO MANAGE A LIBRARY

Library management involves functions such as planning, organising, leading, and controlling. Planning is about systematically making decisions about the library goals. Organising is about assembling and coordinating human, financial, physical, informational, and other resources needed to achieve library goals. Leading is about functions that involve efforts on the part of the librarian to stimulate high performance by employees, and controlling about monitoring various library operations and services. These four management functions are highly integrated, but libraries that excel in organising material resources and in leading their human capital are known to give better performance. Keeping in view the fact that libraries in adult education set ups are, by design, small budget libraries, confined to one room space, and adult education staff manages them manually on part time basis, these four management functions would occur in varying degree. In such a typical set up, the functions of organising and controlling would receive greater attention compared to other two functions.

For managing a library you may take the following step-by-step approach:
- *Step 1:* Defining library policies for collection development

- *Step 2:* Defining library authority and library advisory committee
- *Step 3:* Define procedures for library organisation and administration
- *Step 4:* Defining library space, equipment and tools for library operations and services
- *Step 5*: Defining procedures for maintenance of library collections

STEP 1: LIBRARY POLICIES FOR COLLECTION DEVELOPMENT

Step 1 includes the following task:

- *Define the Objectives of your Library:* State clearly the purpose of its existence;
- *Define your User Community and their Information Needs:* This requires complete knowledge and understanding about library stakeholders. This may include adult education teams, extension workers and adult education professionals, local community members and those who provide funds for the library. Their information needs can be assessed through library surveys, personal interviews, and informal discussions with all stakeholders;
- *Define Library Policy for Building Collections:* The policy states the guiding principles and procedures under which collection development activities, including the selection, maintenance, and weeding of print, electronic, and media library materials will occur. This would also mean specifying subject areas of interest to library stakeholders, their languages preferences, and formats of published and unpublished material. Non-print material could include films, slides, transparencies, photographs, maps posters, charts, etc. The policy must also define the limits in terms of collection size, keeping in view the users strength in a given subject, space available within the library premises, and annual budget earmarked for the purpose. The policy may also specify the subject areas in which the library is going build its

archival collection, if any. Such a policy statement on the part of the library ensures continuity and consistency in selection and revision of materials for the library collections;

- *Define what Different Collections are Required to be Developed and Sustained Keeping in View Users' Information Needs:* The possible options include books collection, reports collection, pamphlet collection, multimedia collection, and reference collection (comprising dictionaries, yearbooks, directories, who's who almanacs, general and subject encyclopaedias), etc. The library may decide on developing some of these collections keeping in view the users' information needs.
- *Define your Book Selection Policy:* State the distribution of library budget by subject and by collection. The policy may also state guidelines for acquiring multiple copies of books, guidelines for accepting books from donors, and guidelines for weeding out material.

STEP 2: LIBRARY AUTHORITY AND LIBRARY ADVISORY COMMITTEE

Libraries in adult education setups are, by design, small budget libraries, confined to one room space, and managed manually on part time basis by adult education staff. The person incharge of the library should be the library authority, responsible for organisation and management of the library. He/she should play a dominant role in decision making, should enjoy the authority to communicate freely with groups across the organisation, and enjoy financial and administrative powers for managing library operations and services smoothly.

The financial and administrative limits of the library authority should correspond to staff of equivalent status in the organisational hierarchy. The library authority should be reporting to the top management in the organisation. There is a need to set up a Library Advisory Committee, which would perform the role of advising the library on its growth and development. It will also act as interface between the library management and the top management in the organisation and between the users groups, for ensuring smooth functioning of the library operations and services without compromising on policies set out for library development. The Committee should comprise members mainly drawn from the organisation, and representing various user groups on the Committee.

Its terms of reference could be worked out on the following lines:

- To formulate policy for developing library resources for reading, reference and projects;
- To develop a general programme of library services to suit the interests and requirements of different categories of users;
- To frame, review and approve library rules;
- To recommend suitable budgetary provisions for the library and resource centre;
- To make recommendations for proper functioning of library as knowledge centre.

STEP 3: PROCEDURES FOR LIBRARY ORGANISATION AND ADMINISTRATION

In any larger set up, library organisation tasks involve assembling, forming logical units of works, defining hierarchical structures, identifying staffing requirements, assigning tasks and responsibilities, coordinating human, financial, physical, informational, and other resources needed to achieve library goals. Administration is another activity required to be undertaken for performance and achieving library goals. It is defined as the process of getting things done through men and materials within the organisational framework.

Library organisation and library administration are closely related to each other. The distinction between the two is very subtle. Organisation comes before administration. The latter starts when the organisation ends. One lays down theoretical principles, whilst the other puts those principles into practice. In the adult education set up, wherein libraries by design are small and are going to be managed on part time basis by adult education staff, not much needs to be done in so far as library organisation is concerned.

In such flat hierarchical structures, the staff has no option but to perform multitasking operations such as administration, technical functions, service support, and library maintenance. For effective performance, it is advisable for the library to opt for outsourcing of library maintenance operations such as stack maintenance, catalogue card maintenance, photocopy services, library up keep, stock verification, gate security, etc. It may also consider outsourcing classification and cataloguing operations if circumstances so warrant.

The libraries in adult education set ups need to undertake planning activities such as strategic planning (*i.e.* identifying library goals, objectives, methods, resources needed to carry out methods, responsibilities and dates for completion of tasks), budget planning (for document collections, library equipments, library furniture, library stationery, media library equipments, if planning for a multi-media library), and library promotion planning. These are not perennial activities and are required to be undertaken once in year.

The extent of budget planning activities would depend upon the size of adult education programmes, network linkages, and staff deployed within the organisation, etc. For building a library from the scratch, it must begin with a small annual budget of ₹100,000/-during the first three years. In the subsequent years, budget requirements may be reviewed and decided based on collection already built and actual requirements. It is a good practice to undertake budget planning exercise in consultation with the Library Advisory Committee for developing collections, library equipments, library furniture, media equipments, etc. It is also a good practice to formulate library plans for promoting and popularizing library services.

STEP 4: LIBRARY SPACE, EQUIPMENT AND TOOLS FOR LIBRARY OPERATIONS AND SERVICES

Bureau of Indian Standards provides that a library should have a stack room, a Librarian's room and a Reading Room having seating capacity of 40 to 120 chairs. The stack room should be big enough to accommodate between 6,000 and 10,000 books. The library-in-charge would need to plan actual library size and seating capacity of 'reading room' keeping in view the optimum number of members in an adult education setup, the variety of library services it is planning to offer, and the members of the adult community who would be coming to visit the library for social interactions. The library equipments and tools like furniture, fittings and accessories should of standard pattern and design, so that users feel comfortable in using them.

The following is the list of essential furniture and fittings for an adult education set up:

- Reading tables
- Chairs for pupils
- Librarian's table
- Circulation or charging desk and chair
- Librarian's shelf list trays
- Card catalogue trays
- Card catalogue cabinet
- Bulletin board and notice board
- Book supporters
- New arrivals display case
- Dictionary stands
- Periodicals display stand
- Newspaper display stand
- Storage cabinet for work room
- Filing cabinets
- Atlas stand
- Wall clock

Besides, the library may acquire radio and television set, tape recorder/player, VCR and VCP, slide and film projector, overhead projectors, computers with internet connection, Xerox machine, etc.

STEP 5: PROCEDURES FOR MAINTENANCE OF LIBRARY COLLECTIONS

You will find that the following procedures help in maintenance of library collections.

Preservation of Library Material

Proper care of library collections is necessary with a view to prolong its life. This requires preserving and protecting books against decay and deterioration. As preventive measures, dusting and cleaning of books and shelves must be carried out on regular basis. Books must be exposed to adequate air and sunlight for a short time in case the library room does not get sufficient sunlight. Avoid keeping books is in damp places. Pest control treatment may be got done on periodic basis. Books and other reading material may be got bound from time to time. Besides, book supporters may be used to keep books upright on the shelves. Reference books such as dictionaries, encyclopedias, directories and picture books are costly and heavy in weight. They must be handled with care.

Organising Reading Materials on Shelves and Their Rectification

Normally, books and other reading display of new books and other reading material received in the library, preparing stack room guides, and shelving volumes returned after use, etc. Library may also perform stock verification on periodical basis, with a view to weed out books, as per its policy, and writing off books, etc.

2

Selection of Library Materials

INTRODUCTION

S.R. Ranganathan's five laws of librarianship:

- Books are for use
- Every book its reader
- Every reader his book
- Save the reader's time
- The library is a growing organism

These laws provide the ideas that decide the principles of effective selection.

Such principles may be summarized as follows:

- The selection process is related to other professional activities and is dependent on them both for policy decisions and practical procedures. Selection is part of the overall collection development process and must be viewed in this perspective;
- One should update professional competence by regular reading in the literature concerning the principles and practices of collection building, selection, publishing, reviewing and acquisitions;
- One must have an intimate knowledge of the library's purpose, its collections and its user groups. These are the key factors in effective, responsible selection of library materials;
- A good selector will develop over time a sound understanding of how the publishing industry and the book trade operate; this includes how library materials of all types are generated, distributed and sold;

- One should become familiar with the publishing policies, advertising media, publicity outlets, names of senior editors and general reliability of those publishers whose lists are most directly relevant to the library's collection building requirements;
- One should become fully familiar with the key reviewing media and should read reviews regularly in order to keep abreast of critical opinion on books and other library materials;
- One should become fully familiar with trade and national bibliographies, and should understand their strengths and weaknesses with regard to the library's collection-building requirements;
- One should always make independent but well-informed judgement about what materials are to be selected for a library, as the competent professional is in the best position to determine the right materials for the specific collection and its users.

THE SELECTION ENVIRONMENT

Selection of library materials occurs within a set of common factors:

- It is done on the basis of existing collection requirements and user needs and wants with regard to subjects, formats and level of content;
- It proceeds within a carefully determined budget, with funds may be allocated to specific areas or other categories to the library;
- It involves a structured approach to the identification and evaluation of potentially suitable library materials.

Within this set of factors there are many permutations, depending largely on the specific variables which apply to the different types of medical libraries:

- In medical libraries within an academic setting, disciplines are being studied at specific levels, from basic undergraduate to advanced research, and both disciplines and levels can be determined accurately from the parent organisation's clearly defined teaching activities. There is generally substantial documentation upon which selectors can draw for information about user interests and needs. Academic libraries use a broader and more detailed range of selection tools, such as trade publications, national bibliographies, reviewing journals, scholarly journal, indexing services.

- Moreover, selection is not restricted to professional librarians, as academic staff are expected to have significant input in the process, particularly if the funds are allocated by departments and schools. This situation is challenged by professionals.
- In non-academic medical libraries, in which collections range from small collection in a single room to large collections in a multi-branch library. In such libraries the subject focus is relatively narrow and emphasizes currency. Here, a high proportion of the collection is devoted to serials. Such libraries are also characterized by the following features:
  - It is most likely for there to be a single professional in charge of the library operation, or at least for collection development not to be the responsibility of professional appointed for this specific purpose.
  - Selection relies heavily on information from publishers and suppliers, and on indexing and abstracting services.
  - Reliance on intimate requirement, because libraries normally build up user profiles, particularly when they offer special dissemination services.

SELECTION PROCEDURES STATEMENT

Selection criteria, as a component of collection development policy. This part does not repeat the information given there, but rather elaborates and complements it. It is looked at as an administration device designed to facilitate implementation of decisions about materials based on collection development policy guidelines. All administrative matters requiring consistency over time, require procedures formalized in a written statement.

The following reasons for advocating the adoption of a formal selection procedures statement, and many of these echo the rationale for having a written collection development policy:

- It sets standards for procedures to be followed;
- It reduces the likehood of bias and personal influence;
- It provides continuity despite staff changes;
- It serves as an orientation device for new staff;
- It provides guidelines for complaint handling;
- It assists in weeding.

SELECTION RESPONSIBILITIES

This addresses two questions:

- Who shall do the selecting?
- How shall the procedure be organised?

The answer to the first question is a combination of library staff and users.

Within the library it may be done by:

- The chief librarian;
- Division or department heads engaged specially for this task (collection development librarian, acquisitions librarian);
- Subject or area specialists; or
- Other professional staff as part of their general duties (re-ference librarians, technical services librarians).

Whichever applies, it should be stated clearly in the written document. Outside the library, selection should involve input from users from all types, and these should be specified clearly: administrators, parent organisation staff, students, teaching staff, general public, etc. To facilitate and encourage participation of these groups, a request form is provided.

This form should have space for all essential information needed to identify an item: author, title, number of volumes or pages, place of publication, publisher, date of publication, series and price, as well as the name of requester. This form is usually an attachment to statement. Copies should be made readily available and accessible to selectors both within and without the library. Figure 2.1 is a sample of such form.

Request Form

Author ....

Title, No. of Vols., Series ....

Edition ....

Publisher .... ISBN ....

Place of Publication .... Date of Publication ....

No. of Copies ....

Reading List ....

Prescribed Text ....

Background Reading ....

Requested by ....

Address ....

Fig 2.1 Request Form

HOW SELECTION IS ORGANISED

It should indicate clearly and precisely who has responsibility for what and who is responsible to whom. If a selection committee is used: who chairs the committee, and who appoints the members? How often does the committee meet? What are its terms of reference? If selection is the responsibility of individuals outside the library: How is this responsibility allocated and monitored? What resource does the librarian have if his external selectors fail to perform adequately? If selection is done jointly by external and internal selectors, what are the lines of demarcation? Who selects reference materials, serials, decides on multiple copies, etc.? All such questions should be addressed in the statement so that there is no doubt about responsibility and so that the newest member of staff has a clear grasp of procedures.

GENERAL GUIDELINES FOR SELECTION

This part turns to what to select. It presents only general guidelines derived from and based on the collection development policy. It lists here general selection sources, together with categories of more specific types of sources (publishers' catalogues, scholarly journals, indexing services, etc.). These listings help ensure that the named sources are used by selectors, and remind selectors of the other types of sources that they ought to be using.

Some libraries may actually name specific sources within each type, but this cannot be done in libraries selecting across a broad range of subjects and types of materials. This part may list languages in which materials are selected, or other limitations which apply across the range of materials. In other words, all selection criteria derived from, or at least compatible with, the collection development policy should be stated here. This will enable all selectors to operate within the same set of guidelines.

HANDLING OF GIFTS AND DONATIONS

Basically, a donated item has to be taken into the collection according to the same criteria applied to purchased item. Therefore, the statement says this and indicates that gifts are received on the understanding that they may be disposed of in a manner deemed appropriate by the librarian. The statement also indicates acceptable conditions of gifts.

CRITERIA FOR WEEDING

The library may well have included a part on weeding in its collection development policy; if so, this needs to be taken into account at this stage. Weeding, often termed 'deselection' in USA and 'relegation' in the UK, involves a number of decisions that should be outlined in the selection procedures statement, involving criteria for weeding, scope of weeding procedures, frequency and purpose, together with a general allocation of staff responsibilities, so that there is no confusion about who is responsible for what and when.

HANDLING OF COMPLAINTS

Complaints about and censorship of library materials have been controversial issues for many years. although this case is less likely to occur in medical libraries than in other types of libraries such as public and school libraries, but it could happen. This part contains a statement of complaint-handling procedures and a standard form to be completed by potential censors. The written statement should be made available, together with a copy of the collection development policy, at the first hint that an item in the collection is being challenged.

The complaint-handling form should be completed only if a formal complaint is lodged. The exact procedure, who is to be involved and the documentation to be utilized must all be stated clearly in this part. The entire statement should be readily accessible not only to selectors, but also to all users, as this often alleviates the need for complaints to go beyond an informal discussion.

SERIALS AND BOOK SELECTION

SERIALS SELECTION

From the eighteenth century, the journal has been an important mechanism for communicating scientific findings, advances in techniques, and changes in accepted practice in medicine and other health professions. Journals continue to constitute the core of health sciences library collections. But biomedical journals now face price increases, dwindling number of personal and institutional subscribers and the threat that print publications will be overshadowed by electronic forms of scientific communication. They also face various changes in the title, the publishers, emerging or splitting, editorship, supercession, ceasing, format or size, numbering, or frequency.

Responsibility for Selection

Because a decision to subscribe to a journal is often a long-term one, with a financial commitment over several years, selection is rarely left to a single person, although the final decision is often so.

Selection Committee

This is the practice in academic medical libraries and in large hospital libraries, as suggestions or requests are brought to the committee for review. Criteria for evaluation are agreed upon and an evaluation form is used to collect data for decision-making and to document decisions. The information should be recorded in a consistent manner on a standard form to allow comparisons.

The information may include the following: Title, publisher, frequency, starting date, cost, coverage of contents by standard indexing and abstracting services and online databases, published rankings or reviews, interlibrary loan data, information about purchase requests, information about other titles in the subject field, evidence of peer review of articles, assessment by faculty or hospital staff, availability in other affiliated library, relevance to the parent organisation's programmes. The frequency to committee meeting may vary from monthly to semiannually.

External Reviewers

These may be faculty or other health professional staff without forming any group. A form similar to the one used for selection committee may be used, preferrably with a sample issue of the journal. The library may use departmental representatives for this purpose. The librarian has to set a plan for follow-up.

Selection Criteria

Although selection criteria previously dealt with apply to all types of library materials, there are some unique characteristics of the journal format that need to be considered:

- *Quality*: Although no single measure will be sufficient to judge quality, there are several factors to be taken into account:
  - *Publisher*: Who is he? How reputable is he as a scientific publisher? Is the publisher a professional society or association? Is the membership of such society or association international? National? Regional?
  - *Editors*: Are they recognized? What is their institutional affiliation? are they themselves writers as well? Does the editorial board include prominent names?
  - Editorial review.
  - *Authors*: Are they members of the editorial board? What is there affiliation?
  - Content.

  a. *Research Journals*: Research journals should

publish articles that follow the accepted format for describing scientific research.

b. *Clinical Journals*: These may be evaluated by practitioners for selection.

c. *Review Journals*: These require more selectivity than the previous types because they do not report new information, and reviews on similar topics may cover much of the same groun*d.*

- Writing and Style:
  - — *Writing Style*: Articles should be readable. The writing should be grammatically correct, well organised and clear.
  - — *Abstracts*: These should be informative.
  - — *References*: These should be pertinent, thorough and up-to-date. Citations should be complete and accurate.
- *Accessibility of Content*: The inclusion of the journal in indexing services may be a criterion for selection. Inclusion in a selective database may also be used for this purpose.
- *Bibliometric Indicators*: Bibliometrics, or statistical bibliography, analyses literature by numerically examining the publications of a discipline. Data can be used to identify journals with the greatest number of articles on a subject or that cover greatest percentage of the literature. But bibliomteric data must be used cautiously as a selection tool, as articles may be cited for multiple reasons and not necessarily to indicate useful research or clinical content.
- *Physical Quality*: It is to be noted here that not all countries have equal access to high-quality paper and printing.
  - — *Illustrations*: Clarity and definition in reproduction of radiographs, photographs and other images. Use of colour may be important in some fields.
  - — *Paper and Binding*: This may not be a factor to be considered as a factor for selection, although using acid-free paper is relevant for material preservation.

- *User Needs*: Patient care and current research needs are driving forces for selection. One indicator of need is the number of requests made to obtain copies of articles through interlibrary loan or document delivery services. The departmental representatives for selection may be a source for identifying department needs.
- Local Availability.
  - Whether the title is available in another library of the parent organisation.
  - Duplication is becoming less likely except for heavily used items.
  - Availability through a network to which the library subscribes.
  - Reliance on remote collections or document delivery services.
- *Cost:* The judgement on the benefit for cost may be difficult, and subject experts should be called upon for advice.

Electronic Journals

Electronic journals may be categorized either by availability of electronic and print parallels or by mode of access.

The first will result in:

- Electronic journals that have an electronic version only, such as Online journal of current clinical trials.
- Electronic journals that are versions of print journals, such as New England journal of medicine.

The second will result in:

- Electronic journals that are available through a commercial vendor.
- Electronic journals that are locally accessible through CD-ROM, floppy disk or other electronic format loaded on a library workstation or parent organisation's network.

The issues that electronic journals pose for libraries are not substantially different than those posed by print journals. Information on availability of electronic journals may be obtained from the Association of Research Libraries (ARL) in both print and electronic format.

Selection Sources

There are several sources or information about journals:

- *Advertising and Announcements*: Advertisements may be sent directly by publishers, or are published in library or medical journals. Vendors also alert libraries in various ways: through lists, order forms, and online information systems. Publishers' catalogues may also be used.
- *Sample Issues*: These are sent by the publisher as sample or trial issues, which often may be requested and sometimes purchased.
- *Core Lists:* Lists of key journals, sometimes together with some other library materials are compiled. The following are examples:
- *User Recommendations:* The library can encourage users to suggest new titles using request form available in the library, whether manually or electronically.
- I*nterlibrary Loan Requests*: Repeated requests from users to obtain articles from a journal should prompt the library to consider a subscription.
- *Reviews:* There are scientific journals that publish reviews of new titles. Among these journals are Nature and Serials review.
- *Indexes*: Lists of journals indexed for major indexing services are used to make a judgement on titles already identified. Announcement of titles added can alert selectors to them. Examples of these lists are:
  - — List of journals indexed in Index Medicus. New titles are announced in *NLM technical bulletin.*
  - — Serial sources for the BIOSIS Previews Database.
  - — Chemical Abstracts Service Source Index.
- *Other Sources*: There are general sources that cover a wide range of subjects. Among these are the following:
  - — Ulrich's international periodicals directory. Bowker.
  - — Standard periodical directory. Oxbridge.
  - — New serial titles. OCLC.
  - — Faxon's librarians' guide to serials.

— EBSCO's librarians' handbook.
— Computer databases such as OCLC, RLIN, SERLINE (an NLM database)
— Serials review. Ann Arbor: Pierian. Quarterly

It has to be noted here that all such sources are also available in machine-readable form.

BOOK SELECTION

Books assist in the dissemination of information by providing a convenient means of access to recorded knowledge. It is true that a medical book is out-of-date when it is published, but this does not invalidate its use as a digest of available knowledge in a physically handy form.

The main categories of books are:

- *Quick Reference Books:* Dictionaries, directories, pharmacopoeias, data book. These are essential items in every collection. Now many of these books are also available in CD-ROM format.
- *Standard Works of Reference*: These provide access to knowledge in depth in subject at an advanced level. They are usually too detailed to serve as textbook guides to their subjects.
- *Postgraduate Textbooks:* The need to specialize is paramount and the number of courses leading to future qualifications is numerous in medicine. This ensures a good market of textbooks at the postgraduate level. They are among the most heavily used materials in the medical library.
- *Texts for Basic Study:* There is virtually no topic in the undergraduate level which is not suitably covered by this type of material.
- *Monographs*: A monograph consists of a treatise on a single subject, and it is always an advanced level work. They may also appear in series.
- *Theses and Dissertations:* Most of the smaller medical libraries do not hold this type of material and larger one will onlyhold those originating in their own parent

organisations. If required, it is usual to have them collected by a central body such as national or depository libraries.

- *Pamphlets and other Ephemera:* Pamphlets are short topical and written with a particular object in view. They may quickly lose their currency. They may be ordered and treatedas books. Many useful pamphlets are available free particularly from pharmaceutical companies.
- *Reports:* A report is a work written by a task force or particular group specially commissioned to study a particular issue or problem. They may be difficult to trace. Reports may also emanate from important bodies in the profession. Research reports in, for example, the pharmaceutical industry may be confidential. Another example of reports is the annual report of a research or teaching institution. Government departments generate a great deal of report literature, of which many are on social and medical subjects.
- *Conference Proceedings:* The quality of this type varies from carefully edited account of important meetings to mere photolithography of the authors' typescripts with little editing and no index.

Responsibilities

- Responsibilities for book selection should be formally agreed upon, and the flow of information and decisions clearly delineated. If most of the selection is distributed among several persons, a manual describing both the responsibilities and the process is useful. This manual promotes consistency and thoroughness in carrying out the functions
- In small libraries, there is little confusion regarding who has what responsibility. But in large libraries the situation is different as procedures need to document how selection tools are handled:
  - Who sees advertising materials, how they are divided, for instance by subject, how they are marked for follow up

- — If books reviews are used, the routing process should be established
  - — Method of transmitting ordering information from the selector to the acquisitions unit
  - — If interlibrary loan requests are to be reviewed, there must be a mechanism for receiving the information.
- The link between selection activity and the budget allocations must be established, whether the individual selectors have any fund management responsibilities or not.

Sources for Book Selection

Selection tools for book selection should be both alerting and evaluative to be convenient for selection. They may be in the form of bibliographies, review or advertising materials, and may be in print and/or electronic formats. Other sources are relevant for selection.

The various sources may be summarized as follows:

- *Publishers' Flyers and Catalogues*: Libraries usually receive a lot of announcements from the publishers about the availability of new books. Moreover, many publishers produce various types of catalogues for their publications, sometimes including previously published editions which are still in print. It is necessary for the library to be on the mailing list of the publishers in the disciplines that concern the library. Visiting their web sites is now enabled as well.
- *Vendors' Flyers and Catalogues*: Many vendors do the same thing as publishers. Make sure that you are regularly informed of their offerings. Some provide altering service, in print or electronically, of new titles.
- *Recommendations from Users*: This should be encouraged. Request forms must be readily accessible. Remember that they themselves receive flyers and catalogues from publishers and sometimes complimentary copies of new titles.
- *Interlibrary Loan Requests:* Although particularly

appropriate for journal selection, they may be also relevant for selecting books that are not brand new.

- *Bibliographies and Library Catalogues:* Bibliographies are of several categories as there are national bibliographies, subject bibliographies both total and selective, author bibliographies, bibliographies of bibliographies, etc. Some of these bibliographies include health sciences while there is one devoted to medicine which is Medical books in print of Bowker.

Another tool that is considered here is what is usually called core lists:

- *British Council*: Core list of library materials: medicine.
- *EMRO*: List of basic sources in English for a medical faculty library. 8th ed. 1999.
- *Royal College of General Practitioners*: Books for general practice and primary health care. London, 1992. Regularly revised.
- *Royal College of Psychiatrists:* Lists of books suitable for a psychiatric library 1988-1993. London, 1993. Regularly revised and updated.
- *Royal College of Psychiatrists:* Key books for a psychiatric library. London. Regularly revised and updated.

Moreover, the most comprehensive catalogue of health sciences books is CATLINE. This is NLM's online catalogue. NLM Locator, which includes CATLINE, AVLINE for audiovisuals, and SERLINE for information on journal titles, is now available on the Internet.

- *Book Reviews*: There are two types of book reviews:
  - — Those published in professional and scientific journals. Examples of such journals are:
    - *a.* *JAMA:* Journal of American Medical Association
    - *b.* Lancet
    - *c.* British medical journal
    - *d.* British journal of hospital medicine
    - *e.* Nursing times
    - *f.* Journal of advanced nursing
    - *g.* New England journal of medicine
    - *h.* Bulletin of the Medical Library Association

There are journals not limited to health sciences such as Nature, and Science, and Library journal:

— Those that are fully devoted as journal to reviews. Some of these reviews cover medicine among the disciplines that they serve. Among them, are the following:

a. *New Technical Books*: New York Public Library (10/year).
b. *Technical Book Review Index:* JAAD Publications (monthly).
c. *Science Books and Films*: American Association for the Advancement of science (5/year).
d. *The Bookseller:* Whitaker (weekly).
e. *Contemporary Psychology*: A journal of reviews. American Psychological Association (monthly).
f. *Directory of Published Proceedings*: Series SEMT-Science, Engineering, Medicine and Technology. InterDok (10/year)
g. *Choice:* Association of College and Research Libraries (11/year).
h. *British Book News*: The British Council (monthly).
i. *American Book Publishing Record*: Bowker (monthly).
j. *Cumulative Book Index*: H.W. Wilson (11/year).

The outstanding example of book reviews is the new publication of Doody Publishing set up in 1993. This publication is entitled Doody's journal: health sciences book reviewing, issued bimonthly and evaluates about 250 titles in each issue. It can be accessed on Internet.

A British version is under discussion:

• *Approval Plan*: Although approval plans are concerned with acquisition. The selection function of the approval plan is summarized as follows:
  — The library supplies the vendor with a detailed profile of its requirements in specific fields, together with any budgetary limits, and the publishers to be considered;
  — The supplier selects and regularly supplies the

materials as specified in the profile;

— The library monitors the materials supplied and have the right to return any item received;

— If the percentage of returns is high then the library should review the plan and take required action, which may include changing the supplier.

— The approval plan does not fit with small medical libraries.

SELECTION IN SPECIAL SETTINGS

Electronic Resources

Selection decisions of electronic resources parallel those of print materials in many ways, but they are treated separately, because their unique characteristics introduce additional factors to collection decision-making and because these formats can affect information delivery, budgeting, equipment, and staffing. Electronic resources play an essential role in every health sciences library. But they are usually expensive, and thus may consume a great portion of a library's budget. So a greater degree of care should be taken in making decisions regarding what the library will provide to its users.

As knowledge-based computer programmes in clinical medicine and other health care disciplines are improved and gain wider acceptance, they appear more commonly as library resources, especially if they can be accessed remotely from offices and clinical care sites. Selection of computer software by students, hospital staff, faculty, clinicians, or researchers should be guided by the library's collection development policy. The policy should address the criteria by which these resources are selected. Scope, depth and audience will define the boundaries.

There are several types of software that may be acquired by health sciences libraries:

- Bibliographic
- *Full Text*: Books and journals
- Numeric or factual databases
- Clinical assist programmes for diagnosis or treatment decisions

- Educational software
- Applications software, such as word processing, analytical or statistical packages, file management, telecommunications, authoring software, graphics software (note here that such software is general purpose not resources)
- Administrative functions or staff support
- Criteria of Resources for Selection
  - *Scope*: The resource must fit the subject scope of the library.
  - *Depth*: The intensity of collecting in a discipline will dictate how many resources the library will acquire, or the degree of specialization needed.
  - *Audience*: The selection should answer the question whose needs should the library intend to serve with the software? Different clientele will require different resources. Computer-based resources for student use should usually be selected with advice and recommendation from faculty or potential users.
- Selection Principles:
  - The resource should fit the mission of the library, and the scope and depth defined in the collection development policy, it should meet users' needs;
  - Specific criteria should address the content, the user interface retrieval software, the format, and the hardware and software required by the resource;
  - Careful investigation and evaluation of the cost-effective-ness of different formats should precede any decisions. An information policy both for the library and for the parent organisation will help guide these decisions.
- Selection Criteria:
  - Content:

    a. Quality of the material presented.

      i. Authoritiveness of content

      ii. Expertise of the authors

   iii. Reputation of the producer
   iv. Comprehensiveness of the information
   v. Quality of the images, if important

b. *Currency*: Regular updates should be provided.

c. *Content Usefulness*: Such as:
   i. Interactive capabilities of testing
   ii. Simultaneously hear and see as required
   iii. Combine text and images, sound and movement
   iv. Highly accurate and up-to-date knowledge
   v. Able to show relationships and probabilities, and suggest possibilities

d. Relationship to Print Publications.
   i. Whether additional material is added
   ii. Convenience of access, amount of demand, need for permanent presentation
   iii. Are updates offered electronically through networks?

— User Interface:

a. Ease of use.

b. Software functions.
   i. The search engine or other control functions should be powerful enough to support the resource;
   ii. Response time should be snappy;
   iii. Use of Boolean operators, adjacency feature, saving searches or search strategies are enabled.

c. Printing and Downloading Capabilities.

d. Duplication of Print Publications. When the software duplicates to a large extent a print publication, the library must determine whether the electronic version offers additional features, such as easier search, use hypertext, reformat information, manipulation or animation of illustrative material, extraction and manipulation.

e. Compatibility with Other Resources.

f. Documentation and Guides.

— *Format*: The library has several formats to choose from:

a. In print
b. On stand-alone CD-ROM
c. On CD-ROM on a LAN
d. By tapes mounted on local institutional network
e. By various routes to a remote utility through a gateway

The following factors should be considered in making this choice:

a. *Users*: Consider the likely users; if they are very few, the cost and support may not be justified.
b. *Expected Use*: The number and frequency of use.
c. *Accessibility*: Convenient access.
d. *Content*: Whether formats differ in comprehensiveness or specialized contents. Compare the interface and performance characteristics. Updating.
e. Costs.
f. *Equipment*: Compatibility with local systems.
g. Legal Issues:
   i. Licensing
   ii. Restrictions to making backup copies, downloading, and printing
   iii. Possibility of sharing

— Hardware, Software, and Space Requirements.

a. Space:
   i. The facilities should be conducive to the types of use that will be made of them.
   ii. Whether the workstation has to be an open area.
   iii. Whether the resources can be used effectively in the available setting.
b. Workstation Configuration.
   i. Networking is to be provided.
   ii. Adequate number of workstations to ensure effective use of the resources.
   iii. Avoid workstations dedicated to single

resource, except for those that will be heavily used, such as MEDLINE, or the library's catalogue.

c. Compatibility.
   i. Is the resource compatible with existing equipment?
   ii. Is the memory sufficient and the machine fast enough for the type of content, such as images?
   iii. Does the new software conflict with any other resources on the same equipment?

d. Additional Software.
   i. Does the resource require specific software such as operating system or database loader?
   ii. Audio and video require additional component.
   iii. Is the existing hardware adequate to accommodate the required software?

Reference Collections

The policy for reference collection should relate to the general collection development policy, whether it forms part of it or written separately. All selection criteria applied to books in general apply here as well. It remains to cover here the types of materials that form the reference collection and the selection sources of reference items.

Types of Materials

Reference collections are used to locate the following:

- *Directory Information*: Brief factual information about people, institutions, organisations, programmes.
- *Data:* Compilations of such information as statistical data, biological facts, chemical compositions, drug descriptions.
- *Definitions:* Collections of medical terminology, foreign language, specialized nomenclature.
- *Descriptions:* Short or encylcopaedic summaries of

diseases, procedures, biological processes, historical events.

- *Bibliographic Information:* References or abstracts by subject, author, citation, historical period, or source.

To enable this, the following types of materials have to be provided:

- *Bibliographies:* Examples include the various core lists and other sources for selection of books, journals and electronic resources mentioned previously.
- *Business or Corporate Information about Health Care Industry:* Examples: The medical and health information directory; the Patersons guides series; Research centres directory; World of learning; Encyclopedia of associations; the Medical and healthcare marketplace guide; the Foundations directory; Directory of medical and health care libraries in the United Kingdom and Republic of Ireland.
- *Dictionaries: Examples*: Dorlands illustrated medical dictionary; Stedman's medical dictionary; the International dictionary of medicine and biology; Taber encyclopedic dictionary; Segen's dictionary of modern medicine; the encyclopedia and dictionary of medicine, nursing and allied health; Jablonski's dictionary of syndromes and eponymic diseases; Mangalini's directory of syndromes; Encyclopedia of human biology; Sloane's medical abbreviations and eponyms; the Acronyms, initialisms and abbreviations dictionary; Mosby's medical, nursing and allied health dictionary.
- *Directories and Biographical Sources:* Examples are the various medical directories published in many countries of the world, such as the UK Medical directory.
- *Drug and Chemical Information:* Examples are the various pharmacopoeias published in many countries.
- *Funding Sources:* Some are listed under the second type mentioned.
- *Handbooks and Manuals:* This also includes style manuals. Examples: Merck index; CRC handbook of

chemistry and physics.

- *Health Legislation, Regulations and Standards:* These are published and documented in various countries.
- *Indexes and Abstracts*: Many are available in both print and electronic formats. Examples include:
  - — Index Medicus (Medline);
  - — Science citation index (SCISEARCH);
  - — Current contents;
  - — Excerpta medica (EMBASE);
  - — Cumulative index to nursing and allied health (CINAHL);
  - Hospital literature index (Health Planning and Administration);
  - — Biological abstracts (BIOSIS Previews);
  - — Chemical abstracts (CA Search);
  - — Psychological abstracts (Psych-INFO);
  - — CANCERLIT;
  - — PDQ;
  - — TOXLIT.
- *Statistical Compilations:* Many countries and health associations publish statistics on different aspects of health. WHO publishes World health statistics annual.
- *Tests*: Examples include: Mental measurements yearbook; stromborg's Instruments for clinical nursing research.
- Yearbooks and annual reviews.
- *General Works:* Most reference collections include a small number of general reference works such as an encyclopaedia, dictionary, almanac, directories of local organisations, an atlas.
- *Textbook Collections:* If the library does not maintain a reserve collection. A representative collection of textbooks in the reference collection may provide convenient access to students who need information for assignments or patient care questions.
- *Electronic Resources:* There is an increasing number of electronic reference sources covering the range of print sources, including bibliographic and fulltext

databases, handbooks, encyclopaedias, directories, and textbooks. The data is stored on CD-ROM, floppy disks, hard drives and mainframe or minicomputers. Some are duplicates or enhancements of printed sources or mainframe sources, such as CD-ROM versions of MEDLINE, others incorporate several publications or resources. Another electronic resource is the OPAC (Online Public Access Catalogue) were one or more workstations are dedicated for them.

- *Ephemeral Materials*: Collection of pamphlets, information sheets, brochures, and even reprints or bibliographies are maintained as adjuncts to reference collections. This collection may also include press clippings. A policy for selection criteria and guidelines for weeding and retention should be developed and followed.

Audiovisual Collections

Audiovisual materials comprise an important segment of many health sciences libraries. But they usually have requirements (such as space, equipment and funding) that make them different from collections of other materials.

Collection development for audiovisuals is different from those for other materials in the following aspects:

- Selection of audiovisuals is more user-driven than that for other formats;
- Previewing is required in the selection process, whether this takes place in the library or at the supplier's place.

Audiovisuals supports all aspects of educational programmes in both academic settings and hospitals (whether for staff or patients).

Selection Criteria

In addition to the general criteria of selection previously discussed, the following additional criteria may be considered:

- *Audience:* The library's interest in the audience which may be professional, academics, or general public including patients and patient families, should be documented in the collection development policy and taken into account in the selection process.

- *Equipment Availability*: The following questions have to be answered: Does the library already own the proper equipment so that users can view or listen to the programme? Are users likely to have access to compatible equipment at home or in their departments? Can the item be used on patient to other broadcast networks?
- *Appropriateness of Format*: Is the format in which the material is presented the most useful one to convey the information? Slides *vs.* videotapes, audiovisual *vs.* print, motion *vs.* still images, audiotape *vs.* printed description.
- *Origin of Format:* does the audiovisual conform to national standards: slides may differ in size.
- *Rental or Permanent Acquisition*: Can the need be satisfied through rental? Is there sufficient recurring demand to justify a purchase? Is it possible to borrow particular items from other library or institution?
- *Restriction on Use:* Are there special guidelines which must be followed regarding the use of the title, such as prohibition on group showings? If it is difficult to monitor and enforce such restrictions, it may not be advisable to procure the item.
- *Cost*: Is the item worth the investment?

Grey Literature

Grey literature is defined as the " literature which is not readily available through normal bookselling channels, and therefore difficult to identify and obtain". Examples of grey literature include reports, technical notes and specifications, conference proceedings and preprints, translations, official publications, supplementary publications and data, trade literature. It has to be noted that not all materials in all these categories are grey.

Grey materials are characterized by the following:

- Poor availability
- Poor bibliographic information and control
- Non-professional layout and format
- Low print run

Types of Grey Literature in Health Sciences

- Government Information.
  - The grey titles issued by government departments. These may outnumber the other normal publications in some countries.
  - The health agency documents, including circulars.
  - Documents produced by national statutory and nonstatutory bodies, academic units and voluntary sector.
  - *Health Authority Literature*: This includes:
    a. Minutes and agenda papers
    b. Annual reports
    c. Public health reports
    d. Strategic plans
    e. Working party plans
    f. Statistical series and bulletins
    g. Medical audit plans
    h. Policy documents
    i. Research and surveys
    j. Health needs assessment surveys
    k. Public opinion surveys
    l. Financial statements
  - Documents of other relevant authorities, such as the ministries of interior, housing, transport, labour, sports and even police service.
  - Grey literature of health service providers in both public and private sectors. This literature also includes research activities and statistics.

Sources for Selection

There are services concerning grey literature in various fields. They are normally with national covering although some may be international.

The following are examples:

- *Government Reports Announcements and Index. Virginia*: NTIS. This publication has three major headings related to health sciences in its subject categories:

- — Biomedical technology and human factor engineering
- — Health planning and health services research
- — Medicine and biology

- Scientific and Technical Aerospace Report (STAR). NASA. This has the following parts concerning health sciences:
  - — Life sciences
  - — Aerospace medicine
  - — Behavioural sciences
  - — Man/system technology and life support
  - — Space biology
- Energy research abstract (ERA). US Department of Energy. It has:
  - — Biomedical sciences, basic studies
  - — Biomedical sciences, applied studies
  - — Health and safety
- British reports, translations and theses. Boston. Spa: The British Library Document Supply Centre. It has: 06 biological and medical sciences.
- System for information on grey literature in Europe (SIGLE). The European Association of Grey Literature Exploitation (EAGLE). It is a bibliographic database holding contributions from 9 European countries.
- For librarians seeking German language grey literature in medical and health care, there are two publications:
  - — FTN (Forschungsberichte aus Technik und Naturwissencha ften). Weinheim: VCH Verlag. This is a bibliography of projects sponsored by the German Federal Ministry for Research and Technology.
  - — Bibliography of medicine. Munich: K.G. Saur. This is a bibliography of German-language publications outside the book trade, and includes literature from Switzerland and Austria.
- PASCAL Bibliographies internationales. Paris INIST. This is an international bibliography with French emphasis covering science and medicine.

- Ethnic minorities health. Bradford: Bradford Community Quarterly bulletin covering conference proceeding, theses and much useful grey literature.
- The Cumulative index to nursing and allied health literature (CINAHL). It is useful for dissertations, standards and conference proceedings.
- *Health Service Abstracts. Oldham:* Department of Health Leaflets Unit. Monthly. It includes books, book chapters, NHS executive publications, reports and periodical references.
- *The European Union Biomedical and Health Research. Brussels:* European Commission. 3/year. It concentrates on national research into medical and health problems in Europe.
- Health Care Literature Information Network (HECLINET). Berlin: Institut für Krankenhausbau, Dokumentation Krankenhauswesen. Bimonthly. It covers the entire range of European literature, both grey and white, on hospitals and health care. It includes conference reports, theses and company publications.
- Conference papers index. Louisville, NY: Data Courier. Monthly. It covers published and unpublished papers.
- WHODOC. Geneva: WHO. Bimonthly. It lists all WHO publications, including periodicals, technical and policy documents, as well as documents emanating from WHO funded programmes.

Other disciplines, such as food and environment, are covered in international databases.

They include:

- *AGRIS. Rome*: Food and Agriculture Organisation (FAO). It has a print version, AGRINDEX.
- CAB abstracts. London: Commonwealth Agricultural Bureau.
- AGRICOLA. US National Agricultural Library. It has a printed version: bibliography of agriculture.
- International register of potentially toxic chemicals (IRPTC). Nairobi: United Nations Environment Programme (UNEP).

- Environmental Chemical Data and Information Network (ECDIN). European Communities at Ispra (Italy) Establishment. This is a factual database.

Consumer Health Collections

During the 1980s and 1990s, increasing attention has been given to the provision of information on health care issues to patients, relatives, carers and wider public. The information provided is called "Consumer Health Information (CHI)'. Development of consumer health information is now a necessity dictated by law in some countries.

It has significant benefits:

- It leads to more truly informed consent
- It leads to increased patient's understanding and satisfaction
- It leads to increased compliance with treatment
- It leads to quicker and less stressful recovery from illness and surgery.

The increased availability of health information for lay people has also been influenced by the WHO declaration of " Health for All by the year 2000 " which says:

- "Health for all will be achieved by people themselves. A well informed, well motivated and actively participating community is a key element for attainment of the common goal".

Consumer health collections exist to serve library users seeking authoritative information, in clearly understood language, about normal anatomy and physiology, diseases, conditions, treatments and other health care topics. Besides the general public users of these collections include medical school students seeking materials to help explain health and disease concepts to patients and their relatives. Others include primary care physicians, nurses and faculty members. It may be part of the reference collection, or on its own. But it is not always the responsibility of the medical library to contain consumer health collections. In some cases it is the responsibility of the parent organisation's public relations unit, while in other cases the responsibility rests with a variety of statutory and voluntary agencies, as it is rather common for the ministries of health and other health authorities to provide this information. Yet in other cases, the responsibility rests with public libraries.

Selection Criteria

The general selection criteria previously mentioned apply here.

But further criteria may be given:

- *Presentation of Information*: This includes the writing style, easiness of use, presence of index and table of contents, illustration, presentation of alternatives and presence of citations and sources.
- *Audience*: The collection development policy should document the audience to be served, to be taken into account in the selection process.
- *Pathway to Additional Information:* The item should have bibliographies, reading list, referral sources and resource organisations.
- Qualifications of the Author and Publisher.
- Currency.

Rare Book, History of Medicine and Archives Collections

Rare book, history of medicine and archives collections, are not found in all health sciences libraries. The difference between collection development in general, and that of rare books derives from the nature of the books themselves. Thus policies governing it are frequently singled out for special consideration in overall collection development policy statements. A distinction is often made between rare book collections and history of medicine collections, under the assumption that the latter are generally comprised of secondary works, the materials are collected in the same manner as other books for the medical library collections, and they are kept in open stacks with the rest of the library's collection.

Rare books are primary research materials, require more proper storage and security controls than the general stack collection, and may also be used as showplace for the parent organisation. The archives collection of the parent organisation is different and is not common in medical libraries as it may be under the responsibility of another department of the parent organisation.

If it exists, it may include: official correspondence, minutes, books of account, publications of the parent organisation, books by and about staff and students including alumni publications, theses from the parent organisation or its staff, records of parent organisation's clubs, associations, and societies catalogue, newsletters, personal papers of the more eminent members of the staff, and photographs. It may also contain records from other local health-related organisations, such as affiliated hospitals.

Selection Criteria

Additional to generic criteria, there are further ones that need to be considered:

- *Presence of other Editions of the Same Work*: In addition to availability of other editions or printings, there may be need for specific edition with special features. Some large libraries may require that all editions of a work be acquired for comparison.
- *Availability of a Facsimile Edition*: Facsimile editions may be useful as reading copies.
- *Physical Condition*: The physical condition may be the reason for selection as the item may be different from modern works. Items that need restoration are not usually acquired.
- *Cost:* This must be appropriate.
- *Research Value of the Artifact over Content:* This concerns signed or annotated copies, special bindings and illustrations. Works of particular publishers may be of interest.
- *Provenance*: Previous owners of the copy. Whether the copy is a stolen copy.
- *The Subject in Context*: This means that the copy may show whether the discipline changed over time.
- *Format:* Formats other than books may figure prominently in rare book and history of medicine collections.
- For archives there must be a policy for retention and disposal of the materials rather than a selection policy.

3

Resources and Services of Libraries

Using Questionnaire-I, for this chapter information was collected from library staff about the administration, organisation, resources, services and facilities of libraries of colleges of education under study. An attempt was also made to ascertain the problems being faced by them in managing these libraries. Questionnaires were personally administered to the all libraries under study. Responses received are analysed and discussed here.

YEAR OF ESTABLISHMENT

Libraries constitute an integral part of colleges. These are supposed to be established simultaneously with their parent institutions. Realizing their crucial role in education, all the libraries have been established together with the inception of colleges. All libraries, except one had been existing for more than 30 years. Library of University College of Education (UCE) came into existence in 2001 along with the college.

LIBRARY STAFF

Library is the trinity of collection, staff and readers, where staff brings together other two elements. Qualified and adequate staff is pre-requisite for effective functioning of libraries.

LIBRARIANS

Libraries need the services of professionally qualified librarians for proper administration of the system. A library having good collection and adequate staff may not essentially provide effective library services, unless it is managed by a professionally qualified librarian having managerial capabilities. All the colleges, except UCE had sanctioned posts of librarians.

The UCE library had a post of an assistant librarian as incharge, which was lying vacant since the establishment of college in 2001. It was being managed by a library assistant. Two Goverment Colleges of Education (GCE) had two posts of librarians each. Out of these, in a college a post was vacant and one librarian was managing library. Table reveals the prevailing position of librarian's posts in colleges under study.

Table 3.1 Prevailing Position of Librarians Posts

Sr. No.	Particulars	No. of Libraries	Percentage
1.	Permanent Librarians	13	72.22
2.	Adhoc based librarians	01	05.56
3.	Post vacant	04	22.22
	Total	**18**	**100.00**

It is evident from table that out of the 18 libraries having sanctioned posts of librarians, 13 (72.22%) libraries had permanent librarians, whereas, a goverment aided college appointed a librarian on adhoc basis. In 04 (22.22%) colleges posts of librarians were lying vacant.

Out of these, a goverment aided college appointed a professional and designated her as an assistant librarian, inspite of the fact that the college did not have any sanctioned post of an assistant librarian. The remaining three libraries were being run by restorers. The National Council for Teacher Education (NCTE) required each college to have a full time librarian. Analysis of the responses revealed that libraries of 06 (31.58%) colleges consisting of 04 Goverment. Aided Colleges of Education (GACE), one goverment college of education and UCE did not meet the NCTE norms about full time librarian.

EDUCATIONAL QUALIFICATION OF LIBRARIANS

Educational qualifications of librarians influence the organisational health of libraries. Higher academic and professional qualification leads to better library management, ultimately better library services.

Table 3.2 Educational Qualification of Librarians

Sr. No.	Qualification		Number of Librarians	%
	Academic	Professional		
1.	M.A./M.Sc./ M.Ed./M.Com.	Ph.D.	01	06.67
2.	M.Phil/Ph.D.	B.Lib.and I.Sc.	01	06.67
3.	M.A./M.Sc.	M.Lib.and I.Sc.	04	26.66
4.	M.A./M.Sc.	B.Lib.and I.Sc.	06	40.00
5.	B.A./B.Sc.	M.Lib.and I.Sc.	03	20.00
	Total		**15**	**100.00**

Table 3.2 shows that out of 15 librarians serving 14 libraries, 06 (40.00%) possessed master's degree in arts/science and bachelors' degree in Library and Information Science (LIS), while 04 (26.66%) librarians had master's degrees in arts/science in addition to masters' degree in LIS. Three librarians had bachelors' degree in arts/science and master's degree in LIS. A librarian possessed Ph.D. degree in the subject of History and bachelor's degree in LIS.

Only one librarian had Ph.D. degree in LIS and master's degree in another discipline. Out of the 07 librarians having master's degree in LIS, 03 had qualified National Eligibility Test (NET) for Lectureship, while a librarian qualified State Eligibility Test (SET) for Lectureship.

It has been found that all 03 librarians serving GCE libraries had bachelor's degree in LIS, whereas all the librarians having master's degree in LIS were serving at GACE.

The NCTE has revised its norms regarding qualification of librarians. These are now only bachelors degree in Library and Information Science, whereas as per NCTE these were "As prescribed by State Government/UT Administration concerned.'

The qualifications laid by State Goverment were as per University Grant Commission. But the qualifications prescribed by NCTE are only B.Lib.and I.Sc. Therefore, this amounts to the degradation of librarians and eventually libraries.

EXPERIENCE OF LIBRARIANS

Table 3.3 Experience of Librarians

Sr. No.	Experience in Years	No. of Librarians	Percentage
1.	Up to 5	02	13.33
2.	6-10	03	20.00
3.	11-15	—	—
4.	16-20	01	06.67
5.	21-25	03	20.00
6.	26-30	03	20.00
7.	More than 30	03	20.00
	Total	**15**	**100.00**

Table 3.3 depicts that out of 15 librarians, 09 (60.00%) had experience of more than 20 years. Out of these, 07 librarians possessed bachelor's degree and 02 had master's degree in LIS. Five (33.33%) librarians had experience of less than 10 years, while a remaining librarian's experience ranged between 16-20 years. All three librarians serving GCE had experience of more than 20 years each. Analysis of the responses tabulated in tables reveals that all the librarians having only bachelor's degree in LIS were appointed more than 20 years ago. On the other hand, all the librarians appointed thereafter had master's degree in LIS.

REFRESHER COURSES ATTENDED

Librarians were asked if they had attended any refresher course, orientation programme, workshop, etc. Responses revealed that out of 15 librarians, 07 (46.67%) attended refresher courses, 02 (13.33) had attended orientation programmes and a librarian also participated in a workshop. It has been found that about 50% librarians had not participated in refresher courses and workshops, which are imperative for updating professionals and essential for Continuous Professional Development.

LIBRARY ASSISTANTS

The UCE and a goverment aided college had a post of library assistant each. Out of the two library assistants serving respective libraries, one possessed bachelors' degree in LIS, while another was only matriculate not having any degree or diploma in LIS.

LIBRARY RESTORERS

Thirteen (68.42%) libraries had sanctioned posts of restorers, while remaining 06 (31.58%) did not. In 12 (92.30%) of 13 libraries, restorers were working against the sanctioned posts, while in a goverment college library post was vacant. Two colleges out of the 06 not having sanctioned posts, appointed restorers on adhoc basis, while remaining 04 had not made such effort. All the GCE had sanctioned posts of restorers. About two-third of the library restorers serving libraries possessed either diploma or bachelor's degree in LIS, while remaining five did not.

LIBRARY ATTENDANTS

Eight (42.10%) libraries did not have sanctioned posts of library attendants. In two libraries, out of the 11 (57.90%) having sanctioned posts of attendants, posts were vacant. All the GCE had sanctioned posts of library attendants. But it was shocking to find that in Desh Bhagat Pandit Chetan Dev Goverment College of Education, Faridkot the previous principal had assigned the job of a 'gardener' to a graduate library attendant and replaced him with an illiterate peon in the library to provide library services to the users. This shows the ignorance and lack of importance of libraries on the part of authorities. Out of the 09 attendants serving libraries, one third had either degree or diploma in LIS, whereas, the remaining two third did not.

LIBRARY COMMITTEE

Generally, library committee comprises of three types of authorities, principal as the chairman of committee, librarian as secretary and teachers and students as members. Keeping in view its significance, librarians were asked about the existence, structure and functions of library committees.

EXISTENCE OF LIBRARY COMMITTEES

Out of a total 19 libraries, 18 (94.73%) had library committees, whereas a goverment aided college did not. In a college it was named as 'Book Purchase Committee'.

Table 3.4 Chairperson of Library Committee

Sr. No.	Chairperson of Committee	No. of Libraries	Percentage
1.	Principal	12	66.67
2.	Librarian	02	11.11
3.	Lecturer	02	11.11
4.	No Chairman	02	11.11
	Total	**18**	**100.00**

Table 3.4 reveals that in 12 (66.67%) libraries out of the 18 having library committees, principals were serving as the chairpersons of the committees, whereas in two GACE libraries, librarians themselves led these. In two colleges, lecturers were the heads of committees. Out of these, a college did not have regular principal. In two colleges, library committees did not have any chairman. In one of these, college principal was the convener of committee and librarian and lecturers were members, while in a remaining library, committee comprised of members only.

Table 3.5 Secretary of Library Committee

Sr. No.	Secretary of Committee	No. of Libraries	%
1.	Librarian	08	44.44
2.	Lecturers	06	33.33
3.	No One	04	22.23
	Total	**18**	**100.00**

It is worth mentioning here that in majority of the libraries *i.e.* 08 (44.44%), librarians were serving as secretaries of the committees, while in 06 (33.33%) libraries lecturers did the job. Four libraries did not have any secretary of the library committees. In a library, it comprised of principal as convener and librarian and lecturers as members, while in two libraries these had only members including librarians. In a remaining library, where librarian was head of the committee, it consisted of lecturers as members. Survey revealed that only one library had students' representatives as members in the committee.

NATURE OF WORK OF LIBRARY COMMITTEE

In majority of the libraries forming 66.67 per cent, library committees were advisory bodies. In remaining one third libraries these were executive in nature because of lack of full time librarians.

COLLECTION DEVELOPMENT

The Working Group on Libraries set up by National Knowledge Commission (2007) emphasized for collection building based on the information needs of users. In its recommendations the Group added "To fulfill its role in the present and changing context, each library must have a well-rounded collection relevant to its user community". A balanced and need based collection, adequate to meet the present as well as future information needs of users depends upon a well prepared collection development policy. Library staff of ten colleges responded that they had prepared and were following collection development policy, while staff of remaining 09 libraries responded otherwise. It was very disappointing to find that none of the libraries had any written guidelines for collection development.

WHO MAKES SELECTION OF SUBJECT RELATED BOOKS

Subject books are meant to meet the curriculum based information needs of users and enable them to explore the concerned subjects in depth. Library staff was asked to give ranking in order of preference to the different authorities mentioned in Questionnaire-I, according to their role in selection of subject books.

Table 3.6 Selection of Subject Related Books

Sr. No.	Persons who Select Books	Scores	Ranking
1.	Teachers	66	01
2.	Principal	60	02
3.	Library Committee	43	03
4.	Librarian	39	04
5.	Others (students and college management)	15	05

Sum total of the scores assigned to different options on the basis of ranking given by librarians reveals that teachers occupied the leading role in selection of subject books, followed by the principals and library committees respectively. Librarians attained the fourth position in order of ranking for subject related document selection, while others (students and college management) earned least scores.

GENERAL AND REFERENCE COLLECTION

As in case of subject books, scores have been assigned to the different authorities involved in selection of general and reference collection also, which are tabulated below:

Table 3.7 Selection of General and Reference Books

Sr. No.	Persons who Select Books	Scores	Ranking
1.	Teachers	62	01
2.	Principal	60	02
3.	Librarian	45	03
4.	Library Committee	43	04
5.	Others (students and college management)	05	05

Table 3.7 shows that teachers have earned the highest scores in selection of general and reference collection too. Principals and librarians were given second and third preferences, while library committees and others attained fourth and fifth positions respectively. Analysis of the responses given in tables makes it clear that the teachers and principals played a leading role in selection of subject related as well as general and reference collection.

DOCUMENT SELECTION TOOLS

Scores have been assigned to the various document selection tools listed in questionnaire-I on the basis of preference ranking given by librarians. Rank '1' was given the highest score '8' followed by others in descending order of 1 score at each stage.

Table 3.8 depicts that teacher's suggestions have earned the highest scores as sources of document selection, while publisher's catalogues and student's suggestions earned the second and third position respectively. Book reviews and other bibliographical tools were given least ranking as document selection tools.

Table 3.8 Document Selection Tools

Sr. No.	Sources of Book Selection	Scores	Ranking
1.	Teachers' Suggestions	132	01
2.	Publishers' Catalogue	101	02
3.	Students' Suggestions	71	03
4.	Books on Approval	54	04
5.	Book Sellers' List	42	05
6.	Book Exhibitions	40	06
7.	Book Reviews	16	07
8.	Other Bibliographical Tools	11	08

COLLECTION OF LIBRARIES

Among three components of libraries *i.e.,* collection, staff and readers, collection occupies the key position. It is collection which determines the use of a library. Collection is a wider term covering books, periodicals, microforms, electronic form docu-ments, etc. Information was gathered about the nature and size of collection of libraries under study.

TOTAL BOOK COLLECTION

Responses received about the total collection of libraries were arranged into different ranges of 5000 each. It is evident from table 3.9 that majority of the libraries under study *i.e.* 10 (52.63%) possessed 15,000-25,000 volumes, while 04 (21.06%) libraries had 10,000-15,000 books. Only two GCE libraries crossed the figure of 30,000 volumes. The UCE library had less than 5000 volumes due to its recent origin in 2001. The GCE were found rich in collection size than GACE and UCE. Main factor affecting this was that GCE received recurring grants for reading material from both the University Grants Commission (UGC) and the State Goverment, while GACE got grants for library from UGC only.

The NCTE (2007 and 2009) require each college to have a minimum 1000 titles and 3000 books for B.Ed. Course and minimum 2000 titles for M.Ed course in libraries to get recognition. The UCE had less than 5000 volumes though it was offering both B.Ed. and M.Ed. courses. The NCTE (2007 and 2009) further mentioned that a library should add 200 titles annually wherever B.Ed. course is being run. In addition it requires annual addition of '100 quality books' where M.Ed. course is also being run. It has been found that libraries of only two GACE were fulfilling the NCTE norms for M.Ed. course.

Table 3.9 Total Book Collection of Libraries

Sr. No.	Total Number of Books Possessed	No. of Libraries	%
1.	0-5000	01	05.27
2.	5000-10000	02	10.53
3.	10000-15000	04	21.06
4.	15000-20000	05	26.31
5.	20000-25000	05	26.31
6.	25000-30000	—	—
7.	More than 30000	02	10.52
	Total	**19**	**100.00**

TEXT BOOK COLLECTION

Table 3.10 shows the textbook collection of libraries of colleges of education in Punjab.

Table 3.10 Text Book Collection of Libraries

Sr. No.	Number of Text Books Possessed	No. of Libraries	%
1.	0-4000	06	31.58
2.	4000-8000	07	36.84
3.	8000-12000	03	15.79
4.	12000-16000	03	15.79
	Total	**19**	**100.00**

Table reveals that majority of the libraries had 4000-8000 textbooks. Six libraries had less than 4000 volumes and 03 possessed 8000-12000 textbooks. Three libraries had 12000-16000 volumes of textbooks. It is evident from the table that textbooks constitute a large part of the total collection of libraries.

REFERENCE COLLECTION

A good reference collection is the soul for sound reference service. It has been observed that all libraries maintained separate reference parts. Responses received about the strength of reference collection are tabulated below.

Table 3.11 Reference Collection of Libraries

Sr. No.	Number of Reference Books Possessed	No. of Libraries	%
1.	0-200	02	10.53
2.	200-500	05	26.31
3.	500-1000	02	10.53
4.	1000-1500	03	15.79
5.	1500-2500	03	15.79
6.	More than 2500	04	21.05
	Total	**19**	**100.00**

Table depicts that 05 (26.31%) libraries possessed 200-500 reference volumes, while other 05 had 500-1500 books. About 21.05% libraries had more than 2500 volumes in reference parts. In majority of the libraries, the reference collection was found to be satisfactory in proportion to their total collection. It was noticed that though the libraries of two GCE were richest in their total collection, still libraries of 04 GACE had more volumes in reference parts.

BOOK BANK

Fifteen libraries (78.94%) had book banks to help poor and needy students, while remaining 04 did not. Out of the 15 libraries, 14 maintained separate book bank parts, while a librarian shared that they did not have any separate book bank part, but lend books to needy students for the full session from text books part. Table 3.12 furnishes the number of volumes in book banks of 14 libraries.

Table 3.12 Size of Book Bank Collection

Sr. No.	Number of Books in Book Bank	No. of Libraries	%
1.	0-500	04	28.58
2.	500-1000	04	28.58
3.	1000-2000	03	21.42
4.	2000-3000	01	07.14
5.	More than 3000	02	14.28
	Total	**14**	**100.00**

Table 3.12 discloses that out of 14 libraries having separate book bank parts, 08 had less than 1000 volumes in their respective book banks. Four libraries had 1000-3000 books and 02 possessed more than 3000 volumes. It was learnt that majority of the libraries added only gifted books to book banks.

NON-BOOK MATERIAL

Non-book material constitutes an important source of information. The NCTE also requires libraries to have electronic publications (CD-ROMs) in collection. But, it has not gained the desired momentum in the libraries of colleges of education. It was found that only 09 libraries had non-book material in meager quantity. Out of these, seven libraries possessed a few CD's and one had cassettes that came free with books. Another library had approximately 400 maps.

DISSERTATIONS

Out of 15 colleges running M.Ed. course, libraries of 13 had dissertations. Eight libraries possessed less than 300 dissertations and 03 had 300-400 titles. Two libraries possessed more than 400 dissertations.

Number of the dissertations possessed by libraries varied according to the year of starting M.Ed. course. The University College of Education, Bathinda and SDS College of Education, Lopon (Moga) started M.Ed. courses during the academic sessions 2006-07 and 2007-08 respectively. Libraries of both of these colleges did not have dissertations.

PERIODICAL LITERATURE

Periodical publications serve the purpose of both information and recreation. These include journals, magazines and all other publications, which are issued at regular intervals.

JOURNALS

Journals are the subject specific periodicals, usually containing primary information. Table represents data about the number of journals on subscription of libraries.

Table 3.13 Number of Journals on Subscription

Sr. No.	Number of Journals	No. of Libraries	%
1.	0-10	04	21.05
2.	11-20	10	52.63
3.	21-30	03	15.79
4.	More than 30	02	10.53
	Total	**19**	**100.00**

Table 3.13 reveals that majority of the libraries forming 52.63 per cent were subscribing to 11-20 journals. Three libraries had 21-30 journals on subscription, while 02 libraries were subscribing to more than 30 journals. Only one library subscribed 02 international journals. A goverment aided college library was subscribing to merely two journals. The NCTE (2007) has prescribed for B.Ed. and M.Ed. colleges to subscribe to a minimum of 10 and 15 journals respectively. But libraries of 02 colleges offering B.Ed. course and 03 colleges offering M.Ed. course in addition to B.Ed. also did not meet these standards. NCTE (2009) provided revised norms regarding journals for M.Ed. course. It requires each library to have subscription to at least one international publication.

BACK VOLUMES OF JOURNALS

Back volumes of journals are the vital sources of information for furtherance of research. All the libraries except one had back volumes of journals.

Table 3.14 Back Volume of Journals

Sr. No.	Number of Volumes	No. of Libraries	%
1.	0-100	08	44.44
2.	100-200	03	16.67
3.	200-400	03	16.67
4.	More than 400	03	16.67
5.	No Response	01	05.55
	Total	**18**	**100.00**

Table depicts that 08 (44.44%) out of a total 18 libraries having back volumes of journals had less than 100 back volumes, while 03 (16.67%) had 100-200 volumes. Three libraries possessed 200-400 volumes, whereas other three libraries were having more than 400 back volumes of journals. One librarian had not specified the number of back volumes of journals available in library. Survey brought to notice that back volumes of journals were not properly organised as six libraries had loose issues, while in 03 libraries these were partially bound.

MAGAZINES

In addition to journals, libraries provide general magazines to users for reading. Majority of the of libraries *i.e.,* 13 (68.42%) were subscribing to less than 20 magazines, while 04 had 21-30 magazine titles on subscription. Two libraries were making available more than 30 magazine titles for users.

NEWSPAPERS

Sometimes, newspapers contain information not available from other sources. Fifteen libraries were subscribing to 05-10 newspaper titles, whereas two had 05 or less newspapers on subscription. A library was subscribing to more than 10 newspapers daily in English, Punjabi and Hindi.

LIBRARY BUILDING

Libraries are dynamic institutions which continue to grow in terms of collection, staff and readers. In order to tackle the resultant growth it becomes necessary to house a library in an independent, functional and modular building. Keeping in view the significance of library building, query was made to ascertain whether libraries have their own independent buildings. Responses revealed that only one goverment aided college library had an independent building used exclusively for library purpose.

The remaining 18 libraries were housed in buildings forming part of college premises. During visit, it was observed that library of GHG Khalsa College of Education, Gurusar Sadhar was sharing building with canteen. Library was located on first floor while canteen was sited on ground floor, causing disturbance to library users. Majority of the libraries *i.e.* 07 (36.84%) were housed in single rooms, while 06 (31.58%) libraries had two rooms each. Three libraries consisted of 04 rooms and one had more than 05 rooms.

It was astounding to find during visit to Khalsa College of Education, Mukatsar that a teacher was taking class in library. When asked, assistant librarian shared that it was a usual practice. That majority of the libraries were housed in one or two rooms, which can not be considered sufficient for effective functioning of libraries. The NCTE (2007 and 2009) norms about library building need to be revised. These require each college to have "a library-cum-reading room.'

SEPARATE READING ROOM

A separate reading room with sufficient seating capacity and free from disturbance is the essence of all types of libraries. Survey revealed that only 05 (26.31%) libraries had separate reading rooms for users, while in remaining libraries chairs were arranged within stack area. Similarly, five libraries had separate librarian's offices to perform the documentary work. In remaining libraries these were in the form of tables or cabins in corners of libraries.

USERS' VISIT TO LIBRARIES

Libraries exist to meet the information needs of users. The strength of users, their information needs and subjects of study, etc. greatly influence the resources and services of libraries. Table reveals the average number of visitors to libraries.

Table 3.15 Average Number of Visitors to Libraries

Sr. No.	Number of Visitors	No. of Libraries	%
1.	0-40	03	15.79
2.	40-80	06	31.58
3.	80-120	06	31.58
4.	More than 120	04	21.05
	Total	**19**	**100.00**

It is evident from the table 3.15 that 06 (31.58%) libraries were being visited by 80-120 users and other six libraries were visited by 40-80 users everyday. Four libraries were visited by more than 120 users daily on an average. In three libraries less than 40 users were visiting a day. The number of daily visitors to libraries varied due to variation in the students' strength with colleges.

SEATING CAPACITY

A library is supposed to provide adequate seating arrangement to users for reading inside library premises. Following table reveals the seating capacity of libraries.

Table 3.16 Seating Capacity for Users

Sr. No.	Number of Visitors	No. of Libraries	%
1.	0-25	03	15.79
2.	26-50	08	42.10
3.	51-75	03	15.79
4.	76-100	04	21.05
5.	More than 100	01	05.27
	Total	**19**	**100.00**

Table shows that majority of the libraries had seating capacity for 26-50 users, while 04 libraries could accommodate 76-100 users at a time. Three libraries had less than 25 seats each for users. A library had seating arrangement for more than 100 users. Six libraries had separate seating arrangement for M.Ed. students, while libraries of remaining 09 colleges offering M.Ed. course did not have such facility. Ten libraries had separate seating arrangement for teachers.

The NCTE (2007) prescribed for each college to provide seating arrangement in libraries for at least 25 per cent of their B.Ed. students and for 10 students of M.Ed. course, but 08 libraries did not meet this requirement. NCTE (2009) has revised norms regarding seating capacity of libraries for B.Ed course. It requires libraries to have seating arrangement for at least fifty per cent of B.Ed students. Only one library had drinking water facility for users. Similarly, Library of DAV College of Education, Abohar had toilet facility for faculty members. Students were not allowed to use that.

LIBRARY BUDGET AND SOURCES OF FINANCE

The impact of Information and Communication Technologies (ICTs) on libraries has brought structural changes to library practices. Effective library management and provision of services depends upon the availability of adequate funds. It was disappointing to find that none of the libraries except one had provision for library budget.

Only UCE, Bathinda had provision of ₹50,000 each year for reading material. But since its establishment in 2001 no increase has been made in this amount. Libraries of GCE and GACE mainly depended up on the UGC grants. Moreover, NCTE (2007 and 2009) is silent about the financial provision for libraries. In libraries of colleges of education under study, the sources of finance varied considerably.

Major sources of finance for purchase of reading material are given below:

- University Grants Commission (UGC) Grants;
- Library Fees;
- Library Development Funds; and
- Amalgamated Funds.

UGC GRANTS

The UGC plays a significant role in funding libraries through out the country. An attempt was made to find whether libraries have received any grant from UGC during the period 2002-2007. Only 13 (68.42%) libraries responded.

Table 3.17 Type of Grants Received from UGC

Sr. No.	Type of Grant Received	No. of Libraries	%
1.	Recurring	10	76.92
2.	Non Recurring	01	07.70
3.	No Grant	02	15.38
	Total	**13**	**100.00**

Table shows that out of 13 libraries, 10 (76.92%) received recurring grants under tenth five year plan, while a library got nonrecurring grant from UGC during the period 2002-2007. Office superintendent of the goverment aided college shared that the college had received special (non-recurring) grant for library meant for 'Backward District College'.

Libraries of two colleges including UCE and a goverment aided college had not received any recurring or non-recurring grant from UGC. The goverment aided college had not demanded grants from UGC because of the conflict between members of college management committee.

AMOUNT OF GRANTS RECEIVED BY LIBRARIES

Librarians were asked to mention the amount of grants received from UGC during the period 2002-2007. Responses received were arranged into different ranges of 1 lakh each.

Table 3.18 Extent of Grants Received

Sr. No.	Amount of Grants Received	No. of Libraries	%
1.	Up to one Lakh	06	54.54
2.	1-2	04	36.36
3.	2-3	—	—
4.	3-4	01	09.10
	Total	**11**	**100.00**

Table 3.18 reveals a considerable variation in the amount of grants received by 11 libraries. Majority of the libraries received less than ₹01 lakh as UGC grant for purchase of reading material under tenth five year plan, while 36.36% received 1-2 lakhs. A library received grant of more than 3 lakhs from UGC.

GRANTS FROM STATE GOVERNMENT

None of the libraries under study received grants from the State Goverment during the period 2002-2007. The State Goverment had earlier given grants to libraries of GCE only, as reported by librarians.

AMALGAMATED FUND

Amalgamated fund is collected from students each year at the time of admission to colleges. This amount is to be used for various purposes *i.e.* cultural activities, games, library and for some other similar purposes. Allocation of amalgamated funds towards library depends upon the discretion of the principals of colleges.

LIBRARY FEE AND LIBRARY DEVELOPMENT FUNDS

As like amalgamated fund, Library Fee and Library Development Fund are also charged from students at the time of admission to colleges. Out of the 13 responding colleges, 08 charged library fee at varying rates from ₹200-400. In 04 colleges it was termed as 'Books and Journals Fee'. Similarly 04 colleges charged library development fund from students at different rates of 100-200. In a goverment aided college it was being charged under the head 'Books Replacement Fund'.

OVERDUE FINE

The negligible amount of overdue fine can not be considered as reliable and sufficient source of funds for libraries. In UCE, the amount of overdue fine goes to the University Account.

TECHNICAL PROCESSING

Technical processing of documents takes place after accessioning. It covers all the activities related with their classification, cataloguing and physical processing. Classification provides systematic order among documents and catalogue guide the users to retrieve needed documents easily from large collection, through various access points.

CLASSIFICATION

Collection has to be classified and the classification scheme has to be user friendly. Survey revealed that out of a total 19 libraries, 18 had classified their collection. On the other hand, in the library of Dev Samaj College of Education for Women, Ferozepur City that was established in 1942, collection was not classified at all. Almirah numbers were written on catalogue cards instead of call numbers. The following table furnishes data about the extent of classification of documents in libraries:

Table 3.19 Status of Classification of Collection

Sr. No.	Extent of Classification	No. of Colleges	%
1.	Fully Classified	11	57.90
2.	Partially Classified	07	36.84
3.	Not At All Classified	01	05.26
	Total	**19**	**100.00**

Table 3.19 reveals that in majority of the libraries *i.e.*, 11 (57.90%) collection was fully classified, while in 07 (36.84%) libraries it was classified partially. In a remaining library documents were not classified at all. It has been found that all libraries were using Dewey Decimal Classification (DDC) scheme ranging from 16th to 21st edition to classify collection.

Earlier UCE library was using Colon Classification (CC), but later on it switched over to DDC. Three librarians responded of facing problems in classifying collection. A librarian having 18th edition of DDC shared that the respective library had an old edition of DDC which did not contain detailed class numbers for the subject of Computer. Librarian of Goverment College of Education, Jalandhar said, "It becomes very difficult to decide the main class of a book in case of interdisciplinary subject books". A librarian stated lack of professionally qualified staff as one of the obstacles in organising collection.

CATALOGUING

Survey revealed that 11 (57.90%) libraries had partially catalogued their collection, not providing access points for all documents in possession. On the other hand, eight libraries had fully catalogued their holdings. Majority of the libraries *i.e.* 11 (57.90%) were following Anglo American Cataloguing Rules-II and remaining 08 (42.10%) libraries were using Anglo American Cataloguing Rules-I for cataloguing. This reflects the popularity of dictionary catalogue over classified catalogue among college libraries.

NUMBER OF ENTRIES PREPARED FOR EACH DOCUMENT

Users may approach a document through different access points *i.e.* subject, author, title, etc. Table shows the number of entries prepared for each volume in libraries to provide access to their holdings.

Table 3.20 Number of Entries for Each Document

Sr. No.	No. of Entries Prepared	No. of Libraries	%
1.	One Entry	06	31.58
2.	Two Entries	09	47.37
3.	Three Entries	01	05.26
4.	All Possible Entries	03	15.79
	Total	**19**	**100.00**

Table 3.20 reveals that in 09 (47.37%) libraries, only two entries (Author and Title), and in 06 libraries only one entry for each document was prepared. Three librarians responded that they prepared all possible entries for each book in possession. Librarians were further asked to state the time taken to process new arrivals.

Table 3.21 Time Taken to Process Books from Date of Acquisition

Sr. No.	Average Time Taken	No. of Libraries	%
1.	Less than a Week	08	42.11
2.	1-2 Weeks	08	42.11
3.	More than Two Weeks	03	15.78
	Total	**19**	**100.00**

Table 3.21 depicts that in 08 libraries, it was taking 1-2 weeks to process new arrivals, whereas, in other 08 libraries books were being processed with in a week. Three librarians responded of

taking more than two weeks to process documents, due to inadequate staff. All libraries maintained card catalogue. Eight libraries using computers also prepared computer-based databases of books.

Five librarians mentioned the problems they faced in cataloguing, whereas, remaining majority responded otherwise. Three librarians complained of lack of professional staff and one of them further added that his college principal did not sanction funds even to purchase catalogue cards and cabinet. A librarian responded that they did not have catalogue code to get clarity in case of any doubt about cataloguing rules, while another shared that their library did not have standard subject heading list and they faced problem in assigning subject headings.

STOCK VERIFICATION

Stock verification, also known as physical verification brings to light the number of volumes missing from a library. It also helps to rectify the misplaced documents, and enable to take out books for repairing and binding. It has been found that 18 libraries were undertaking stock verification regularly, whereas in the library of UCE it was done since its establishment in 2001.

FREQUENCY OF STOCK VERIFICATION

Responses revealed that out of 18 libraries, 11 (61.11%) undertook stock verification once in two years, whereas in 07 (38.89) libraries it was undertaken every year. Majority of libraries *i.e.* 15 did stock verification during vacations and a library carried out it during the period of examination. A librarian responded that, 'It depends upon the availability of time' and another preferred to perform this job before the commencement of the new academic session. There are various tools to undertake stock verification *i.e.* stock taking registers, accession register, separate sheets with accession numbers, computers etc. Table depicts that out of the 18 libraries, 88.88 per cent were using stock verification register for this purpose. A library was using accession register for stock verification, while in a goverment aided college library computer was used for the purpose.

Table 3.22 Method Used for Stock Verification

Sr. No.	Method of Stock Verification	No. of Libraries	%age
1.	Stock Verification Register	16	88.88
2.	Computer	01	05.56
3.	Accession Register	01	05.56
	Total	**18**	**100.00**

AVERAGE LOSS OF BOOKS

Librarians were asked to mention the quantum of loss of documents suffered annually on an average. Responses received are tabulated below:

Table 3.23 Quantum of Loss of Books

Sr. No.	Average Loss of Books	No. of Libraries	%
1.	0-20	05	27.77
2.	21-40	07	38.89
3.	41-80	01	05.56
4.	No Loss	01	0.56
5.	Loss Not Calculated	01	05.56
6.	Not Specified	03	16.66
	Total	**18**	**100.00**

It is obvious from table that out of 18 libraries, in 07 (38.89%) libraries average loss of collection per year ranged from 20 to 40 books, whereas in 05 libraries it was below 20 documents. In a library average loss of documents went beyond 40. Three librarians had not specified any number representing loss of book, but responded that it was very low. A librarian responded that they never found any book missing from library. Another shared that they did stock verification every year, but never calculated the loss of books because of shortage of time and adequate staff, which makes stock verification useless.

RESPONSIBILITY FOR LOSS OF BOOKS

Responses revealed that in 14 libraries out of the 18 undertaking stock verification, missing books were written off against loss of books, while staff of four libraries responded that they were held responsible for the loss. On asking about the policy for writing off books, staff of 16 libraries responded that maximum three books were being written off for every thousand books with the permission of library committee. Whereas two librarians responded, "there is no such policy, library committee takes the decision for writing off books".

CIRCULATION SERVICE

Circulation is highly used service of a college library. Survey revealed that in 02 libraries 'demand boxes' were placed for B.Ed. students. The students were required to put slips in demand box giving details of needed books and their identification. The demand boxes were being opened next day morning to take out the needed books from almirahs for lending to students. Similarly, a library adopted slip system for lending books to B.Ed. students. In these libraries the M.Ed. students were entitled to borrow books at any time. The remaining 16 libraries had practice of lending books on the spot when demanded.

NUMBER OF BOOKS USERS WERE ENTITLED TO BORROW

An attempt was made to find the maximum number of books that a user could borrow from library at a time. Responses received are organised according to category of users.

B.ED. STUDENTS

No uniformity was found among libraries on the number of books that users were entitled to borrow at a time. Majority of the libraries *i.e.* 11 (57.90%) entitled users to borrow 03 or less books at a time, whereas remaining 08 (42.10%) libraries had this limit between 04-06 books.

M.ED. STUDENTS

Table 3.24 Number of Books Entitled to Borrow (M.ED. Students)

Sr. No.	No. of Books Being Issued at a Time	No. of Libraries	%
1.	1-3	02	13.33
2.	4-6	12	80.00
3.	7-10	01	06.67
	Total	**15**	**100.00**

Total 15 colleges were offering M.Ed. course in addition to B.Ed. in libraries of 12 (80%) of these colleges, users were entitled to borrow 04-06 books, whereas in two libraries they were allowed to borrow up to 03 books only at a time. In a goverment aided college library M.Ed. students were entitled to borrow up to 10 books at a time.

TEACHERS

Table 3.25 Number of Books Entitled to Borrow (Teachers)

Sr. No.	No. of Books Being Issued at a Time	No. of Libraries	%
1.	01-05	—	—
2.	06-10	06	31.57
3.	11-15	03	15.79
4.	15-20	01	05.27
5.	20-30	01	05.27
6.	No Limit	08	42.10
	Total	**19**	**100.00**

Table reveals that 08 libraries had no limit over the number of books a teacher could borrow at a time. Six libraries entitled teachers to borrow 06-10 books, while a library gave privilege to teachers to borrow up to 30 books at a time in case he or she was guiding M.Ed. students for dissertation.

LOAN PERIOD

Students

It has been found that majority of the libraries were lending books to B.Ed. and M.Ed. students for 14-15 days. In a goverment aided college library users were entitled to keep books with them for 07 days only. In case of M.Ed. students, a library had practice of lending books for a month.

Teachers

Ten (52.63%) libraries had not fixed any loan period for teachers. They were entitled to keep books with them as long as desired. Four libraries had practice of lending books for one month, while in 03 libraries teachers were privileged to retain books with them for the full session. A library had practice of lending books to teachers for the period of one year, while another fixed loan period as three months.

Table 3.26 System of Circulation

Sr. No.	System of Circulation	No. of Libraries	%
1.	Ledger System	17	89.48
2.	Browne System	01	05.26
3.	Computer	01	05.26
	Total	**19**	**100.00**

It is evident from the table 3.26 that 17 (89.48%) libraries were using ledger system for circulation of books, while one was using Browne system. In library of a goverment aided college computer was being used for circulation. In two libraries, B.Ed. students were allowed to borrow books during particular fixed time only.

In a goverment aided college library books were issued to students during the period of tea break and lunch break only, while in another library circulation time was fixed as 11 a.m. to 3.30 p.m., though the library was kept open for 9 a.m. to 4 p.m. In remaining libraries there was no such restriction of time for lending books to students. A few libraries had fixed days for different parts of students for circulation.

OVERDUE FINE

Sixteen (84.21%) libraries were charging overdue fine from users for return of books after due date, whereas remaining 03 libraries did not. Out of the 16 libraries charging overdue fine from students, 15 could not dare to charge it from teachers. Only UCE library was charging overdue fine from teachers for late return of books.

RATE OF CHARGES

Majority of the libraries were charging overdue fine from users at a nominal rate of ₹1 or less per book per day. It is interesting to mention here that in a goverment college library overdue fine was being charged from students @ Rs.10 per book per day.

RESERVATION OF BOOKS

Librarians were asked whether they had provision for reservation service in case the needed books were already issued to other users. Response revealed that majority of the libraries comprising 17 (89.48%) were providing reservation service to users, while remaining two libraries did not.

MOST USED COLLECTION

Responses revealed that in 17 libraries textbooks were used by students and teachers more frequently than other documents. Of remaining 02 libraries, a librarian responded that books of all categories were used equally, while, another shared that text books and reference books were used more frequently.

EXPECTATION OF THE INTERNET CONNECTIVITY

Responses of the library staff revealed that the users of 12 libraries did not expect the Internet connectivity in libraries because of its availability in computer labs, whereas 07 librarians responded that users do expect this service. Six libraries were already providing the Internet service to users. Librarians responded that users expect the Internet in libraries for academic purpose *i.e.* to access research papers and articles in the subject of education.

SERVICES

Our education system is becoming more and more complex. The classroom instruction alone cannot be considered sufficient to attain educational objectives. College libraries exist to supplement their parent institutions in achieving educational goals. Therefore, these are expected to provide the necessary services and facilities to users. Services provided by libraries under study are discussed here.

OPENING HOURS OF LIBRARIES

Opening hours of libraries have direct bearing on the use of their resources and services. Survey brought to notice that 15 (78.94%) libraries were being kept open for 6-7 hours a day, while remaining 04 (21.06%) libraries were being opened for 7-8 hours daily. Working hours of majority of the libraries coincided with class hours.

All libraries remained closed with colleges on Sunday and holidays, but were kept open during vacations. It has been found that during vacations also majority of the libraries were kept open for 6-7 hours a day, while a library remained open for 4-5 hours only. Three librarians shared that there was no specific timing for opening libraries during vacations.

REFERENCE SERVICE

Responses revealed that all libraries were providing reference service. Librarians were further asked to indicate the type of reference service being rendered.

Table 3.27 Provision of Reference Service

Sr. No.	Type of Reference Service	No. of Libraries	%
1.	Short Range	17	89.48
2.	Short Range and Long Range	02	10.52
	Total	19	100.00

Table 3.27 makes it clear that 17 libraries were providing only short-range reference service while two librarians accepted of providing long-range reference service also in addition to short-range reference service.

CURRENT AWARENESS SERVICE (CAS)/SELECTIVE DISSEMINATION OF INFORMATION (SDI)

Current Awareness Service is aimed at keeping users abreast with the latest developments in concerned field. As reported by librarians, 11 libraries were providing CAS, while remaining 08 did not. None of the libraries had provision for SDI service. Librarians were further asked about the methods of providing CAS. The responses received for multi-choice options are tabulated below:

Table 3.28 Method of Providing Current Awareness Service

Sr. No.	Method of CAS	No. of Libraries	%
1.	Display of List of Recent Acquisitions	03	27.28
2.	Recent Acquisitions Display	06	54.54
3.	Routing of Periodicals	05	45.46
4.	Verbal Discussion with Users	01	09.10

Table 3.28 reveals that majority of the libraries were providing CAS through display of recent acquisitions and 03 were rendering it by display of recent acquisition lists. Five libraries were circulating periodicals among teacher. A librarian shared that he provided CAS through verbal discussion with the users. But on the other hand, only one student of a college was familiar about this service.

BOOK EXHIBITIONS

Only 04 libraries were organising book exhibitions. Two librarians responded of organising these on the 'important occasions' *i.e.* Gandhi Jayanti, Maharishi Dayanand Anniversary etc. A library organised book exhibition on the occasion of annual convocation, while remaining one arranged that on the college functions. A few librarians invited booksellers to organise book exhibitions in their libraries. Three librarians responded of providing bibliographical services, while remaining responded otherwise.

PHOTOCOPY SERVICE

The NCTE provided in its norms and standards that a college library shall have photocopying facility. Only 08 (42.10%) libraries had provision of photocopy service, while remaining majority *i.e.* 11 (57.90%) did not. In majority of the libraries it was offered at a genuine rate of 50 paise to ₹1 per copy, whereas in a library photocopy charges were fixed @ ₹1.50 per copy for students and ₹1 for teachers. All libraries except one had no limit over number of pages a user could get copied at a time. The remaining library had fixed this limit to a maximum of 20 flashes.

RESOURCE SHARING

Resource sharing enables libraries to provide access to the users to the resources and services beyond their means and help to overcome the problem of paucity of funds. Only five libraries of GACE were participating in resource sharing programmes with other libraries. It has been found that resource sharing was limited to books only. These libraries were co-operating with the libraries of other institutes run by the same management.

REFERRAL SERVICE AND NEWSPAPER CLIPPING

Referral service is very useful as no library can acquire all the available information. Survey revealed that 14 libraries were providing referral service, while library staff of remaining 05 libraries responded otherwise. Staff of all libraries except one library had maintained newspaper clipping files of important newspaper articles on education and of news related to NCTE and their colleges.

ORIENTATION

Responses revealed that library staff of all libraries, except one was giving orientation to users towards libraries. Library staff was asked about the method of providing orientation. It is evident from table that in 55.56 per cent of the 18 libraries giving orientation to users, it was provided through lecture method, while in 03 (16.67%) libraries users were taken around libraries. In three libraries, a combination of the aforesaid methods was used to give orientation. In UCE library users were given orientation individually at the time of giving them membership. Response received is tabulated below:

Table 3.29 Methods of Providing Orientation

Sr. No.	Method Used	No. of Libraries	%
1.	Lecture	10	55.56
2.	Visit Around Library	03	16.67
3.	Notice Board	01	05.55
4.	Lecture and Visit Around Library	03	16.67
5.	Other Method	01	05.55
	Total	**18**	**100.00**

ACCESS

Open access is essential to facilitate maximum use of library collection. It gives users opportunities to browse documents on their own and enable them to find most relevant information. Survey brought to notice that only 05 libraries had open access system and 08 libraries were providing partially open access. The remaining 06 libraries had close access to collection. Fear of theft and lack of adequate number of staff members were the main reasons for following close access. During visit to DAV College of Education, Abohar it was observed that books were kept in almirahs touching the ceiling of library, leaving no scope for browsing.

USE OF COMPUTERS

The ICTs has greatly enhanced the efficiency of library services. Computers are used to provide various library services and perform the routine, repetitive and clerical jobs. The functioning of all types of libraries is influenced by this vital machine. Libraries of college of education are also adapting to this need of the day. It was found that out of total 19 libraries, 10 libraries had computers, while remaining 09 did not. Eight libraries were using computers for automation, and one had two computers to provide the Internet service.

In a library computer was kept aside in a corner without any use as library did not have any library automation software and the Internet connectivity. Librarians were further asked to indicate the softwares being used for library automation. The responses received from library staff of 08 libraries using computers for library automation are discussed here.

Table 3.30 Softwares being Used for Automation of Libraries

Sr. No.	Name of the Software	No. of Libraries	%
1.	SOUL	01	12.50
2.	CDS/ISIS	01	12.50
3.	WINSIS	01	12.50
4.	Alice for Windows	01	12.50
5.	Local	02	25.00
6.	Not Use Any Software	02	25.00
	Total	**08**	**100.00**

Table 3.30 shows that out of a total 08 libraries using computers for automation, 02 libraries were using locally developed softwares, while another implemented SOUL for automation. A library has implemented CDS/ISIS and other two were using WINSIS and Alice for Windows respectively. Two libraries had not used any library automation software but prepared databases of documents in 'Microsoft Word' and 'Microsoft Access' respectively. It was observed that majority of the libraries were using computer to perform housekeeping operations. All libraries were using computers to create databases of books. Five of these also created databases of journals, magazines and newspapers in addition to databases of books.

INTERNET

Majority of the libraries did not have the Internet connectivity, though the NCTE requires a library to have computer with the Internet facility for the use of faculty and student-teachers. Only 06 libraries were providing the Internet service to users.

ATTEMPTS TO PROMOTE USE OF LIBRARIES

Library staff of 17 libraries responded of making efforts to promote use of libraries, whereas in remaining two libraries no such attempts were being made. Both of these libraries did not have librarians and these were being run by restorers.

Library staff of 17 libraries responded of ascertaining information needs of users to improve the resources and services to promote use of libraries. Responses revealed that in three libraries, the library staff displayed the lists of recent arrivals and in six libraries they displayed the recent acquisitions to promote use of libraries. Librarians were further asked to indicate the methods used to ascertain information needs of users.

Table 3.31 Methods Used to Ascertain Information Needs of Users

Sr. No.	Methods of Ascertain Information Needs	No. of Libraries	%
1.	Discussion with Users	17	100.00
2.	Maintain Suggestion Box	06	35.30
3.	Record Queries	03	17.64
4.	Conduct Survey	02	11.77

It is obvious from table that discussion with users was the most useful method to ascertain their information needs, as the staff of all 17 libraries ascertaining information needs of users was using this method. In addition, 06 libraries had maintained suggestion boxes. Two librarians reported about conducting user surveys to ascertain the information needs of their users and take necessary action wherever applicable. Three librarians responded of maintaining record of users' queries. Inadequate staff was the major problem faced by librarians in promoting use of libraries. Nirie librarians expressed the need to appoint more staff to serve users effectively. A librarian of a goverment aided college not having adequate supporting staff in library commented "I remain busy in locking and unlocking almirahs throughout the day and do not get time for this.'

PROBLEMS FACED BY LIBRARIANS

Librarians were asked to express the problems being faced by them in managing libraries.

INADEQUATE STAFF

Lack of adequate staff was the major obstacle in functioning of libraries, influencing their organisation and administration. Nine librarians responded that they did not have adequate staff to serve the users. It has been found that three libraries were being run by restorers. Many GACE did not have the sanctioned posts of library restorers and library attendants. Librarians were overburdened with the non-professionals jobs due to lack of adequate staff.

PROBLEM OF SPACE

Some libraries including library of Goverment College of Educa-tion, Jalandhar were suffering from the problem of insufficient space. Only five libraries had separate reading room for users whereas, in remaining libraries chairs were arranged in stack area. A librarian complained of shortage of furniture.

PAUCITY OF FUNDS

Funds are the nerve centre of an organisation. Responses of the library staff of four colleges revealed that they were facing the problem of scarcity of funds for purchase of reading material.

Purchase of documents largely depended upon the UGC grants. The administration of colleges contributed less towards libraries. A librarian shared that they did not have funds even to purchase catalogue cabinet and cards.

STATUS

Society has not recognized librarians equivalent to teachers. Three librarians complained that they were not given equal recognition with teaching staff. In spite of the higher academic and professional qualification they were thought as a part of clerical staff. One of the librarians went to the extent of saying that they were on a par with the teachers in terms of salary only but not in status.

SUGGESTIONS OF LIBRARY STAFF

Library staff was required to give suggestions to improve the services of libraries to make them more effective. Library staff of 10 libraries made suggestions for the provision of more staff in libraries to serve the users, as majority of the libraries did not have adequate staff.

A restorer serving at a goverment aided college library, where post of librarian was vacant responded that college should appoint librarian to relieve her from the responsibility of managing library. Four librarians expressed the need for supporting staff to assist them in proper organisation of libraries.

Staff of five libraries suggested that libraries should be provided independent buildings to accommodate the growing collection and users. A librarian demanded the provision of adequate furniture in library. Library staff of four colleges suggested for the provision of adequate funds for purchase of reading material, furniture and equipment to make library services more effective. A librarian responded that he has computer in library, but it was not being used for any purpose as the authorities had not sanctioned the requisite funds to purchase library automation software. Three librarians suggested for computerization of library operations for effective functioning.

FUTURE PLANS

Librarians of only five colleges expressed their future plans regarding libraries, whereas library staff of majority of the colleges had not responded to questions. Librarians of DAV College of Education, Hoshiarpur and Dev Samaj College of Education for Women, Ferozepur City had plans to develop local area network with in college campus. They also planned to introduce the Internet service in respective libraries.

A librarian responded that he want to develop library as per the requirements of National Assessment and Accreditation Council (NAAC). Library of Khalsa College of Education, Amritsar had two computers to provide the Internet service. Its librarian was planning for automation of library operations using standard software. Similarly, two more librarians had plans to implement computers in libraries. One of them was interested in using SOUL software for library automation.

SUMMARY

To conclude, libraries did not have adequate staff leaving librarians overburdened with the semi-professional and non-professional jobs. Six libraries did not have regular librarians, having its influence on the organisation and administration of libraries. Moreover, the NCTE has not provided any detailed norms regarding library staff. It has been found that the functioning of library committees was restricted to acquisition and writing off missing books rather than the overall development of libraries.

Student's involvement in committees was almost absent, as only one college library had students' representatives as members of library committee. By and large libraries did not have any collection development policy. Analysis brought forward that teachers and principals were playing leading role in selection of documents, while librarians had little say in selection of subject related books. Availability of financial support influenced the collection size of libraries. Libraries of GCE had more volumes than libraries of GACE and UCE.

Non-book material was almost absent in libraries. A few libraries had CD's that came free with books, though the NCTE prescribed for colleges to have 'electronic publications' in collection. Many libraries did not meet the NCTE norms regarding annual addition of books and minimum number of journals on subscription. Only 05 libraries had separate reading rooms, while in remaining libraries chairs were arranged with in stack area.

The NCTE norms about library buildings need to be revised, as it requires each college to have library-cum-reading room. It was observed that in a goverment aided college library books were arranged on shelves touching the ceiling. When users need books they express their demand to library staff and then library attendant take out books from shelves using ladder. Except UCE, none of the colleges had provision for library budget. The UGC grants, library fee, library development fund and amalgamated fund constituted the regular source of finance.

The NCTE remained silent about financial provision for libraries. Survey revealed the lack of standardization for technical processing of collection. In 07 libraries, collection was partially classified, whereas in the library of a college established in 1942, collection has not yet been classified. Eleven libraries had partially catalogued collection. Eight libraries gave the privilege to the teachers to borrow as many books as they wish, while 10 libraries allowed them to keep books with themselves for as long as desired.

Shockingly, 02 libraries were using demand box system and another was using slip system for lending books to B.Ed. students. Majority of the libraries were being opened for 6-7 hours a day, leaving users with little time to use libraries. In addition to circulation, reference service was the only service provided by all libraries.

Eleven librarians admitted of providing Current Awareness Service (CAS), but on the other hand only one student and a few teachers were aware about this service. Eight libraries were rendering photocopy service. Libraries did not provide any advance library services. Only 08 libraries were using computer for automation of their operations. In addition, a library had 02 computers to provide the Internet service.

Only six libraries had the Internet connectivity, though the NCTE prescribed that college library should have computer with the Internet connectivity. Library staff of 17 libraries responded of ascertaining information needs of users to improve resources and services to promote use of libraries. Discussion with users was the most useful method to ascertain information needs of users. In addition, two librarians reported about conducting user surveys to find information needs of users.

Lack of staff and paucity of the funds were the major problems faced by librarians. Another major problem is related with the status of library staff *viz.*-a–*viz.* teachers, they feel that that they are not on a par with the teaching staff and this leads to frustration and apathetic mind set of library staff. It is in the hands of the library staff also to change this attitude and make a place for 161 themselves in the college. It was good to find that many librarians were planning to implement computers and provide the Internet services in libraries.

4

Building Library Resources and Services

INTRODUCTION

Like any other library in academic setup or research institutions, resources in adult education libraries have also to be planned, developed, and organised for access and retrieval. Besides, such libraries need to offer library and information services such as instructions in the use of library catalogue and reading materials, reference service, information dissemination, etc.

The procedures for building library resources and rendering library services and explains the procedures for library management. It discusses the techniques for classification and cataloguing of books and other reading material for information access and retrieval. In addition, it describes the services that a library in an adult education set up needs to offer its clientele. Let us now begin with a discussion on building library resources and services for adult learners.

BUILDING LIBRARY RESOURCES AND SERVICES

The libraries in adult education set ups are, by design, small budget libraries, confined to one room space, and adult education staff manages them manually on part time basis. Such members of adult educators who do not have any formal education and training in library and information science would find it easy and simple to learn library skills and apply them for building library collections and rendering library services.

They can take the following step-by-step approach:

- *Step 1:* Acquisition Procedures
- *Step 2*: Classification and Cataloguing Procedures
- *Step 3:* Library Services

STEP 1: ACQUISITION PROCEDURES

Library acquisition is about procedures for selection of published material for library acquisition, procedures for placing orders for purchase books and other reading material, their accessioning as well as of material received as gratis. It also about procedures for payment of bills, and about upkeep and maintenance of records as required for the purpose.

Procedure for Book Selection

The first step in book selection operations is to invite recommendations from users for purchase of new books and other reading material. For this, the library could take initiative by inviting books on approval from booksellers, or give users publisher catalogues for selection, or send them to visit book exhibitions. Based on this exercise, a tentative listing of useful books is complied.

The second step is to get the compiled list of books approved by the Library Advisory Committee. The Committee might approve it in total or shortlist it as per their judgement. While finalizing books and other reading materials for purchase, the Committee should pay special attention to the usefulness of the selected material, currency of information given in the books, their cost and availability of funds. The book selection exercise should be undertaken on regular basis through out the year, and not towards the end of the financial year once, just to exhaust book budget.

Procedure for Book Purchase

The second step in book acquisitions is to initiate action for placing orders with the approved vendors or booksellers for selected books. In this regard, the Library needs to obtain first the financial sanction of the competent authority in the organisation. It could be either head of the organisation, or its deputy or any other designated person for the purpose. For operational performance, it will be useful if the In-Charge Library is given financial authority to sanction expenditure, say, up to ₹5000/-only in respect of such books and other reading material as recommended by the Library Advisory Committee.

The library should by default purchase only latest edition of a book, unless desired otherwise specifically. Sometimes cheap editions of foreign books are printed. In such cases, it is advisable to go for cheaper editions only. However, if one of the roles of the library is to archive books for future, in such a case the library should purchase books printed on good quality paper. The Library may draw up a panel of vendors/booksellers as per following criteria.

It may purchase books from booksellers on the panel:

- Bookseller must have membership of the Delhi State Booksellers Association/Federation of Indian Publishers;
- Bookseller must have experience in the line for at least two years;
- Must have PAN Number from the Income Tax;
- The panel may be reviewed every year for performance on the parameters of relevance, quality and comprehensiveness of the books displayed for approval or on the parameter of efficiency and effectiveness with which the bookseller supplied books against order.

The next step is to place formal orders with approved for purchase of books. There is no need for inviting quotations since as per financial rules of the Government of India books are not store items. Purchase orders can be placed on the catalogue price of the book. As per standard practice, booksellers offer discount on the catalogue price of books, ranging from 10 to 15 per cent.

Books priced in foreign currencies are to be paid in Rupee currency. The foreign currency conversion is done as per bank's TT selling rate as prevalent on the day of the supply of books. Information about bank conversion rate can be had from newspapers such as The Economic Times, and The Financial Times. The booksellers are required to supply books along the bill in triplicate. One copy of bill is to be returned to the bookseller duly signed as a token of receipt of books supplied. The library should insist on price proof of the book and bank conversion rate from the booksellers before accepting the supply of books.

Accession of Books

Libraries need to maintain records of the books acquired in accession register. This register constitutes a permanent record of the library. Figure 4.1 below shows a sample outline of columns of an accession registers. Printed accession registers are also available in the market. Before accessioning, the library needs to physically check the books supplied against order in terms of latest edition, year of publication, and price. The next step in book acquisition is accession of books by making record entries in the accession register, wherein each book is assigned an accession number.

This number is reproduced later on several different pages in the book accessioned such as:

- Back of the title page–bottom portion,
- Secret page in a book. (This is a discrete page in a book which invariably carries its accession number. The secret page number is known only to the library staff and hence it is known as a secret page); and
- On the last page of the book; and on all the copies of the bill/cash memo.

Date	Accession Number	Author	Title	Ed	Place and Publisher	Year of Publi-cation	Vol	Pages	Cost	Vendor	Bill No and Date	Remarks

Fig 4.1 A Sample Outline of Columns of Accession Register

Printed accession registers are available in multiple of 1000 entries per register with a minimum of 5000 entries. Accession register starts from accession number 1 and goes up to 5000. Additional accession register, if required, should begin in continuation of the last accession number in the previous register. Avoid overwriting and cuttings of any kind in the Accession register.

The competent authority in the Library must affix a certificate in the beginning pages of the Accession Register certifying that

'This register contains...(so many) pages in which accession number run from...to....." While making entry in the Accession register it is advisable to use ink of lasting quality so that its colour doesn't fade away with the passage of time. The Accession register is a valuable document and must be kept under lock and key when not in use. After accessioning, books stamped bearing the name of the library. Book tag, book plate, book card pockets and due date slip are to be pasted at the appropriate places in the book as decided upon by the library.

STEP 2: CLASSIFICATION AND CATALOGUING PROCEDURES

Each accessioned book is classified, for assigning it a unique (numeric or alphanumeric) call number and catalogued to facilitate its access and retrieval from the card catalogue by author, title, subject and call number. The call number of the book is reproduced on the back of the title page, book plate and on the book card. The book card records necessary information about the book such as its accession number, author, and title. After verifying all these details, the book is released for circulation.

Classification

One of the major management tasks of the librarian is to organise the reading material for browsing, searching and retrieval by subject and language. The job of classifier involves giving each book in the library a unique numeric or alphanumeric number called 'Call Number'—as per library parlance. This number defines placement/shelving position of the book in the stacks. The other objective of call number is to bring books on the same subject together for browsing and retrieval.

According to Ranganathan a classified arrangement should be such that the library staff is able to:

- Locate a book demanded by a reader immediately even if the library has miles of shelves of books;
- Replace the book at its correct place on the shelf;
- Find out a proper place for a newly purchased book among other books on the same subject;

- Find a place for a new book on a new subject among the already existing books on related subjects.

Choice of the Scheme of Classification

Quite a few schemes of classification have been in use in libraries. These include Colon Classification, Dewey Decimal Classification, Universal Decimal Classification, and Library of Classification, etc. Some of the small libraries design and develop their local scheme of classification. Applying an established and widely used scheme of classification is always better than designing and developing a local one. This gives the library the benefit of continuity in experience in classifying documents and to build thereby the foundation for the future.

Most libraries use *Dewey Decimal Classification* (DDC). It is now running into 22nd edition. This speaks volumes about its popularity amongst libraries throughout the world. One of the advantages of using DDC is that it can be adapted to the needs of any large or small library. Its abridged editions are designed to meet the special requirements of small libraries. This schedule alone may not be found adequate to represent all the facets of a subject. Therefore, the use of the Standard Subdivisions of 1000 classes at times may be found necessary to separate a book from other books having the same ultimate class. These standard subdivisions are not in themselves class number and hence can't be used in isolation, but may be suffixed/and added to any number from the schedule.

Cataloguing

A library catalogue is a vital link between the reader and the book. It serves as the key to ascertain the availability of wanted book in a library and its physical location in the stacks. Conventionally, cataloguing of books in libraries is done by using standard cataloguing codes such as *Anglo-American Cataloguing Rules* (AACR), Classified Cataloguing Code.

According to these cataloguing codes, the levels of cataloguing differ from library to library. For example, a major library may apply for highest level of cataloguing, in which information that goes into the cataloguing entry is very extensive and detailed.

However, a small library set up—like the one in adult education organisations—could consider going in for lowest level of cataloguing, in which the elements that go into the cataloguing entry are minimal to ensure access and retrieval of a book by author, title, and subject. A sample catalogue entry using AACR2 code is given below for illustration. This entry is made on a model on 5"x3" cataloguing card.

Main Entry and Added Entry Cards

The cataloguing can be done by using cataloguing software or manually. If a library plans to go in for manual cataloguing, cataloguing entries are to be made on 5"x3" card catalogues. For every book, main entry as per sample given above is made. Additional entries are made in case the book has more than one author. Additional entries are also made for access by title and subject. For making added entry cards, main entry card is made in duplicate, and search element such as second author, title, or subject heading is imposed on the top of each duplicated card. For example, if there are two authors then there would one added entry card for the second author, the first author has already been given access point in the main entry card.

Catalogues are of different types such as author catalogue, title catalogue, or subject catalogue. Each catalogue type has catalogue entry cards arranged alphabetically. These different types of catalogue entries can also be merged together and filed in a single sequence. Such a catalogue is known as dictionary catalogue. For convenience in searching information from the cataloguing tray, for every bunch of 100 cards, guide cards is inserted. Appropriate starting letters in the alphabetical sequence are inscribed on the guide cards. The cataloguing tray can hold 1000-1500 catalogue cards.

***STEP 3*: LIBRARY SERVICES**

The services offered by libraries can be grouped as conventional library services and the services for promoting library use:

- Conventional Library Services
  - Library Rules

  - Circulation: Issue and Return of Books
  - Inter-Library Loan Service
- Service Promoting Library Use
  - Initiation/Orientation Service
  - Reference Service
  - Current Awareness Service
  - New Books Display
  - Thematic Display
  - Press Clipping Service

Let us first discuss conventional library rules and then deal with service promoting library use.

Conventional Library Services

Library Rules

Every library frames a set of rules for regulating its services to members. Rules are framed keeping in mind the library objectives and members interests. As far as possible rules should be explicit, free from any ambiguity.

The basic issues addressed in framing library rules are the following:

- Who can use the library?
- Opening and closing hours of the library
- How many books can a member borrow at a time?
- For how long can the member retain borrowed books?
- Conditions of loan, find for the late return of books, loss or damage of books during the loaned period
- Reservation of books
- Recall of issued books
- Renewal of loans
- Suspension of membership privileges
- Personal books/property counter, etc.

Circulation: Issue and Return of Books

Circulation means issuing books to valid members on loan, and canceling loans them from issue records upon return of books by members. It is one of the most important activities of a library from users' perspective. For managing circulation, the library needs a proper circulation system designed and developed for the effective control of circulation operations in terms of time per transactions, manpower deployment requirement, and accuracy in record keeping.

The manual systems currently in use are:

- 'Newark' system,
- 'Browne' system,
- 'Passbook' system.

Of all these systems, Browne system of issue and return is most popular for its efficiency in time per transaction. It is therefore important that a library in the adult education set up may apply Browne system for managing its circulation operations.

Browne System

In Browne system, the members are given Reader's Ticket(s) to enable them to borrow books from the library. The design of the reader ticket is such that it has a pouch on its front side. The pouch is used to hold Book card when a book is issued to a member. For every library book, a Book card is made. It is kept inside the 'Book Pocket' provided in the book. While issuing a book the Circulation-in-Charge simply removes the Book Card from the Book Pocket and inserts it in the Reader's Ticket pouch, puts in due date stamp on the date slip provided in the book.

The 'Book Card' coupled with the 'Reader's Ticket' is arranged behind date guides in the charging tray. This is the simplest of all the methods for issue and return of books. It reduces paper work in managing circulation transactions to the bare minimum. At the time of receiving books from the borrowers, Book card is separated from the Reader's Ticket and it is inserted back in the Book Pocket of the book received. At the close of the day, the issue record is got rearranged and filed behind Due Date guides. For books not received by due date, it is a good practice to send reminders to the borrowers for returning the overdue books. Secondly, the library may consider giving grace period to members before issuing such reminders.

Late Fine

Though it may be unfair to impose fines for the late return of borrowed books, yet it is essential in a library to enforce discipline amongst members. This is done mainly as a deterrent since the amount collected as fine is always very trivial. Formal receipt is, however, issued after realizing late fee money from defaulters in cash. As far as possible, a library in an adult education set up may not resort to this system unless it is warranted by circumstances.

Conscience Box

An alternative to fine system for late return of books is Conscience Box. This concept was designed and developed by Dr S R Ranganathan. In this method no formal receipt is issued to the borrower, instead money as overdue charges is dropped in the Consciences Box. The key to this Box always remains with the authority in the organisation. The Conscience Box is opened at a convenient time in the presence of several officials. The distinct advantage of this method is that it saves time and develops in members a feeling of civic sense and responsibility.

Reservation of Books

Books in heavy demand usually remain in circulation. Members in the waiting list could reserve such books so that they could get the priority in borrowing them upon their receipt in the library. The library informs the member in the waiting list about the availability of the reserved book.

Loss of Books

Books reported as lost by borrowers are required to be dealt as per library rules. Usually, the borrower is advised to replace the book with a new copy. If, however, the book is out of stock in the market, he may be asked to pay the current price of the book after getting it verified from the Publisher's catalogue or from trade bibliographies. The price may also be got ascertained from the Accession Register and formal receipt issued to the borrower. Necessary postings may be done in the Accession Register indicating in the Remarks Column about the 'Lost and cost realised vide receipt no…dated….'

Inter-Library Loan Service

Every library has a liaison with other libraries in the vicinity.

In case of urgent requirements, the resource of such nearby libraries could be harnessed for borrowing books on inter-library loan, or get a photocopy made of the wanted material. The library in the adult education set up could consider building such type of cooperative networks for the purpose.

Service Promoting Library Use

You can use the following devices to promote the use of library by adult members of a community.

Initiation/Orientation Service

For most of users, a visit to the library is the first encounter with the world of books. The users have to be made aware of the privileges they are entitled to as also the rules they are to follow to derive full benefits from the library. There are certain 'do's and don'ts which need to be explained to users at the time of their first formal visit to the library. This information is given to new members upon registration during initiation/orientation service. This service is also important for inculcating reading habits in neo-literates.

Reference Service

Reference service is a reactive service given to members on demand. In an adult education set up, the emphasis in reference service should be on giving knowledge and not just information or documents.

Current Awareness Service

For promoting library services, the library needs to offer proactive services such as current awareness service, selective dissemination of information service, etc.

Display

All the books added into the library stock must be put on display for limited period so as to bring them to the notice of all library users. On special occasions, such as birth day of an important author or leader, festivals, sport events, relevant books may be separated from the general sequence and put on a display to bring them to the notice of users.

Press Clipping Service

Newspapers are the most important sources of latest information. It would be most appropriate if the relevant cuttings of write-ups, editorials letters, statements, news items, events etc. are organised in some logical order for future reference and use.

TIPS FOR IMPROVING LIBRARY VALUE

The following useful tips may help you improve library value at your adult learning setup:

- The library collection must be kept relevant (*i.e.* it must be need based, and irrelevant material if any must be weeded out), current (*i.e.* it must offer latest and novel information), accessible (*i.e.* it must provide tools for such as catalogues, databases for access to information), and available (*i.e.* document wanted by users must be available on the shelf and success rate of the library in this regard should be at least 80 per cent);
- Organise customized information services and give information to users in the form that they can understand and use. For example, audio-visual media is most suitable form of information delivery to adult community lacking in literacy;
- Customized information services include information repacking (such as rehashing technical information for non-technical audience), information condensation (such as preparing abstracts, digests, summaries of useful documents for information dissemination), and information consolidation (such as state-of-the-art information giving an overview of the trends in the literature);
- Customized information services should aim at disseminating information for adding and updating knowledge of individuals, increasing their awareness on issues of interest to them;
- Use customized information services as a tool to enable the library to play its role as knowledge gatekeeper on topics of interest to the organisation and its clientele;

- Make library as a place for social interactions by organising discussions on issues of topical importance;
- Follow the best practices in library management, operations and services;
- Library operations and services must kept be efficient and library response time must not exceed users expectations;
- Increase the library penetration by enlarging its users base;
- Develop a special collection of books and publications frequently in use;
- Keep the library circulation current so that books do not remain with the borrower for more than a prescribed period of loan;
- Books not in circulation or not in use must be removed from the shelves and be considered actively for weeding them out;
- Organise library collections in classified sequence to facilitate information browsing, searching and retrieval by subject;
- Publish bibliographies on hot topics of interest to users
- Undertake user survey of library services on periodical basis to ensure that library services are focused and effective;
- Keep the library ambience pleasant and inviting;
- Develop networking with other libraries for sharing resources;
- Ensure regular training of library staff on library skills and procedures;
- For collections exceeding 10,000 volumes, the library must consider using any library management system for library automation.

LIBRARY AND RESOURCE CENTRE SERVICES

DEPARTMENT FOR THE BLIND AND VISION IMPAIRED

The Library and Resource Centre is a component of the Department for the Blind and Vision Impaired (DBVI) from which two fundamental programmes are administered. Library services are offered to persons, who are physically disabled, visually disabled, hearing impaired or reading disabled. Resource Centre services are provided to local school divisions to support education of visually impaired and blind children.

Library services are provided free of charge to eligible visually, physically and reading disabled persons by the DBVI Library, which is a member of the National Library Service for the Visually and Physically Handicapped network of the Library of Congress. The books and equipment are provided free to the affiliated libraries from The Library of Congress. Services are administered at the state and local level. The library collection includes books and magazines covering a wide range of topics and reading levels. Required playback equipment and accessories are also furnished. Books and equipment are mailed to and from eligible persons using the "free matter for the blind" mailing privilege.

A variety of Resource Centre services are provided to blind and visually impaired children and vision professionals in the Commonwealth. The Centre houses an inventory of adaptive equipment that is distributed to blind and visually impaired infants, children and youth throughout the state. The Resource Centre also provides textbooks and novels for use by blind and visually impaired students in their local school districts. Textbooks are produced or purchased from another state, and loaned for the school year. Services also include transcription of special materials, and the provision of resource and reference services for instructional materials.

The Reading Room of the Library and Resource Centre is open for public use. It offers materials in adapted formats for browsing and research, a collection of professional materials, computer work stations with adaptations for visually impaired and blind individuals, an adapted internet connection, closed circuit televisions for enlargement purposes, and scanning capabilities.

5

Administration of Circulation Services

The circulation department's primary function is to supply the library user the books, pamphlets, serials, and other materials wanted. Jennie M. Flexner reports that four major functions comprise circulation work: the staff must have a familiarity with the holdings of the library, a knowledge of the needs and interests of the users, an appreciation of the techniques employed in carrying out the service policies of the institution, and a willingness to cooperate with the other departments of the library.

In many respects, the circulation desk is the library's reception room as well as its book distribution and information centre. Indeed the users frequently judge the library and its administration by the general atmosphere and level of service at the circulation desk. It is curious that, despite its nerve centre role, the circulation desk has been accorded relatively little attention by writers on library techniques. The lack of information regarding the service requirements of students and faculty members in colleges and universities has been noted by L. W. Dunlap.

Circulation work is discussed in a stage in G. R. Lyle: while L. R. Wilson and M. F. Tauber use a single part to treat reference, circulation, stack, extension, and other services. *Technical Services in Libraries* devotes but three out of twenty-two stages to circulation work.

The circulation department, being responsible for loan services, usually maintains a record of all loans, keeps a file of registered borrowers, provides machinery for the recall of overdue items and for reserving titles in demand, supervises the shelving of material in the stacks, and arranges extension, interlibrary, and public relations services.

The organisation of the circulation department depends upon the size of the library, the scope of its work and the degree of departmentalization. Each type of library-public, college, university and special-has particular needs and the organisation must reflect these needs. While every circulation department must be organised to give speedy and efficient service, this goal must be regarded as a means rather than an end in itself.

In the college and university, the end is to advance the instructional and research programmes; in the special library it is to further the successful operation of the business or profession; in the public library field:

- To facilitate informal self-education of all people in the community;
- To enrich and further develop the subjects on which individuals are undertaking formal. education;
- To meet the informational needs of all;
- To support the educational, civic, and cultural activities of groups and organisations;
- To encourage wholesome recreation and constructive use of leisure time.

In small libraries all the administrative duties, including those of the circulation department, are assumed by the librarian. He selects and organises the staff, establishes the policies, outlines procedures and routines, and supervises the work of the staff. In larger libraries a department head, responsible to the librarian, assumes these administrative duties. In the very large libraries the circulation chief may report to an assistant librarian or a division supervisor, representing the circulation staff in dealing with the public and with higher library authorities.

The traditional library, with its large central stack, has a central circulation desk which takes care of most circulation routines. The college or university library in this type of organisation usually has supplementary service points including a periodical room, reserve desk, and departmental libraries. The large public library has its branches, deposit stations, and bookmobile service. The divisional type of library has major service posts in each division as well as a central loan desk for general circulation. Whatever the type, of library there should be a centralized organisation to provide uniform loan and public service practices in all parts of the library system.

The librarian in charge of the circulation department, no matter what the size or type of organisation, must be aware of the latest ideas and techniques employed in this field. He must constantly examine the methods used in his own library, in relation to new developments and to the quality of service called for in his particular situation. Indeed the entire circulation staff should be encouraged to make recommendations for simplifying records and operations. The layout of the department-lighting, furniture, supplies and equipment—will demand the attention of the department head.

Policies regarding service to users, including hours of opening, borrowers' privileges, interlibrary loan privileges, fines, lost books, and similar factors should be set down in writing. The department head should be thoroughly conversant with the basic aims of the library as well as with the community or institution it serves. Changes in methods or policies should be made with the help of the best advice within the department. At all times he must consider the effect of proposed changes on interdepartmental relations and on the basic aims of the library as a whole. Internal department rulings should be made after appropriate staff conferences, but changes affecting other departments or the library as a whole should not take place until there has been full discussion by all the staff members involved and until the new policies have been approved by the librarian.

While the importance of circulation work and its role in influencing the users' opinion regarding the quality of the library's service has been acknowledged by writers from Melvil Dewey to Bernard Berelson's there is need for the circulation chief to organise the work of the department so that the professional and clerical aspects of the work are kept separate. The routine work of charging and cancelling books, filing cards, shelving books, as well as the handling of reserves, overdues, and renewals can best be assigned to the clerical staff. The professional staff should be engaged in establishing policies, working with and advising the users, improving relations with the public or, in the case of the college or university, with the faculty and departments. The supervision of the staff and the maintenance of good inter-departmental relations within the library are key responsibilities of the professional worker.

The qualifications necessary for the department head and the other professional members of the staff will vary depending upon the size and type of library. Standards for college and university libraries are noted in *Classification and Pay* Plum *for Libraries in Institutions of Higher Education.* The new public library guide sets forth principles and standards of service. The clerical and part-time workers of a loan department should be selected for their ability to get along with people as well as for their competence in performing the necessary routine tasks. The public relations function of people working at service points must constantly be kept in mind.

There should be active cooperation between the members of the circulation staff and the other units of the library system. Each person on the staff should be given an opportunity to get a good over-all picture of the workings of the entire library. A training programme should be arranged to broaden the experience of the staff so as to insure maximum flexibility. Some libraries arrange for a regular interchange of staff between departments. Because the circulation staff represents the library to the users from whom it receives complaints and suggestions, it can be helpful to other units in the library's organisation.

In a well integrated library the members of the circulation staff will regularly lend assistance to the reference, acquisition, and catalog departments. Well-trained clerical and professional assistants can take care of the quick reference, informational, and directional service, thus relieving the reference staff so that it can devote its time to the more serious and time-consuming questions. Such cooperation will also eliminate to some degree the all-too-frequent complaints of library users who dislike being shunted back and forth between service units to get answers to simple requests.

The circulation department workers can assist the acquisition department by sending along promptly the titles of new books recommended by the borrowers. In the course of readers' advisory work, formal or informal, the circulation staff learns of new areas of subject interest which might not be covered adequately by the library's holdings.

Prompt referral of these deficiencies to the acquisition staff and fast action in supplying these lacks result not only in good service but also in doing much to increase the library's prestige. In the public library field these requests can come from individual citizens, organised clubs, or from the needs of a vigourous adult education programme. In the college and specialized libraries similar requests come from new course and research needs as well as from individuals.

The public service person is in a very good position to help the library to interpret the catalog. If the problems and difficulties encountered in the day-to-day use of this important bibliographical tool are passed along to the catalog department, adjustments and improvements can be made. An integrated approach to better service might well produce suggestions for new subject headings and references.

The chief administrator in the department must see that sufficient instruction is given to accomplish the tasks. The achieving of this goal requires a careful analysis not only of duties but of personnel if satisfactory assignments are to be made. Each new staff member must be given a clear understanding of working conditions, work week, weekly schedules, vacation and sick-leave benefits, regulations regarding time lost by tardiness and other causes, social security, and the availability of hospital and surgical benefit plans.

The level of public service depends upon the punctuality of staff members and their careful carrying out of all assignments. Attendance records should be kept for tax as well as for administrative purposes. Staff morale will depend upon the fair and equal enforcement of all rules and regulations. Each employee should be made aware of the proper channels for making complaints and criticisms.

In addition to the initial instruction and in-service practice, the use of a staff manual is recommended. Here one finds outlined the circulation procedures, samples of all forms used, as well as a record of decisions made. Staff meetings should be held regularly to discuss problems and matters of policy. In larger libraries it might be desirable to have meetings of part heads in addition to meetings of the entire professional staff. Separate meetings of the clerical staff and of the part staffs can also be useful to administrators. In every size library, benefits can be derived from general meetings of the entire circulation staff especially if everyone is encouraged to comment freely.

Statistics play an important part in helping the administrator, governing board, or appropriating body to measure the success of the library. While librarians stress the fact that quantitative statistics of transactions, books, periodicals, records, and micro-films, tell only a partial story of circulation operations, nevertheless it is frequently the only method of demonstrating the library functioning to the general public. Regular review of the types of statistics kept should be made to ensure that they serve a clear and useful purpose. Spot checks can be made for information not needed regularly. In addition, libraries should be prepared to gather and report statistics on circulation services to recognized statistics gathering agencies.

Data recorded by the circulation department should include controlled studies to provide unit costs for the various activities in the department. For example in the college and university field one might want to know what it costs to circulate a reserve book; in another library the comparative costs of servicing different types of materials, books, periodicals, and recordings, could be found useful. Basic work statistics are useful in charting the flow of work; a word of caution is always in order regarding the danger of valuing statistics for their own sake, a costly and time-consuming occupation.

If comparatively little has been written about the circulation desk itself, less has been done concerning the role of the staff as public relations representatives for the library. Quite apart from *the* normal courtesy, tact, and service, we must accept the fact that all library users are public relations conscious whether they are aware of it or not. A faintly cynical article, "Public Relations—the Invisible Sell" should serve to remove the blinders from even the most naive librarians. In the public service area the problems of overdue books, fines, lost books, and mutilation afford many opportunities for the staff to concern itself with the library's public relations.

It requires patience, undoubtedly, to explain to the borrower that fines are not money-making schemes, that lost books must be replaced, that mutilation (if detected) is the equivalent of a lost book. It requires even more patience to explain to an interested borrower that his recommendation for a book must be denied. The careful explanation for the denial, whether verbally or in writing, is the library's responsibility to itself; a peremptory 'no' is a loss in good public relations, a failure on the part of the library to make known its needs and its problems.

Fines are considered by some librarians as a source of income but generally the purpose of a fine system is to ensure the prompt return of books by the end of loan period. The non-return of books when due interferes with the right of other borrowers and results in a poorer level of service. There is no standard fine schedule in use in public libraries. A rate of from two to five cents per volume per day (holidays and Sundays generally excluded) has been generally adopted, and many libraries establish a maximum fine. Children are frequently assessed a smaller fine, and some communities have experimented with grace periods during which overdue books may be returned without penalty.

The administrator of the public service unit must have the training and experience necessary to evaluate the latest technical advances, to establish satisfactory policies for the use and the care of the book collections, and to select and supervise the staff required for this job. Above all he must have the ability to instill in his staff those qualities which make the library a dynamic institution.

Much of his concern will involve him in the supervision of routine; it may be even more difficult for him to preserve his sense of the human equation. He would do well to remember that: 'The only excuse for the perfection of routine processes is that they shall contribute to a fuller and better development of the library's essential services.' This means not the custodianship of books nor the mere providing of books as they are wanted but also, as noted by Justin Winsor, "...in inducing an improvement in the kind of reading."

6

Conservation Book Repair

INTRODUCTION

Most of a public library's resources are spent on collecting, cataloguing and circulating material. While much effort goes into acquiring books and paper materials, little follow-up occurs in caring for that same material. Book and paper materials receive a great deal of use: they are pulled off the shelf roughly, stuffed into backpacks, forced onto photocopiers and dumped into book drops. In addition to ongoing patron and staff use, the books in a library collection are constantly aging; many are expensive and difficult to replace.

Caring for a library collection is a large task. Each library, regardless of size, must choose how to care for its collections. Successful book repair is an important component of a collection development and maintenance programme. In the past, maintaining a library collection was usually accomplished with plastic tape and household glue. Unfortunately, these products do not lead to successful repairs. Books return for repairs again and again or are discarded when they are damaged beyond repair.

In many cases, the fault lies with the repair choices, not the book. The basic concepts used in conservation book repair, such as using materials that are stable and reversible, were originally introduced to care for rare book collections. These same practices and materials can be successfully adapted to repairing non-rare books, and it is the intent of this manual to teach these techniques for use in circulating and reference collections.

USING THIS MANUAL

While it can be difficult to learn practical, hands-on skills from a book and tempting to jump right into a repair technique without reading the introduction, Please resist the urge. The introduction to each technique explains how to choose a particular technique and why that technique works while others do not. With a solid understanding of these principles and techniques, it is possible to quickly evaluate damaged books and choose the treatment that will lead to a successful repair.

CHOOSING BOOKS TO REPAIR

Choosing which books to repair is the first step in any successful book repair programme. Because each library is unique, one library's guidelines for retaining or repairing books may be very different from another's, Taking the time to create guidelines that are realistic and consistent with the needs of a collection can insure the well being of library materials and the effective use of staff time.

Before choosing to repair a book, ask questions such as:

- Is this book a candidate for weeding? Is the information misleading or has it been superseded by a new edition or a better book on the subject? Is the information trivial, of no discernible literary or scientific merit or irrelevant to the needs and interests of the library's patrons?
- Has the book previously been repaired using improper or damaging techniques? Is the book worn beyond mending or rebinding? Should this book be replaced or sent to the bindery? Is it easier and cheaper to purchase a replacement copy rather than repair the old volume?

It can be a difficult decision to not repair a book. However, the urge to save every book is unrealistic because some books cannot be effectively repaired and should be replaced. Learn to choose the books that can be repaired and those that cannot so the library collection will be in better condition and staff time will be better utilized. Choosing the proper repair for a book and carrying out that repair takes knowledge and skill. In a small library, the person who makes the repair decision will probably be the person who repairs the book.

In a larger library, that process might be shared by two staff members, in which case, both people need to understand the principles of book construction and repair. After deciding to repair a book, choose the best kind of treatment.

If a volume is to be replaced or withdrawn after one more circulation or when a replacement is purchased, mending it quickly using non-conservation repair methods such as clear plastic tape, might be an option. If the book is needed for a longer period of time or is part of a permanent collection, always repair it using conservation repair techniques such as those outlined in this book.

DETERMINING WHY A BOOK NEEDS REPAIR

It is important to determine why a book needs repair:

- Has it been damaged through carelessness or simply through use?
- Was it manufactured in a way that caused the damage?
- Has an old repair failed or caused more damage?
- How have previous repairs hindered the mechanics of the book?

Look at the kind of paper used in the book and how the book is constructed:

- Is the book constructed in signatures?
- Is the book constructed in single sheets glued or over sewn together?
- Is the paper coated and shiny?

All these factors should be considered when choosing to repair a book and deciding what techniques to use.

PLANNING REPAIRS AND THE WORKSPACE

- Read the directions for any repair thoroughly before attempting the repair.
- Make sure the workspace is large enough to work comfortably. Clear away excess objects and have the tools and materials needed close at hand.

- Think about where the repaired books will dry. Materials that are glued or pasted must dry under weight or the paper will buckle.
- If the book has several problems, start with the simplest and work towards the most complex. In general the text block is repaired first then the cover. The last part of the book to be repaired is the attachment of the text block to the cover.
- Try to group similar types of repairs together. In addition to saving time and materials, repeating the same repair several times is a good way to improve repair techniques.

PRACTICING REPAIRS

- Initially, it's a good idea to practice each repair either on a book that has been withdrawn from the collection or on plain paper. Different types of paper and different book structures will react differently to the paste or glue. For instance, shiny, coated paper will not absorb as much moisture as uncoated paper so less paste is used on the latter kind of paper.
- Read the explanation and instructions before beginning a repair. Take time to assemble all the tools and materials called for in the instructions.
- Reread the instructions after practicing a repair two or three times. They will probably be more understandable and some questions that came up during the repair may be answered. Once it is clear why and how a repair works, it is easier to choose a technique to match a particular repair need and not rely on the written instructions.

The materials and techniques used in conservation book repair should not damage books and, if a repair is not successful, it can usually be reversed and repeated. Be aware of your skill level and limitations. If a repair is too advanced, wait until you have more experience. Practice these techniques to improve your skills. Above all, keep working.

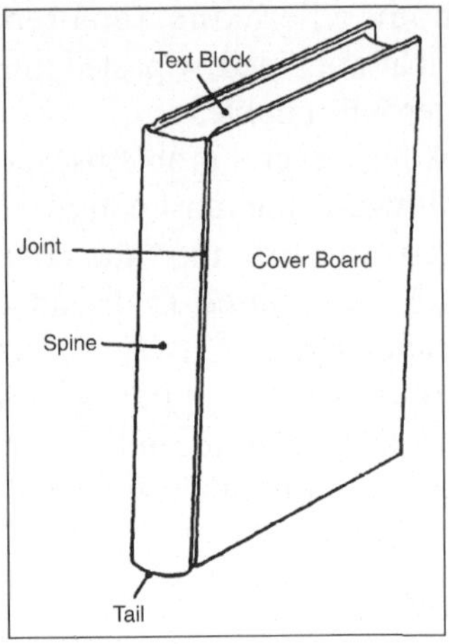

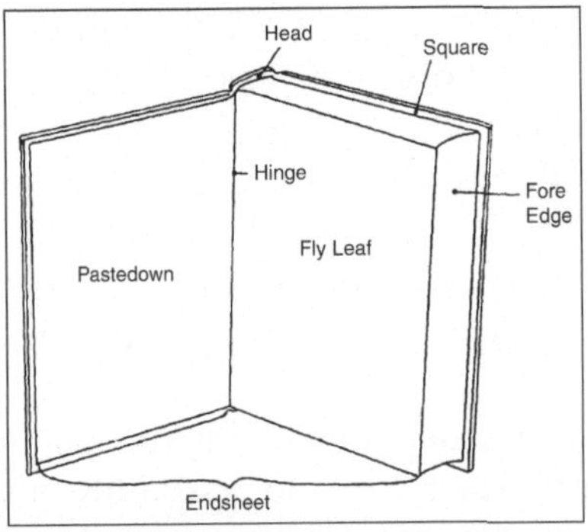

THE BASIC INFORMATION

Understanding book construction, the materials used to repair books and the proper way to handle tools are important components of a successful repair programme. Books are constructed in several ways. Many repair materials work best on certain kinds of paper or in specific parts of a book. "The right tool for the right job' is an axiom that applies to book binding as well as other fields. Having a few specialized tools and understanding how to use them will save time and energy.

BOOK STRUCTURE AND CONSTRUCTION

The pages of a book, whether they are sewn or glued

together, are called the text block. The covers of a book are called the case. The case is made of the front cover, the spine and the back cover.

Text Blocks in Signatures

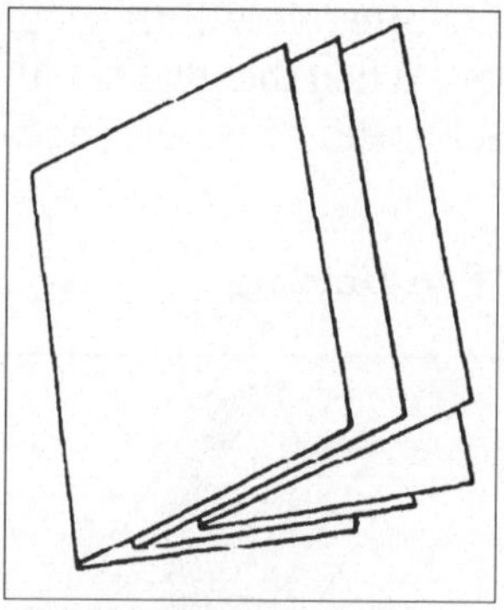

When the text block is sewn, the pages are gathered together in groups; then each group is folded in half.

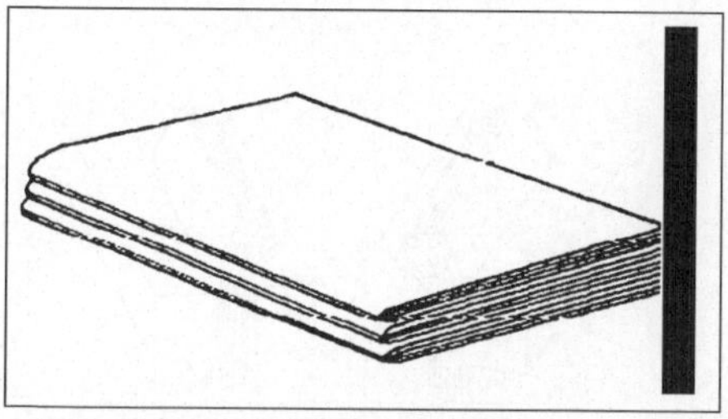

A group of folded pages is called a part or signature and is usually four to eight pieces of paper. Books that are constructed of sewn signatures tend to function best because the pages are securely attached to one another and they open flat. Modern manufacturing techniques enable book manufacturers to create a text block with signatures, cut small notches in the folded edge and insert glue to hold the pages together instead of sewing thread. These books look like they are sewn, but they are not. Open the text block to the centre of a signature and look for the thread, if it's not there, the book is glued.

Text Blocks in Loose Sheets

Text blocks can also be single sheets glued together in a

process called adhesive, perfect, or fan binding. In this process, fast drying glue is applied to the spine of the text block. Adhesives that dry very quickly are often brittle and that is why the spine of a book cracks when the book is opened. Once the spine glue is cracked, the pages will begin to fall out. In addition to the problem of brittle glue, there is often very little glue attaching each page to the adjoining pages. When the glue is only in contact with the very thin edge of each sheet of paper, pages can easily separate over time.

Single and Double Fan Binding

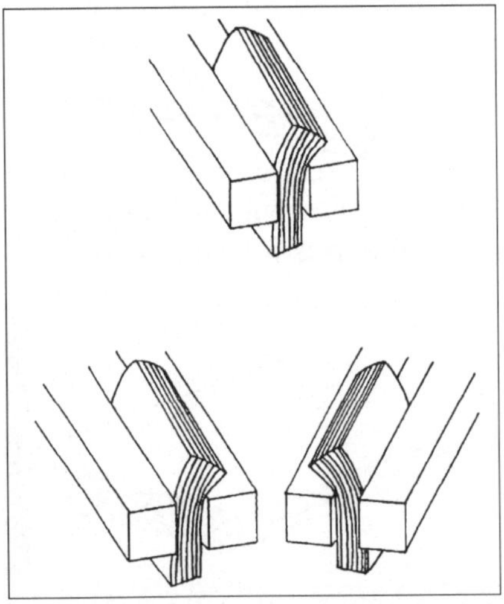

In single-fan binding, the pages of the text block are fanned in one direction and glued along that fanned edge. In this style of binding, a thin line of glue penetrates the inner margin of each page, not just the spine edge. Double-fan adhesive binding goes another step beyond single-fan binding. After the pages are fanned in one direction and glued, they are also fanned in the opposite direction and glued along the second fanned edge.

Double-fan binding applies glue on the inner margin of each side of the page, not just on the spine edge or the inner margin of one side of the paper. It is much stronger than single-fan binding. When library binders bind a book using double fan binding, they use adhesives that dry slowly and flexible. In addition, they usually reinforce the spine edge of the adhesive bound text block with cloth and paper so it is stronger and the text block opens flat. A library binder can be a good source of information to understand the binding processes.

Keep in mind the bindery is selling a product and as the customer, you can question the binder until all the techniques are fully explained. The services offered must meet the specifications that a library has defined for its collections. In order to set minimum levels of excellence in library binding, the Library Binding Institute has published the Standard for Library Binding. This booklet explains the different types of bindings and what standards should be met in library bound books. The Guide to the Library Binding Institute Standard For Library Binding written by Jan Merril-Oldham is a plain English explanation of the Standard.

Oversewn Text Blocks

Before library binderies began to fan bind books, the most common form of library binding was oversewing. In the oversewing process, the folds of the signatures are trimmed off and the pages of the text block are oversewn to one another with a diagonal whip stitch.

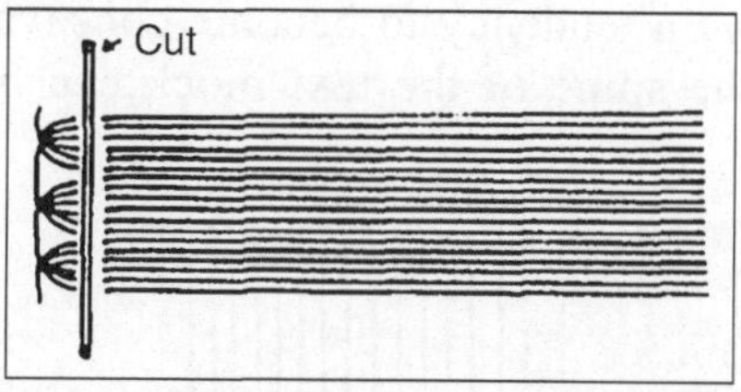

Since the sewing threads tend to pierce deep into the inner margin, the pages are restricted from turning easily.

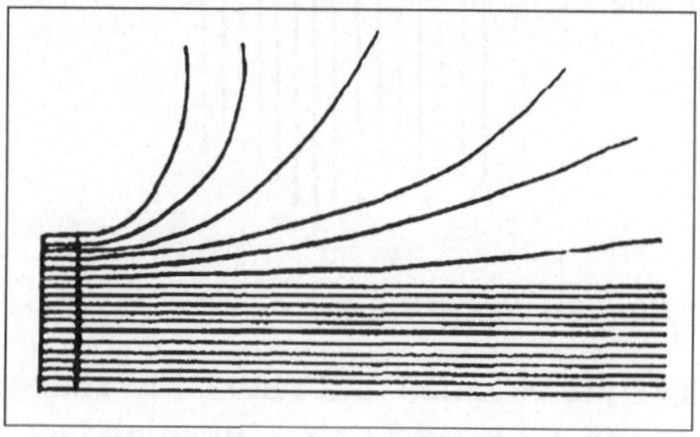

Oversewing is a strong form of binding, but it is often so strong that over time the pages can break out of the binding as they are forced to turn against the sewing threads. Oversewn books may not be candidates for rebinding since much of the inner margin was trimmed off or damaged by the oversewing threads.

Books should not be oversewn unless they are very heavy and have wide gutter margins to accommodate the sewing threads. Many libraries stipulate their binders must have permission to oversew a volume.

Sewn Text Blocks: Flat Back and Rounded and Backed Text Blocks

The pages of a book attached together by sewing or gluing is called a text block. Before a text block is attached to a paper or book board case, it can be treated in several ways.

Flat Back Text Blocks

Flat back books are a type of binding which has a flat text block spine. The case spine of flat back books is usually a piece of book board covered with book cloth. The spines of flat back text blocks have a tendency to become concave over time. To prevent this, the spine of the text block can be rounded and backed.

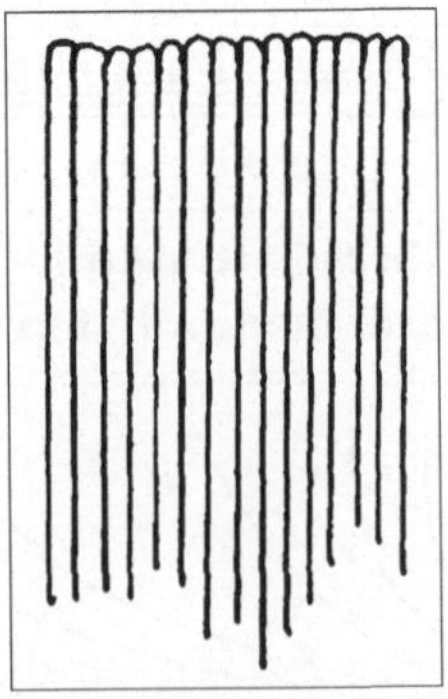

Rounded and Backed Text Blocks

Text blocks are rounded and backed to shape the flat spine of a text block into a curved spine with shoulders

Reprinted from
Bookbinding and the
Conservation of Books

Rounding a text block is the process of molding the spine of a text block into an arc of approximately onethird of a circle. Rounding takes place after the pages of the text block are attached to one another by sewing or gluing. A light coat of adhesive is applied to the spine which is then worked into shape with light pressure, applied with your fingers or a special hammer called a backing hammer. Backing is the process of shaping a ridge or shoulder on each side of the spine of a text block prior to attaching the spine lining material.

Reprinted from
Bookbinding and the
Conservation of Books

Using a backing hammer, the folds of each signature or glued pages are bent over from the centre to the left and right until shoulders are formed against which the boards will fit. The width of the shoulders is determined by the thickness of the cover boards. In addition to providing space for the cover boards, backing also distributes the swell caused by the sewing threads or adhesive and helps maintain the round of the text block over time.

Book Case Construction

Regardless of how the text block is assembled, modern books are usually manufactured in two stages.

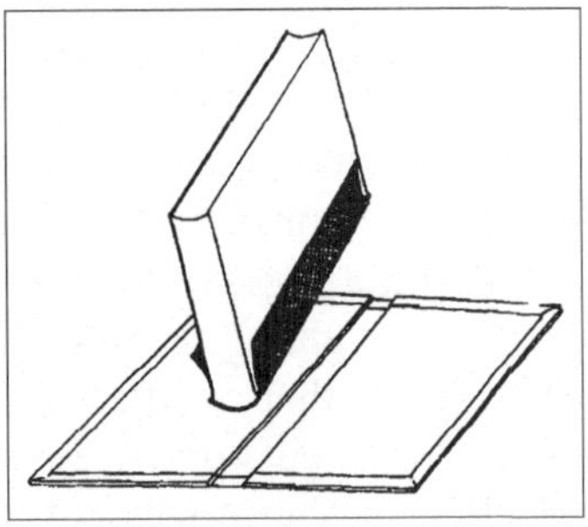

The text block is constructed in one operation where the pages are attached to one another, the spine covered with a cloth liner, called crash, and a paper spine liner is added over that. The book case, consisting of a front cover, a spine and a back cover, is constructed separately in a second operation and the two parts of the book are attached by gluing the crash and end papers to the case covers. The crash holds the text block into the case while the end papers cover up the crash.

PAPER AND BOOK CLOTH

Many types of paper or book cloth can be used in manufacturing, binding and repairing a book.

Paper

Although many different types of papers are used to print and manufacture books, three important types of paper to be familiar with in book repair are uncoated paper, coated paper and acid-free paper.

Uncoated Paper

Uncoated paper is the most common type of paper and is made from plant or tree fibres that are processed into sheets. Originally, most uncoated paper was handmade from linen or cotton rags. These older papers age very well because they contain few damaging chemicals. In the 1860s, a process was developed to turn cellulose fibre from trees into paper. This type of paper can be made in large quantities but contains some very damaging chemicals that cause paper to become brittle more quickly than paper made from cotton or linen.

Coated Paper

A sheet of paper can be impregnated with very fine clay to produce a very fine printing surface. Introduced at the end of the 19th century, coated papers is ideal for printing halftone illustrations. Unfortunately it is not very strong and is highly susceptible to water damage. Often the text pages of a book are printed on uncoated paper while the pages that contain illustrations are printed on coated paper. The coated paper may be part of the signature or tipped onto a page uncoated page.

Acid-free Paper

Acid-free is a designation given to paper that has a pH value of 7.0 or greater on a scale of 1 to 14. Fibres from any source can be made into paper that is acid-free. Both coated and uncoated papers can be acid-free. Acid-free paper used in conservation book repair includes photocopy paper and Japanese repair tissue.

Book Cloth

Book cloth is a specially woven cloth backed with thin paper. The paper backing gives the cloth support, minimizes stretching and allows the material to maintain a crease.

There are three main categories of book cloth:

- Starch-filled book cloth in which the weave of the cloth is filled with starch. This type of cloth is sometimes called sized book cloth;

- Acrylic-, pryoxylin-, or vinyl-impregnated book cloth;
- Plastic coated book cloth.

Heavier book cloth is sometimes called buckram.

Paper and Book Cloth Grain

Paper and book cloth have a grain just as fabric does and it is important to understand how that grain affects repairs.

Reprinted from Library Materials Preservation Manual

When the grain of the paper and book cloth runs parallel to the spine of the book, the cover and pages open freely and stay open without much effort. This is called 'with the grain'. Paper that is bound into a book with the grain running perpendicular to the spine of the book is called 'against the grain'. Modern publishers often print the pages of a book against the grain to get more pages on a large sheet of paper.

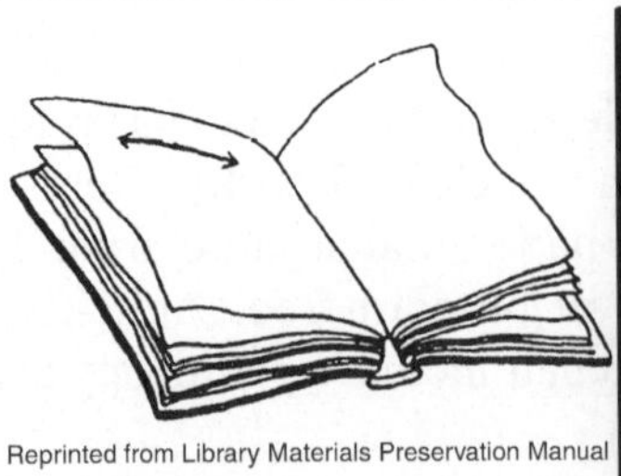

Reprinted from Library Materials Preservation Manual

When the grain runs perpendicular to the spine of a book, the book can be difficult to open and it will not remain open without a great deal of pressure. Books printed against the grain are easily damaged since patrons must force the book open to read or photocopy it. When pages or the case of a book are repaired, the grain of the repair materials should always run parallel to the spine of the book.

Determining the Grain of Paper or Book Cloth

All paper and book cloth has a dominate grain. Paper can be tested for grain using the bend test, the tear test or the water test. The grain of book cloth usually runs parallel to the selvage or bound edge of the fabric. If the selvage of the book cloth has been cut off or if there is any doubt about the grain of book cloth, the bend test or the tear test can be used to determine the grain.

Bend Test

The quickest way to test the grain is to bend the paper or cloth slightly in each direction.

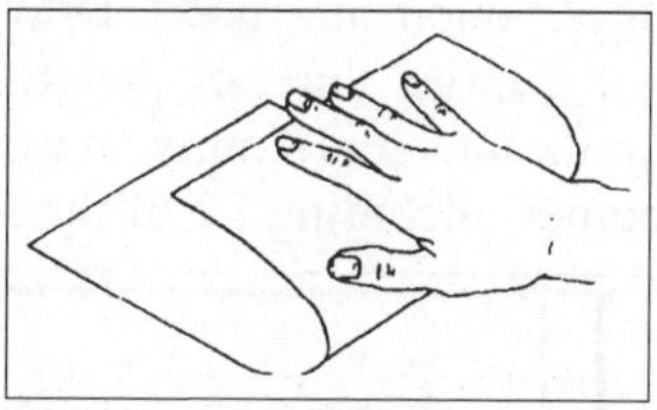

Bring two opposite edges of a piece of paper or cloth together but do not crease. Instead, gently press down on the bend with minimal pressure. Feel any resistance Now bring the other two opposite sides of the paper or cloth together and repeat the process. In one direction there is more resistance than the other. The greater resistance means the paper or cloth does not want to bend in that direction because it is bending against the grain. When the paper or cloth is bent in the opposite direction, there is much less resistance. The bend that offers the least resistance is the bend that goes with the grain of the paper or book cloth. Mark the direction of grain on the paper for future reference.

Tear Test

Another way to test for the grain is to tear the paper or cloth.

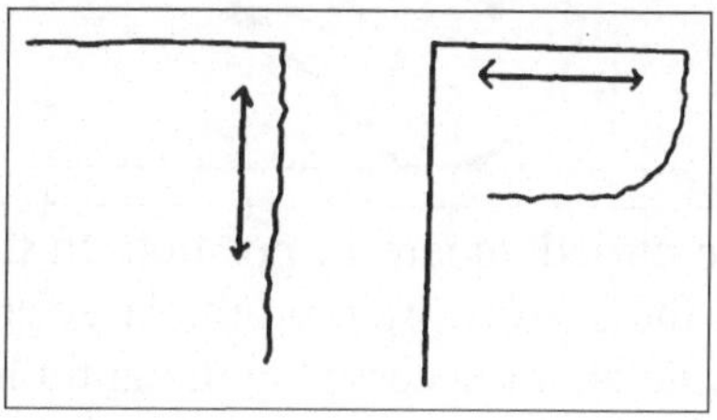

Paper or cloth will tear easily and straight along the direction of the grain. When forced to tear against the grain, the paper or cloth will be difficult to tear and the tear will tend to curve until it meets the grain. Tear the cloth or paper close to a comer and then pencil a small straight line in that comer indicating the direction of the grain so it won't need to be determined every time it is used.

Water Test

When grain is particularly difficult to find, a water test can be used. Use this test only to test paper being used to repair a volume, not on pages bound in a book. Draw a 4" straight line along one comer of a large sheet of paper. This line will not necessarily be the grain line, it is simply an orientation line. Cut a square out of the comer, including 1/2 of the line.

Moisten the small square of paper and lay it on a work surface. As the water is absorbed into the paper fibres, the square will begin to curl. The two edges that curl towards one another are parallel with the grain. Mark the correct grain on the square.

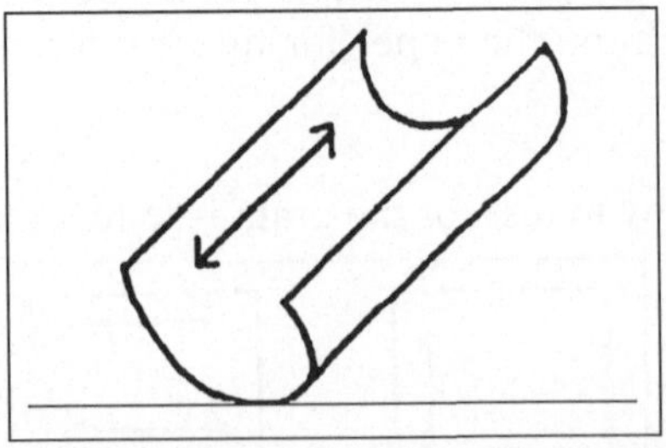

Replace the curled square in position on the large sheet of paper and mark the correct grain on the large sheet. Remember, the first pencil line is not necessarily the grain line.

PAPER REPAIR MATERIALS

Conservation book repair generally usesJ apaneser epair tissue, wheat paste, and heat-set tissue or archival repair tape to repair paper tears.

Japanese Repair Tissue

Japanese repair tissue is sometimes called 'rice' paper, but this thin paper is made from the fibres of the mulberry tree, not from rice as the nickname implies. The strength of Japanese repair tissue comes from its long fibres which make the paper very strong, even though it is very thin. Hand made Japanese repair tissues are made on a mold and have mold or 'chain' lines which can be seen in the paper. These lines generally run the same direction as the paper grain. The lines are visible when the paper held up to a light or held down to let the light shine from above.

The grain can also be determined by using the tear, bend or water test discussed previously. In general, Japanese repair tissue is torn rather than cut. A piece of torn Japanese tissue has a delicate feather that blends into the repaired paper, so there is no sharp edge for the repaired page to turn against. Different methods of tearing Japanese tissue are discussed later in the Book Repair Tools and Techniques part. Japanese repair tissue can be purchased in different weights and colors. Generally, three weights will cover most repair needs.

Since most paper is not truly white, buy the 'natural' or 'toned' colours:

- TENGUJO light weight for working over type or illustrations
- KIZUKISHI medium weight for most repairs
- S~KISHU heavy weight for heavier paper

Although Japanese repair tissue may seem very expensive, only a small amount is used on any one tear. One sheet of Japanese repair tissue will last a long time.

Heat-set Tissue

Heat-set tissue is a thin tissue that has been coated with a heat activated, acrylic adhesive. The tissue is tom or cut to fit the tear or paper loss, laid in position and covered with silicone release paper. The tissue is adhered to the paper with a heated iron. A standard household iron or tacking iron from a book repair supply house or hobby store can be used to adhere heat-set tissue.

Heat-set tissue is sold with the silicone release paper. Heat-set tissue tends to be more brittle than Japanese repair tissue as it does not have the long, strong fibres of the Japanese tissue. It is not recommended for use on the folds in paper or areas that need to flex and bend. Since heat-set tissue is not applied with moisture, it works quite well on shiny, coated paper that can buckle when wet.

Document Repair Tape

Document repair tapes differ from common clear plastic in several ways. The carrier is thin, acid-free paper, not plastic. It is not as stiff as plastic tape so a page can turn and bend more easily. The adhesive used is a neutral acrylic adhesive that should not dry up, yellow over time or seep out the edges of the document repair tape. Because this adhesive is neutral, it should not react chemically with the paper.

The manufacturers of these tapes have tested the materials using artificial aging tests and they believe these tapes will remain stable over time and can be removed easily. Actual experience is not always so positive. Some libraries are finding that these tapes dry hard and crack or that the adhesive dries up and the paper carrier falls off leaving the paper discoloured.

In addition, some tapes are not reversible over time. Because of these problems, document repair tapes should not be used on valuable books or books that are a part of a long-term permanent collection. Document repair tape has become accepted for use in some circulating collections and is definitely better than clear plastic tape.

Some libraries choose to use document repair tape on materials that will not remain in the collection for a long time, such as reference books or children's books. Document repair tape can be a quick way to repair paper tears, and staff can use it easily after very little training. Document tape is sold under several brand names. Some of these are Fihnoplast P, Filmoplast P-90, and Document Repair Tape.

Clear Plastic Tape

Many library books are repaired with clear plastic tape. What appears to be a quick solution can become a long term headache in a library repair programme. Before using plastic tape, it is important to understand how it works and how it affects books. Plastic tape is dangerous to use in books because it is unstable and causes a great deal of damage. Often two or three layers of tape will cover a single repair. The first repair did not work and additional layers of tape were added to correct the problem.

Unfortunately, adding more layers of tape only creates a thick pile of tape; it does not repair the book.. Plastic tape has two main parts: a clear plastic carrier and an adhesive that sticks to the paper. As the tape ages on a piece of paper, the adhesive penetrates the paper fibres of the page and causes a chemical reaction that stains the paper and makes it brittle. Once the adhesive has dried, the plastic carrier falls away and the stain remains. The adhesive on the tape seeps out the edge of the plastic carrier, attracting dirt or adhering one page to another.

Once tape is in a book it is very difficult, if not impossible to remove. Simply lifting the tape off the page will damage the paper because the top layer of paper is removed with the tape. If the tape covers the text, it cannot be removed without damaging the print. Removing plastic tape is difficult even for trained conservators who work with chemicals and special tools. Using tape to reattach a loose page restricts the page from turning freely. The tape has a sharp edge and makes the original paper heavier than before so the paper tends to turn against the edge of the tape and not at the hinge.

Soon the paper breaks against the edge of the tape and falls out of the book. Now a second repair is needed and if the page is repaired a second time with plastic tape, the same problem occurs. Wide, clear plastic tape is also used to repair the cover spine or corners of a book and special 'repair wings' are sold to repair comers as well. While tape covers up the problem but it does not repair it.

Often the tape slides out of position or detaches entirely while the adhesive remains on the book cover attracting dirt or sticking books to one another on the shelf. Some libraries that practice conservation book repair may use plastic tape in very specific instances.

Plastic tape might be used when a book will not remain in the collection for a long tune, such as children's books, reference books that are updated regularly, or books that need 'one more circulation' before they are discarded. Decisions regarding when and how to use clear plastic tape should be made ahead of time. Be certain a book is not important in a long term collection policy before repairing it with plastic tape. Keep in mind that once the tape is in the book, it cannot usually be removed without damaging the book.

REPAIR ADHESIVES

There are two main kinds of adhesives used in conservation book repair: paste and glue. Each has special properties and should be used in specific instances.

Paste

Paste is generally a cooked mixture of water and vegetable starch, such as wheat or rice. Repairing paper with paste will give a stronger bond than repairing it with glue because the paste soaks into the paper fibres and bonds them together. Since paste contains water, it can stretch and cockle paper. It dries slowly and can usually be reversed with water.

Wheat Paste

Wheat paste is used to mend tom paper, attach Japanese tissue or soften old paste and glue. It is not usually used on book cloth or the case of a book. Wheat paste can be purchased uncooked, instant or pie-made. Wheat paste prepared from scratch will last for 3-4 days before it begins to mold. Prepare a small amount of paste and keep it refrigerated. Instant commercial or prepared pastes can be convenient in some situations.

Thick Wheat Paste:

- 6 TBS wheat starch
- 2 Cups cold water
- Place the wheat starch in the top of a double boiler.

- Mix the water into the starch stirring constantly.
- Bring the mixture to a boil.
- Lower the heat and stir constantly as the mixture simmers.
- Cook until mixture thickens.
- Remove from heat and cool.
- Put through a sieve and store refrigerated for 3-4 days.

Thin Wheat Paste:

- 3 1/2 TBS wheat starch
- 2 Cups cold water
- Follow the instructions for Thick Wheat Paste above.

Microwave Wheat Paste:

- One tablespoon wheat starch
- Five tablespoons distilled water
- Place the wheat starch in a deep container, add distilled water and place in microwave. Microwave on high setting 20-30 seconds, remove paste and stir. Return to microwave and cook another 20-30 seconds. Remove and stir again. Continue this process for 3-4 minutes depending on the power of your microwave. Paste should stand a few minutes before using.

Glue

Several types of glue have been used in bookbinding over the years, the most common being animal hide glue. In recent years, animal-based glues have been replaced with synthetic vinyl resin glues, the most common of which is polyvinyl acetate emulsion.

Polyvinyl Acetate (PVA)

PVA is a good all-around adhesive. It has a low moisture content and dries quickly. It dries flexible, so it can be used to tighten hinges, repair book cover comers and reattach loose book cloth to book board. PVA is not affected by mold or fungi. However, it is damaged by freezing, so most book repair supply houses will not sell PVA by mail from October to March. If PVA freezes, it separates and loses its adhesive properties.

PVA can be thinned with water or thin wheat paste for different consistencies and effects. Thinning PVA with water adds moisture and does not add any additional adhesive properties while thinning with wheat paste adds the adhesive qualities of the paste to the glue. Many book binders or repair technicians use a 50/50 mixture of PVA and wheat paste strained through a sieve.

Other books may describe different adhesives or mixtures of adhesives. PVA glues cover a wide range of brand names and not all are used to repair books. For instance Elmer's glue is technically a PVA but is not flexible when dry so it has limited use for repairing books. Two common brand names for PVA glues used in book repair are AT-l 100 from Colophon Book Arts Supply and Jade 403 available from Talas. These companies are listed in the Supply Sources.

Working with Adhesives

Most people learning to repair books use too much adhesive. The belief seems to be that if a little is good, a lot is better. In book repair, that just isn't true. A thin, even coat of adhesive makes the best bond. Too much adhesive will ooze out of the edges of a repair and bond to the pages. Also, too much adhesive causes the paper to wrinkle and takes longer to dry. Watch each repair carefully. If there is excess glue or paste, wipe it away. Next time, try to use less paste or glue. When applying adhesive, choose a brush that matches the size of the surface. When pasting or gluing a small area, use a small brush. When the area is larger, use a bigger brush.

LINEN THREAD

Books are traditionally sewn with linen thread which is very strong and can be purchased in several sizes. Choosing the right thread is important for a successful repair. Using thread that is too thick can damage a book because the text block may not fit back in the original case. Thread that is too thin can tear through the folded signature paper. In general, it's best to use as thin a thread as possible, but choosing the right thread depends on the kind of paper and how many signatures are being resewn.

Thread Sizes

Common sizes of linen thread are 12/4,18/3,25/3,35/3 and

60/3. The first number is the thickness of the strand or ply and the second number is the number of strands or ply per thread. So 12/4 is composed of 4 strands that are 12 thick. The 12 refers to an industry designation that relates to the weight of the wholesale quantities of thread. In this sizing system, the smaller the number, the thicker the thread so 12 thread is thicker than 60 thread. 35/3,30/5, and 18/3 are a good assortment of thread to have on hand. It can be hard to recognize a particular thread size so it's a good idea to mark the size of thread on the inner cardboard spool before discarding the paper wrapper.

Waxing and Threading Linen Thread

Like all thread, linen thread has a tendency to tangle. Waxing sewing thread with beeswax keeps the thread from tangling and helps the thread 'grip' the paper. Run the thread through a cake of beeswax two or three times to coat it with wax, then run the thread through your fingers. The heat generated from the friction will melt the wax into the thread.

Measuring Thread Length

The length of thread needed depends on the height of the book and how many signatures need to be resewn. Save time by measuring the thread directly on the book. For instance, a book with one unattached signature will need a piece of thread that is at least three text block heights long plus one text block height for tying knots.

Adding Additional Lengths of Thread

It's not a good idea to try to work with more than 4-5 book heights of thread at one time. There are two ways to add additional lengths of thread discussed in Tying Knots In Thread, which follows.

Locking the Thread onto the Needle

It can be very frustrating to have a needle fall off the sewing thread in the middle of a repair. Lock the needle onto the thread before beginning a repair to assure the needle will not fall off during the repair. Thread the needle as usual.

Grasp the leading end of thread and wrap it around your thumb:

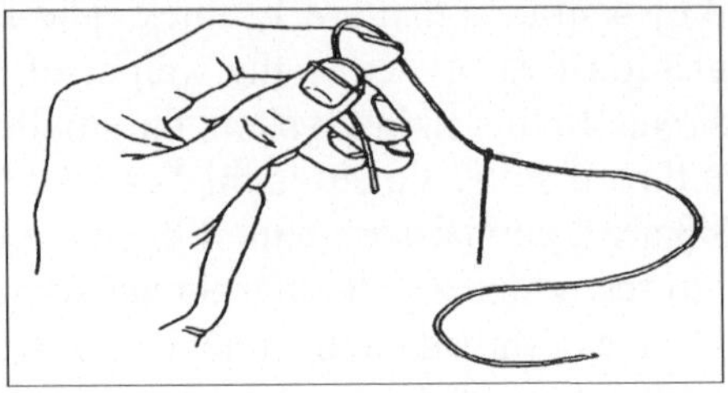

Carefully pierce the thread with the needle against your thumbnail:

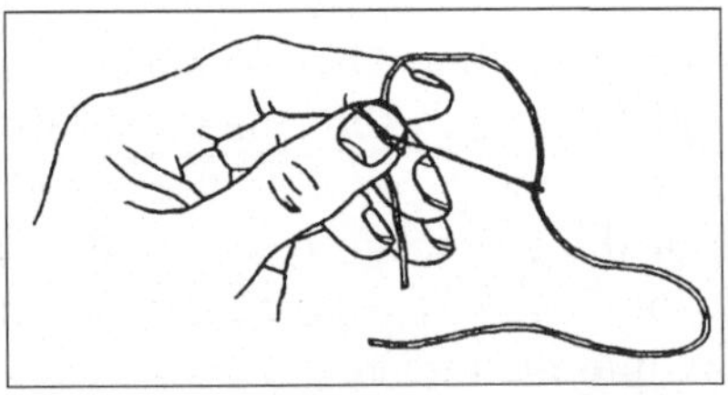

Pull the needle through the pierced thread:

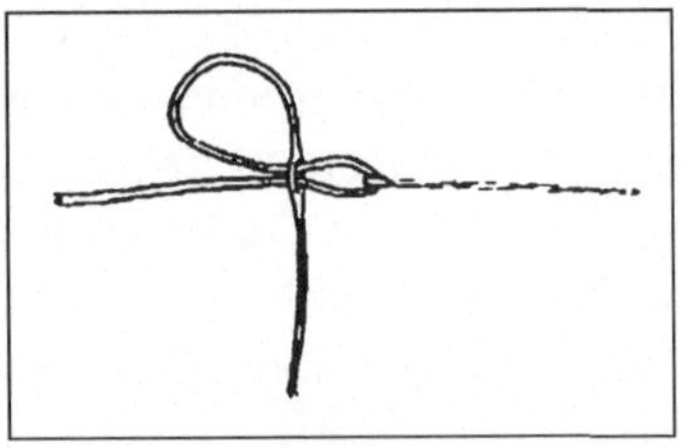

Hold onto the sewing thread and pull until the pierced thread is tight against the sewing needle.

Tying Knots in Thread

There are two basic knots used in book repair, the weaver's knot and the square knot.

The Weaver's Knot

Since sewing with a very long piece of linen thread can be difficult, the weaver's knot is used to tie on additional lengths of thread so shorter lengths can be used. Tie on additional thread when there is about 6" of thread left on the needle. Tie the knot inside the signature, as close to the last sewing station as possible.

A knot cannot easily pass through a sewing station hole so it should lie between the sewing station holes on the inside of the signature:

- Make a loop of the remaining thread and hold it in your left hand, with the short end of the loop on the bottom.
- With a new thread, make a loop with the short end on the bottom and hold it in your right hand.
- Insert the left-hand loop underneath and into the right-hand loop and hold both in place with your left thumb.
- Take the short end of the right-hand loop under and through the left-hand loop as illustrated.
- Pull the short end of the left-hand loop and both ends of the right-hand loop away from each other until the knot is secure. Trim both ends.

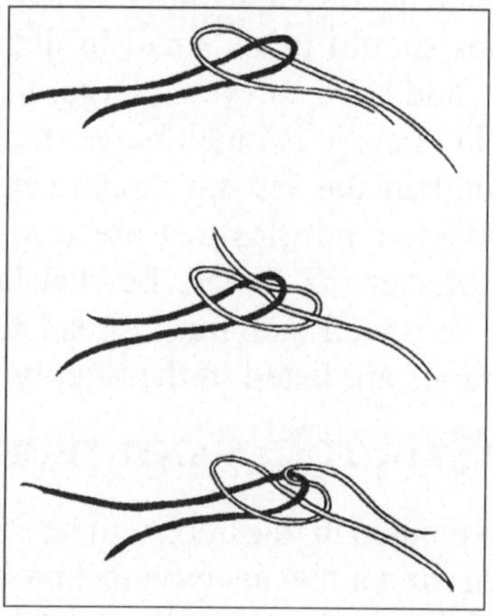

The Square Knot

Square knots are used to tie off sewing thread when resewing a text block or attaching materials into pamphlet binders:

- Take one end of thread in each hand.
- Pass the right-hand thread over the lefthand thread and through the loop. Pull tight.
- The original right-hand thread is now on the left side. Place it over the right-hand thread and bring it through the loop. Pulltight. Trim the end of the original thread. Do not cut the added thread..

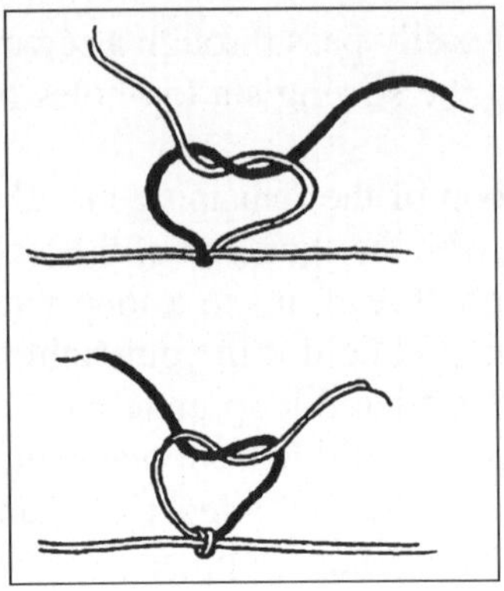

SEWING NEEDLES

Using the right needle will make sewing easy and more successful. Needles should be as small in diametre as possible, have a blunt point, and have an eye no larger than the shaft of the needle. If the sewing needle is much bigger than the thread used, it will make a hole that the sewing thread cannot fill up. Many book suppliers advertise needles that are very large, sometimes much larger than the sewing thread. Leather harness called Egg Eye needles work very well with most thread and are available in leather shops. Sources are listed in the Supply Sources list.

BOOK REPAIR TOOLS AND TECHNIQUES

The repairs explained in this book will be easier to accomplish using the right tools and a few specific techniques. If you already have tools and techniques that seem to work, practice each repair using the tools and techniques given in the instructions, then decide which is better. If a tool or technique does the same job and doesn't harm the book, feel free to use it.

BOOK REPAIR TOOLS

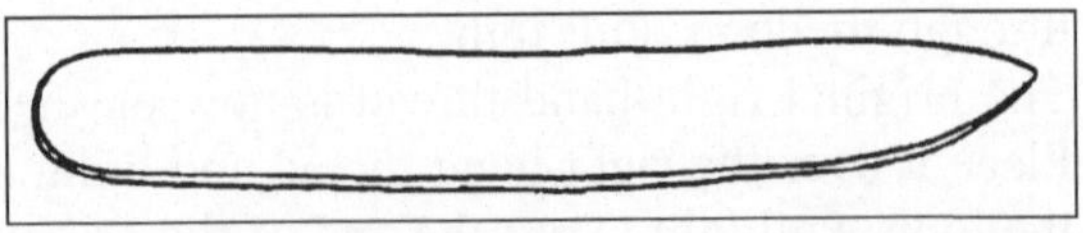

A folder is a tool approximately 6-8" long and about 1-1 1/2"

wide. A typical folder is approximately 1/8" thick, smooth with one pointed end and one rounded end made from animal bone or plastic. Folders are used for many things such as creasing paper, smoothing down repair tissues and working cloth into a joint area. Some plastic folders are available with two round ends. When purchasing a folder, try to buy one made of bone with one rounded end and one pointed end. That tool will be much more versatile. Bone folders can also be filed to a desired shape and size while plastic folders cannot.

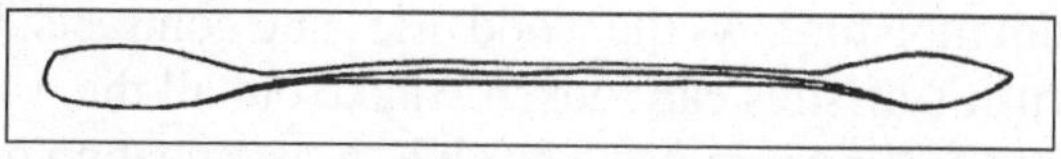

A microspatula is a metal tool, approximately 6-8" long with one rounded end and one pointed end. Use a microspatula to pick up pasted strips of Japanese repair tissue, lift book cloth or end papers away from the book board, or apply glue or paste in a very tight area. Microspatulas are manufactured very thin and many book binders file or sand them even thinner.

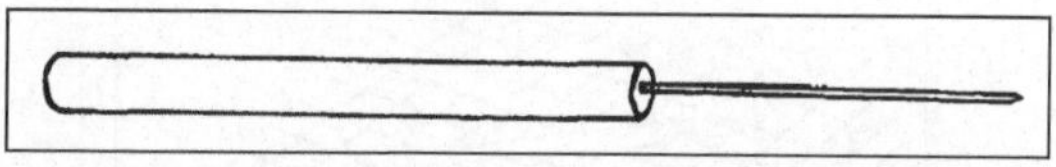

A needle-in-a-stick can be used to apply glue to small, tight areas, mark cutting lines or score tear lines on Japanese repair tissue. This kind of tool can be purchased from a pottery material supply house or botany material supplier. It can also be constructed by drilling a very small hole in the end of a wooden dowel and inserting the needle into the hole. The needle should fit tightly into the hole in the dowel. A small drop of glue on the end of the needle will help it hold better.

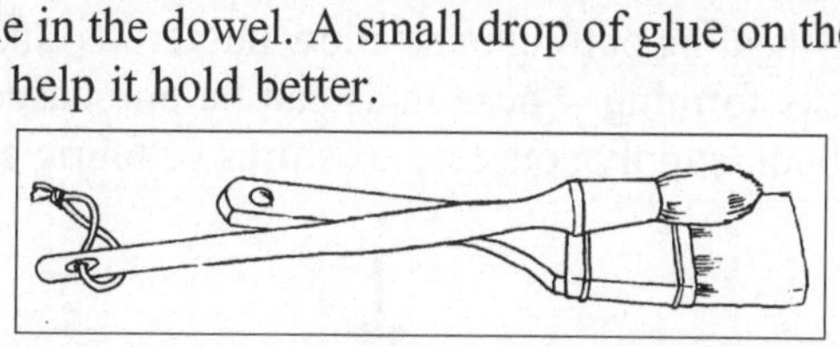

A good assortment of brushes makes repairing books much easier. The size of the surface to be pasted or glued determines the size of the brush used, so keep a variety on hand. Round or flat bristle brushes be used. While natural bristle brushes are usually best for performing repairs, some libraries recommend using a synthetic bristle brush for PVA glue as it can be difficult to wash all the glue out of a natural bristle brush. A buildup of PVA glue can ruin a brush. Some people like to use separate brushes for paste and glue.

A brush should never be allowed to dry with the adhesive on it. Keep the brush in the adhesive or water and always wash a brush out when finished. Mild hand soap or dish washing liquid can be used to thoroughly clean brushes. When storing a brush in water, use only enough water to cover the bristles. If the water extends above the ferrule of the brush, the wood of the shaft can expand with moisture. As the wood dries and contracts, the ferrule and the brush's bristles can loosen. Shake out all the water from a brush before putting it in paste or glue. A self-healing cutting mat and sharp Xacto knife, scalpel or breakaway utility knife such as Olfa Silver makes precise cutting easy and fast. It is important to always work with a sharp blade when cutting or trimming repair materials. Attempting to cut with a dull blade will usually result in a torn edge that needs even more repair.

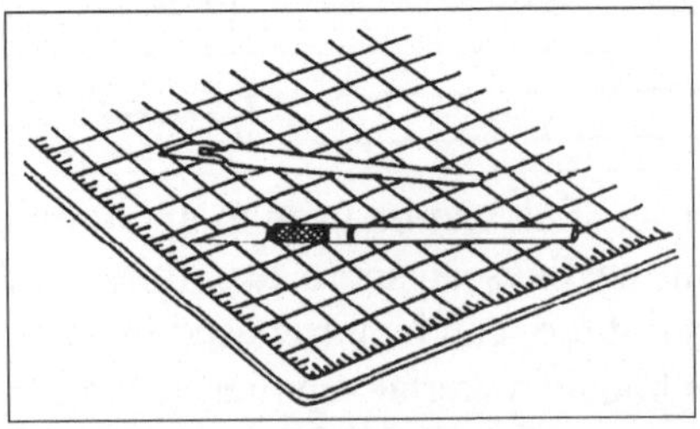

Cutting on cardboard is not always a good idea because the knife blade can be caught in the 'track' of a previous cut and ruin a repair. Self-healing cutting mats allow numerous cuts to be made without tracks forming. These mats can be purchased in various sizes from book supply sources, art stores or fabric stores.

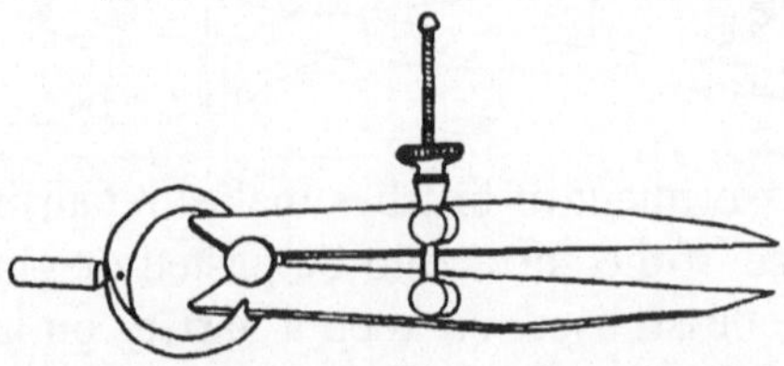

Dividers can be used to transfer and mark measurements from one place to another. Other basic tools include sharp scissors and a rigid, metal straightedge. Punching sewing holes in folded signatures can be tricky. Using a punching jig and a signature punching cradle will make the job much easier. To construct a punching jig, simply fold a piece of paper in half lengthwise and clip one end diagonally. This diagonal cut marks the top of the printed page.

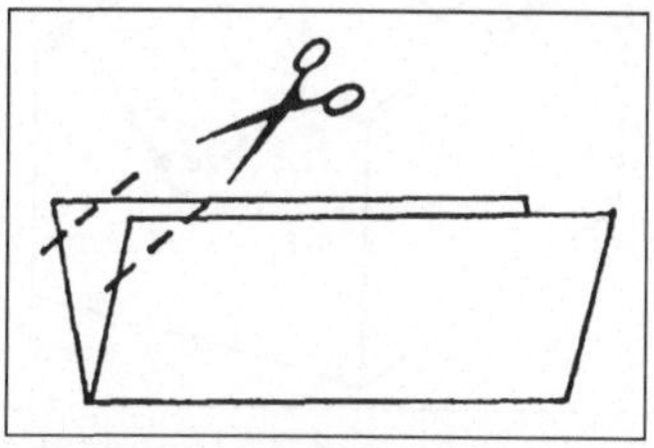

Mark the desired sewing hole stations on the outside of the fold in pencil.

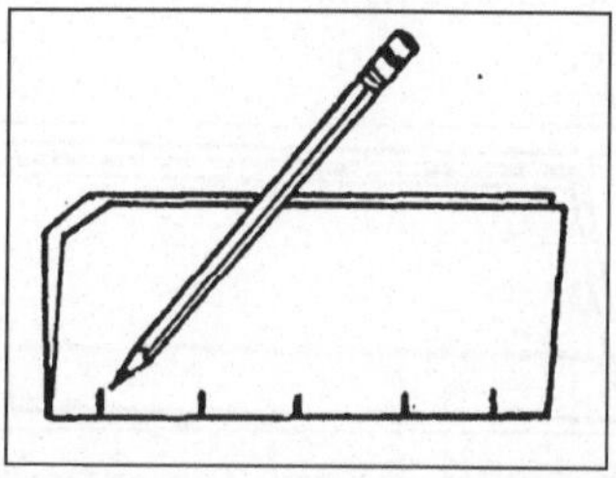

Turn the jig inside out so the pencil marks are on the inside of the fold. Place the punching jig inside the pamphlet or folded signature. The jig should be seated all the way down into the fold and lined up with the top edge of the book.

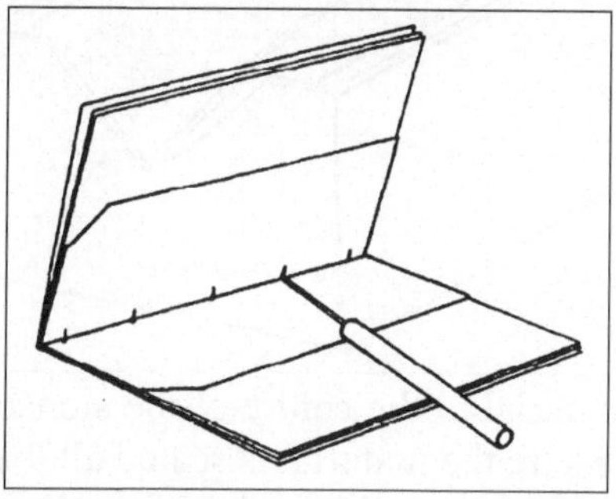

Lay the pamphlet/signature flat on the table and carefully punch holes through the fold with the needle-in-a-stick. A signature punching cradle helps control placement of the sewing stations and can be constructed out of thin plywood, mat board or cardboard. To construct a simple cradle from a cardboard box, make a 45 degree angle 'V' cut in both ends of a box.

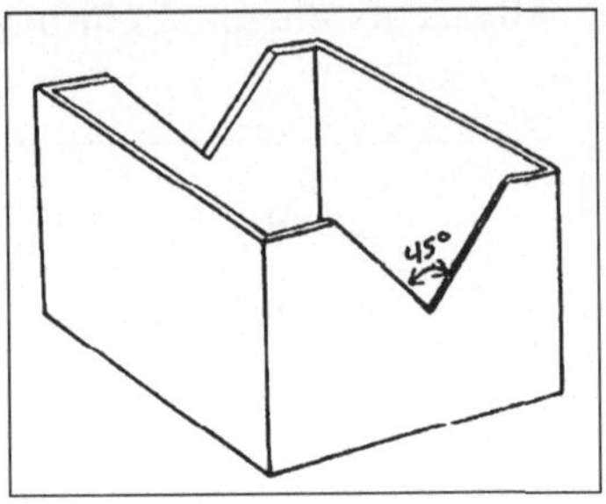

Cut two pieces of cardboard 2" longer than the length of the box and 1" wider than the length of one side of the 'V' cut. Glue a 1 1/2" strip of book cloth connecting the two pieces of cardboard along one long edge.

Glue the cardboard strips into the cut out 'V' with PVA.

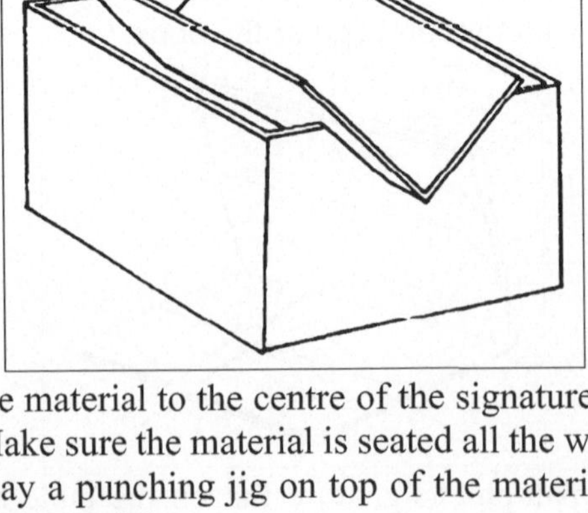

Open the material to the centre of the signature and lay it in the cradle. Make sure the material is seated all the way down into the cradle. Lay a punching jig on top of the material and punch with a needle-in-a-stick.

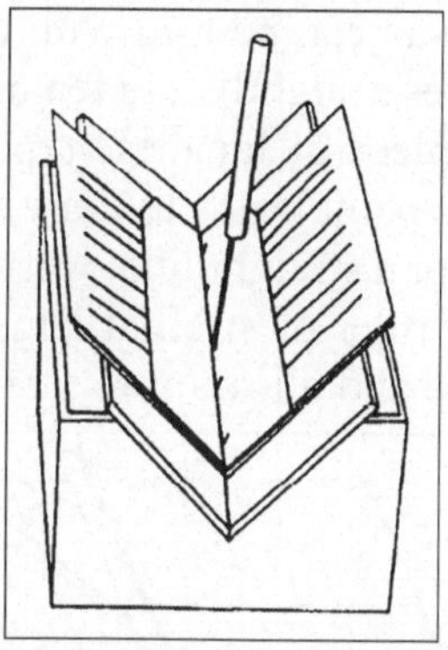

Paper wrapped bricks or jars filled with coins or buckshot can be used as weights while a repair is drying.

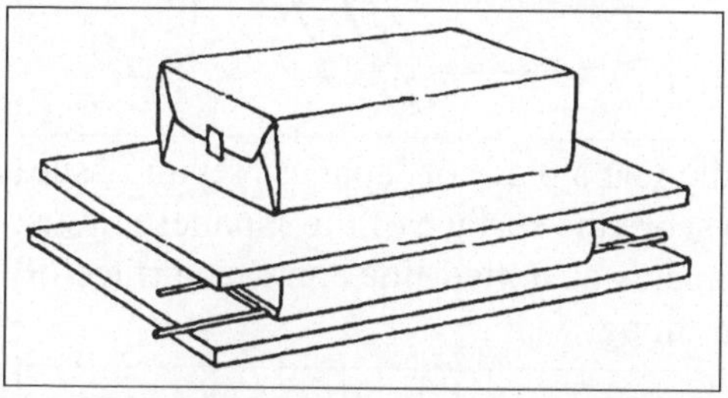

1/4" glass with ground edges makes a perfectly flat work or drying surface. The glass should not be larger than 18" x 18" or it can be difficult to move from one place to another. Thin pieces of plywood or Formica can also be used.

Caring for Tools

It is very important to keep book repair tools clean, especially tools that are used to apply paste or glue. Wash folders, knives, needle-in-a-stick and brushes with warm soap and water. If adhesive is left to dry on a tool, it can build up over time and damage the tool. This is especially true for brushes.

BOOK REPAIR TECHNIQUES

Tearing Japanese Repair Tissue

Japanese repair tissue is usually tom so that the edges are feathered, not cut sharp as they would be with a knife or scissors. The feathered edge allows the repair tissue to 'blend' onto the text paper. Repair tissue can be tom with a water tear or needle tear. A needle tear gives a slightly less feathered edge than a water tear. To water-tear a piece of Japanese repair tissue, use a small, pointed natural bristle paint brush to draw a wet line or shape on the Japanese tissue. For a straight line, wet a piece of repair tissue against the edge of a ruler or straight edge. The water weakens the fibres of the tissue and allows it to tear along the wet line.

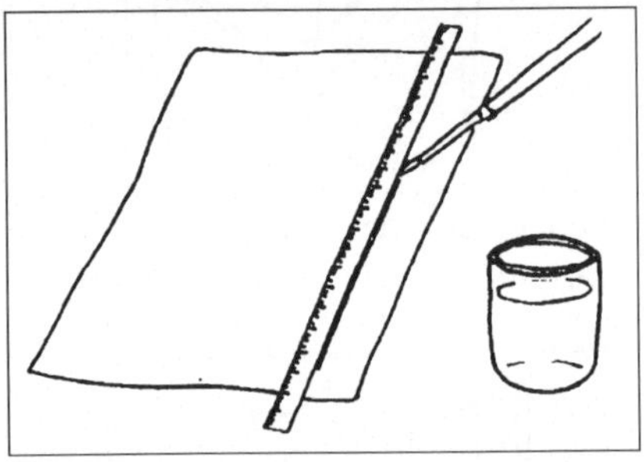

To needle-tear a piece of Japanese repair tissue, use a needle-in-a-stick to score the surface of the Japanese tissue. The point of the needle creates a 'dotted line' on the surface of the Japanese tissue to tear along.

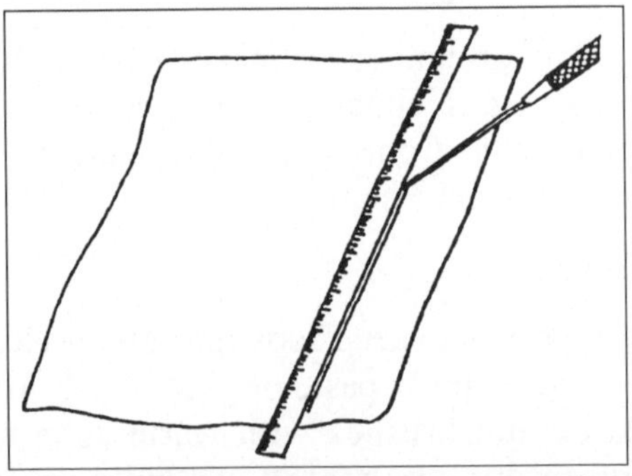

To tear a piece of Japanese tissue to a specific shape, such as to repair a missing comer or mend a hole in the middle of a page, tear the tissue as follows:

- Lay a piece of black mat board or paper under the missing area to make the outline of the loss more visible.
- Put a piece of Mylar polyester film over the loss to protect the page from the water and needle; then lay

two layers of Japanese repair tissue over the Mylar and water tear or needle tear the patches to fit the loss. One patch will go on each side of the loss.

If the damaged page is not attached to the text block, it is possible to use a light table or the light from a window to see the area that needs to be patched. Put the text page on a light table or window, cover with Mylar and repair tissue. With the Mylar film protecting the page, needle or water tear the Japanese repair tissue to the desired shape.

Applying Adhesive to Japanese Tissue

When applying adhesive, choose a brush that matches the size of the surface. If the area is small, use a small brush; a bigger area needs a bigger brush. A thin, even coat of adhesive makes the best bond. Too much adhesive will ooze out the edges of a repair and can stain other surfaces. Apply paste or glue to paper or cloth by brushing from the centre of the materials being glued towards the outer edges in a star burst pattern.

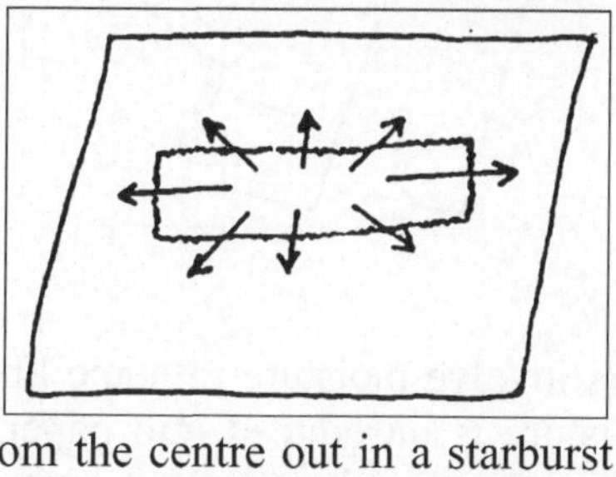

Brushing from the centre out in a starburst pattern protects the edge of the paper or cloth. There might be small tears at the outer edges of a piece of paper or cloth that the brush could catch and tear or the brush might 'grab' the edge of the paper and turn it back on itself, sticking the two surfaces together. In addition to applying adhesive directly to a piece of paper, it can also be applied indirectly. This method is especially useful when working with very small pieces of paper or cloth. Brush the adhesive onto a piece of glass or plastic then lay the paper or cloth on top of it. The paper or cloth acts as a sponge and absorbs the adhesive from below. Use the bristles of a brush or fingers to work the paste into the Japanese tissue. When Japanese repair tissue is transparent, it has soaked up all the paste it can.

Masking is another technique used to apply adhesive to paper. By using a strip of waste paper to protect most of a sheet of paper, you can apply adhesive to a very specific area in a controlled way. This is especially helpful in operations such as TIPPING-IN A PAGE.

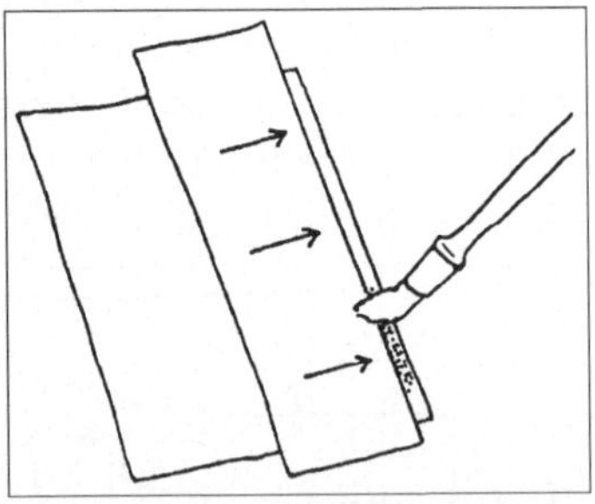

Drying Repairs

Most repairs involve moisture of some kind, be it paste or glue. When moisture is introduced into paper, board or cloth, special precautions need to be taken. A wet repair should be isolated from other pages in a book or it can adhere itself to adjacent pages and the book will not open correctly. Repairs to the cover of a book must also be protected until dry.

The simplest way to isolate and protect a paper repair is with a moisture barrier, such as wax paper, Mylar or by using a combination of a non-stick, porous material such as Hollytex or Pellon with blotter paper. Since moisture cannot pass through a barrier such as wax paper the repair can take longer to dry. Non-stick, porous material, such as Hollytex and Pellon, a woven polyester material can also be used to protect a repair. Both these materials allow moisture to pass through so repairs dry faster, but keep in mind the moisture has to go somewhere.

When using porous materials, be sure to use blotter paper to absorb the moisture so it does not travel to the pages of the book. Blotter paper is a thick unsized paper made from rag or cotton Enters. Because it does not contain size, it can absorb moisture easily. When blotters are used to absorb moisture in a book repair, they should be replaced with dry blotters periodically so the moisture of the blotter will not remain in the book.

Repairs must always dry on a smooth surface under weight so that they do not buckle and curl. 1/4" glass with ground edges or pieces of plywood covered with Formica can be used to create a smooth surface anywhere. Glass or plywood can be stacked so that several repairs take up very little space. Paper wrapped bricks, jars filled with coins or buckshot can be used on top of the glass for weight.

Measuring Books

Measuring books accurately can be a challenge since books are not always square or flat. It's standard practice in book repair to take most repair measurements with a piece of scratch paper rather than a ruler.

Measuring the Height of a Book

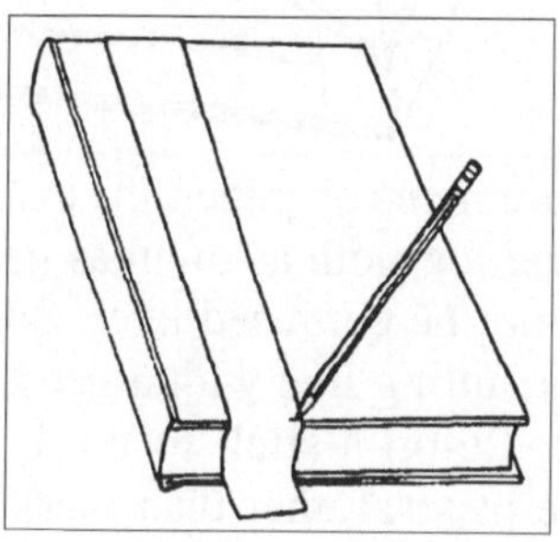

Lay the scratch paper in position and mark one or both ends of the measurement. Add direction arrows to indicate where the measurement starts and stops.

Measuring the Spine Width

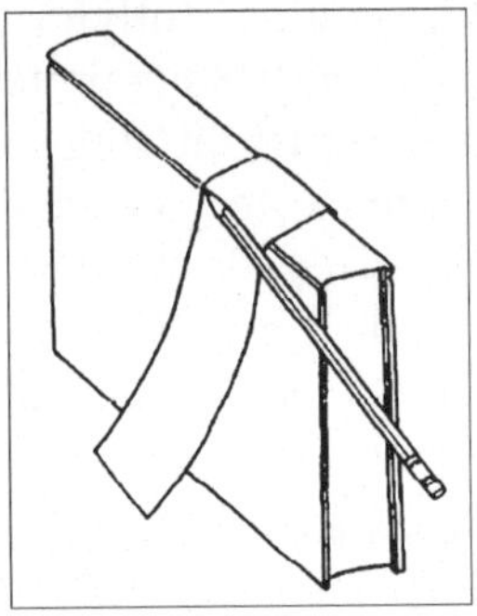

The spine can be measured in two ways:

- Measure actual distance across the spine from shoulder to shoulder;
- Measure the actual thickness of the spine by laying the book flat on the table and measuring vertically across the spine.

Be sure to measure the thickest part of the book. It might be the spine, the fore edge or part way in between.

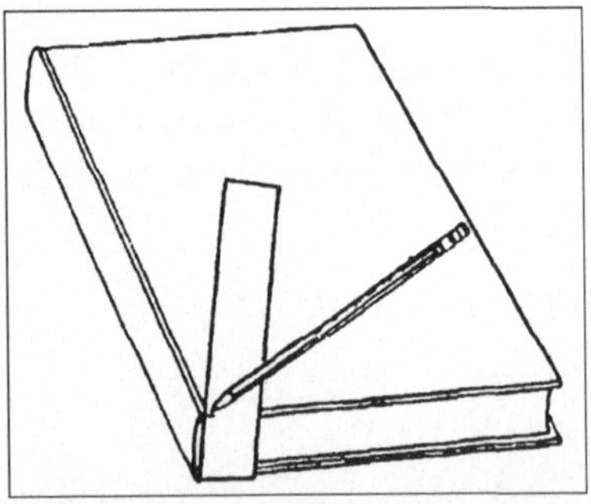

With the measurements on paper, the exact measurement can be transferred to paper or cloth as often as necessary. Label each measurement so as not be confused later. Sometimes it is easier and faster to mark a cutting line with a needle point instead of a pencil. Use the needle-on-a-stick to mark a measurement by slightly piercing the paper, rather than marking it with a pencil.

Dividers can be used to mark and transfer measurements from one place to another.

SIMPLE BOOK REPAIRS

Most book repairs begin as simple problems. If a simple problem is ignored or handled incorrectly, it becomes a complex repair. When a book is repaired early, there is much less work and the volume stays in circulation longer.

CLEANING PAGES

When attempting to clean paper, always start with the least abrasive cleaning method before trying others. Keep in mind that cleaning library materials be a time consuming task. Evaluate each book before attempting to dry clean it. Make sure that cleaning a particular volume is a good use of time.

Dry Cleaning

Dry cleaning is any kind of cleaning that does not use water or liquid cleaners. Done correctly, dry cleaning will not damage library materials. Some dirt can be swept off the page using a soft, natural bristle brush. Always brush from the centre of the page out towards the edges in a star burst pattern and up and down the hinge area to remove dirt or eraser crumbs.

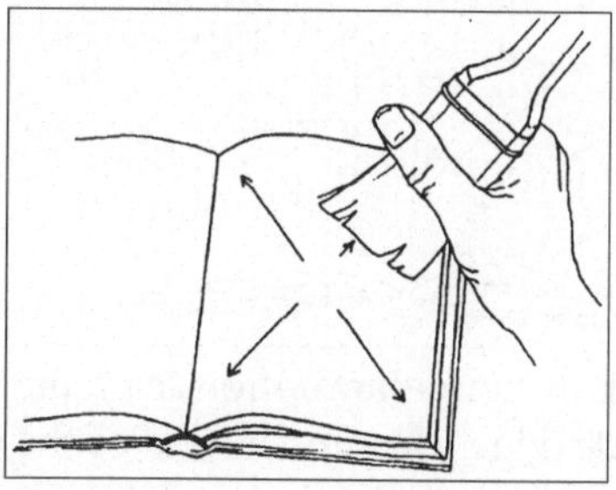

Brushes can be of any size but should have soft, natural bristles. Plastic or nylon bristles can scratch the paper. Brushes used for dry cleaning should not be used for water, paste or glue so it's best to designate a brush just for dry cleaning. Watch out for paper tears that can catch on the brush and NEVER brush from the edge of the paper towards the middle. The brush could 'grab' the edge of the page, pull it back on itself and cause a tear. This is especially important to remember when there are small tears on the edge of the page. After using a dry brush to sweep off the surface dirt, products such as Opaline or Skum-X can be used to remove more stubborn surface dirt. Opaline and andurn-X are both eraser products.

Opaline comes in a bag and Skum-X in a shaker dispenser. Opaline is applied by kneading the bag above the paper until the paper is covered with a fine powder of tiny eraser crumbs. Skum-X is applied like salt from a salt shaker. Using clean fingers, rub the paper lightly in a circular pattern.

Do Not Rub The Paper With The Opaline Cloth Bag or the bag will become soiled quickly and transfer that dirt onto the page. It is possible to protect the page from skin oil by rubbing through a soft cloth or a piece of polyester film, such as Mylar.

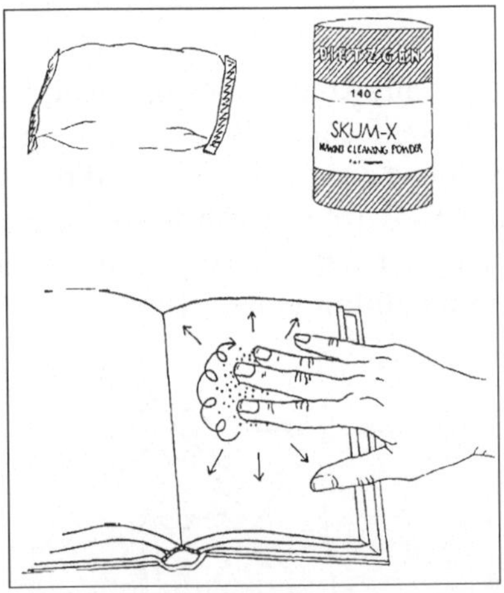

Always work in a circular motion from the centre of the page towards the outside edge. Be very careful of the edges of the page; they tear easily.

The eraser crumbs change colour as they pick up dirt. Once they seem to have picked up as much dirt as possible, brush the eraser crumbs off the page. Use a natural bristle brush to sweep the eraser crumbs off the page. Brush from the centre of the page towards the edge of the paper and don't forget to sweep the eraser crumbs out of the hinge area.

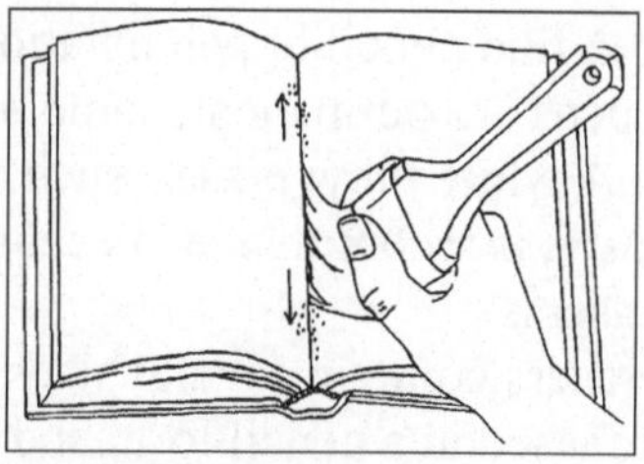

TIGHTENING OR REPAIRING CASE BINDING HINGES

Case binding is a general term for the process of constructing a hard cover book in two parts: the text block and the case or cover. As detailed in Book Case Construction, the major point of attachment between the text block and the cover is the crash cloth that covers the spine of the text block and is glued to the cover boards. The text block is usually attached to the case so that it sits approximately 1/8-3/16 above the shelf.

This means that gravity is constantly pulling the text block down. The adhesive in the hinge area can dry up over time and become weak while the spine and endpapers are still intact. When the glue dries up, the crash separates from the book board and the hinge area becomes loose. Often the end paper will split along the hinge and the crash will be visible underneath. The common repair practice of applying plastic tape to the hinge area does nothing to reattach the crash to the case board, it only adds a layer of tape in the book.

Tightening Loose Hinges

When the hinge area is loose and the endpaper is not tom, use a wooden stick such as a bamboo skewer or thin knitting needle coated with PVA to feed a small amount of PVA into the joint area. Carefully insert the PVA-coated knitting needle or stick into the hinge area at the top of the book, rotating as the stick is pushed down.

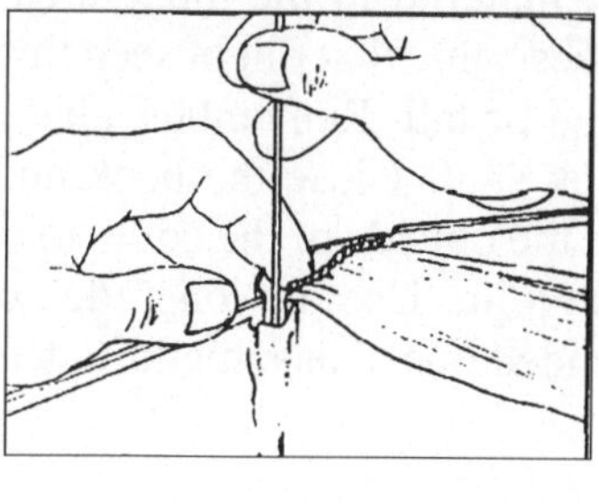

Librarians often find pencil or pen notations on the page of a book. While most pens are permanent, some pencil marks can be erased from paper. A white vinyl eraser, such as Faber Castelblr and Magic-Rub eraser, is recommended because it is less abrasive than most other erasers.

These vinyl erasers come in several sizes and can be shaped with a knife or purchased in a pencil form and sharpened to reach small areas or between lines of print. Erase in one direction, working from the centre of the paper towards the edges of the paper. DO NOT rub the eraser back and forth or erase from the edge of the paper towards the centre of the book. Use a natural bristle brush to sweep away the eraser crumbs, paying special attention to removing eraser crumbs from the inner margin of the page. Remember to brush from the centre of the page towards the edge.

Other Types of Cleaning

Dry cleaning will only remove surface dirt. More advanced cleaning techniques include taking the book apart and washing each page. That is a time consuming and costly process. If simple dry cleaning does not seem to be successful, it may not be feasible to clean the book.

If the book is still usable as is, return it to the shelf. If it is not usable, consider replacing the book. Keep in mind that staff time is valuable and many books need attention. Consider educating patrons with a 'Keep Our Books Clean' campaign. Pull the stick out, turn the book over and repeat on the opposite end. Be careful not to get any glue on the spine of the text block.

After both ends of the hinge are glued, put a piece of wax paper or non-stick material in the hinge area to protect the end paper from any excess glue that might seep through the tom hinge area or out the head or tail. Remember, glue in the wrong place could glue the book shut! Close the book and use the long thin edge of a folder on the outside of the cover to work the book cloth down into the case joint. Use the long edge of the folder as the ends, even the rounded one, can sometimes tear through the book cloth.

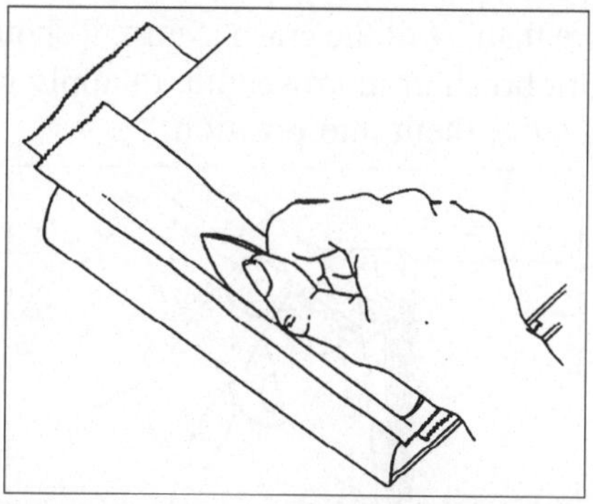

Work from the centre to the top of the book, then from the centre to the bottom of the book. This will adhere the crash, end paper and book board and move any excess glue out of the hinge area.

Open the book cover and use a folder to gently work the end paper back into the hinge. Again, use the long flat edge of the folder as the ends can tear through the paper. Replace the wax paper in the hinge, close the book and rub the folder in the outer joint once again.

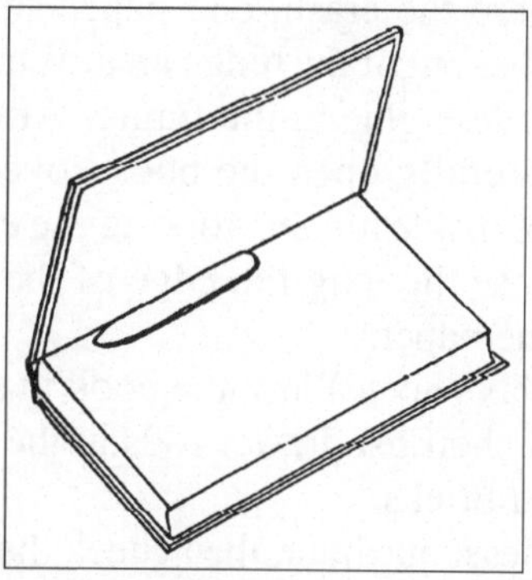

Place the book in a book press to dry. If a book press is not available, put knitting—needles or shelf list drawer rods in the hinge areas of the case and place weight on the book. Let dry overnight and return to the shelf.

Tightening/Repairing Damaged Hinges on a Case Bindings

A variation of the Tightening Loose Hinges technique can be used when an endpaper is split at the hinge. Check the crash carefully, if more than l/4 of the crash is torn, it should be replaced. Use a small paint brush or microspatula to apply glue to the split end papers and work them into position.

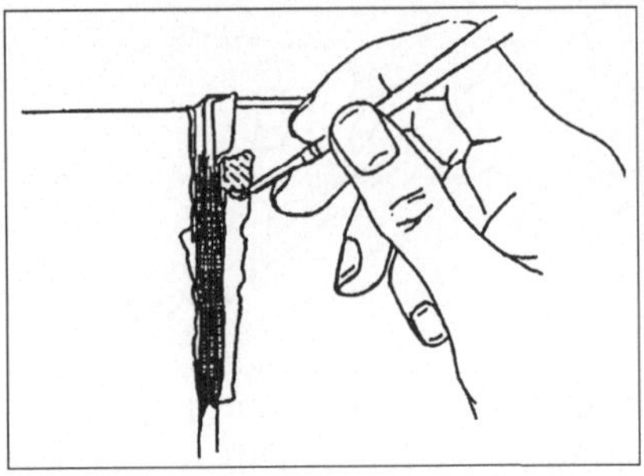

Put a piece of wax paper or non-stick material in the hinge area to protect the paper from any excess glue and close the book. Use the long thin edge of a folder on the outside of the cover to work the book cloth down into the case joint. Remember the rounded ends of the folder can sometimes tear through the book cloth. Work from the centre to the top of the book, then from the centre to the bottom of the book.

This will adhere the crash, end paper and book board and move any excess glue out of the hinge area. Wipe away any excess glue and try to use less glue in the future, After setting the joint with the folder, carefully open the book cover and gently work the folder along the inside hinge, working the end paper back into the hinge. Again, use the long flat edge of the folder as the ends can tear through the paper.

Replace the wax paper. Place the book in a book press or put knitting needles or shelf list drawer rods in the hinges and weight with paper covered bricks.

Let dry for at least one hour, then check the repair. Sometimes the repaired end papers will not quite meet. This space will not affect the strength of the repair but it can be covered with a strip of Japanese tissue and wheat paste for a cosmetic touch. Tear a piece of Japanese tissue the height of the text block and wide enough to cover the hinge repair.

Apply paste to the Japanese tissue and gently lay the tissue on the hinge. Use a folder to carefully work the tissue back into the hinge.

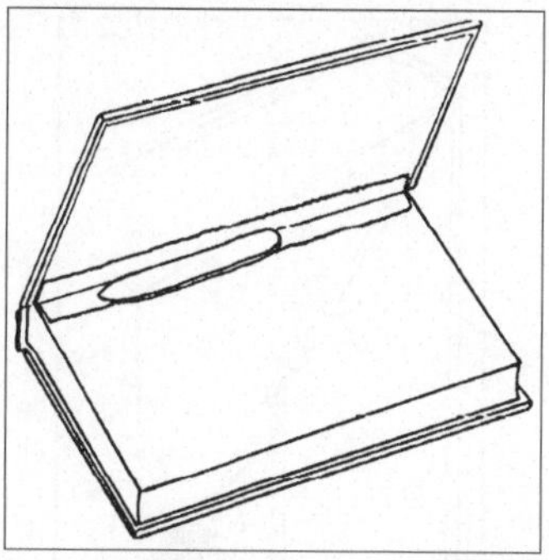

Insert a piece of wax paper or non-stick material, close the book and use the long edge of the folder to work the cloth into the cover joint. Place the repaired book in a press or insert rods or knitting needles in the joints, add weight, and dry overnight before returning it to the shelf.

MENDING BOOK CASE CORNERS

The corners of a book take a great deal of stress and can be damaged while the rest of the case is still in good condition. This is another repair that is often handled with plastic tape or purchased 'repair wings.' Applying tape or wings does not repair the comer; instead it adds a layer of tape on top of the problem. The adhesive on the tape can seep out or dry up over time, causing the plastic carrier to fall off. That can leave behind a sticky residue that is often impossible to clean up.

Repairing Book Boards Corners

The book board used in book case construction consists of many layers of board. If the book cloth is damaged or tom open at a corner, the different layers of board are often visible. When damaged comers are repaired with plastic tape, the book board is not repaired, it is only covered up. To truly repair the book corner, the various layers of book board must be glued to one another and the book cloth repaired or replaced. In some cases the corners are damaged while the book cloth is still intact. Other times the book cloth will be tom or missing. In either case, cut through the book cloth on the top and fore edge of the board. Cut well past the damaged board into sound board and cloth.

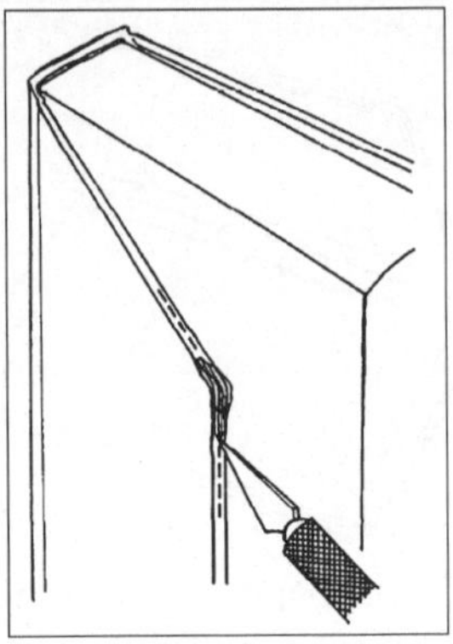

Separate the layers of board and use a microspatula or knife to apply PVA glue to several of the book board layers. The PVA will seep through the thin layers of board so every layer does not need to be glued. The number of glued layers depends on the condition of the book board.

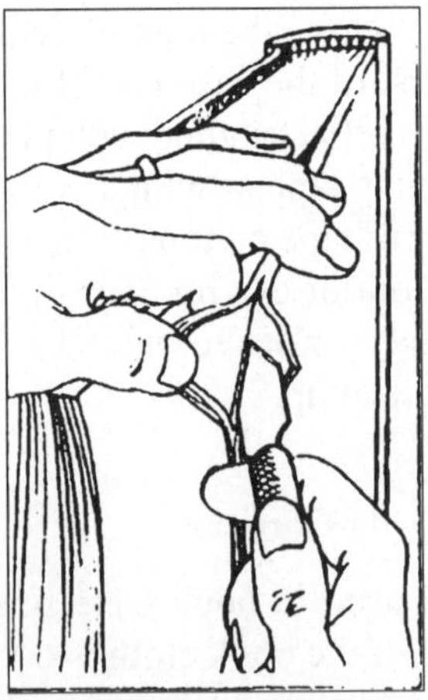

If the original book cloth covers the comer, paint a small amount of glue on the wrong side of the book cloth and smooth it over the comer.

If the book cloth needs to be replaced, follow the instructions for Attaching New Corner Book Cloth. With fingers or a folder, press the book cloth onto the board, moving from the base of the repair up towards the comer edge. Wipe away any excess glue with a cloth or paper towel.

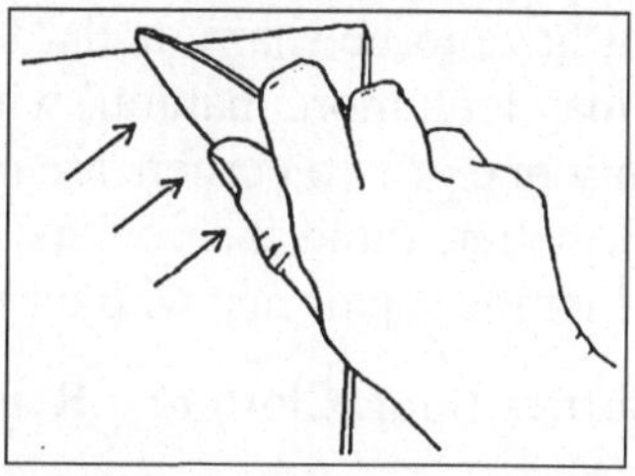

Note how much excess glue came out of the corner and use that as a gauge to decrease or increase the amount of glue used. A small amount seeping out is good because it means that the glue has reached all the layers of cardboard. Too much adhesive seeping out is wasteful and makes a mess to clean up. For sharp flat comers, cover each side of the comer with wax paper or non-stick material and clamp between two pieces of book board using Binders or Bulldog clips. Use dense mat board or book board, not corrugated cardboard that will compress under the pressure of the clips.

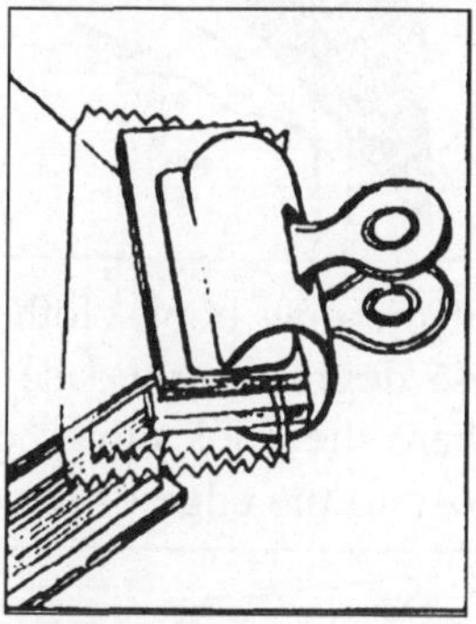

Another way to achieve flat comers is to lay the repaired comer flat against the work table and weight it down with a paper covered brick.

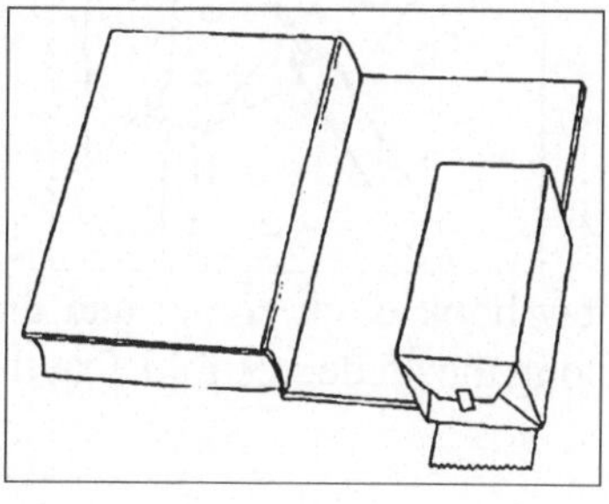

Comers do not have to be sharp or flat to protect the book. Some older books may look more 'natural' with rounded corners, especially when only one or two corners are repaired. If rounded comers would look better, mold the comers into position while the glue is wet and let the repair dry without weight or pressure.

Attaching New Corner Book Cloth to a Repaired Corner

After the corner book board is repaired, cut a piece of new book cloth to cover the repair. The grain of the book cloth must run parallel with the spine of the book. Glue the book cloth patch in place on the outside of the book cover. Dry under weight.

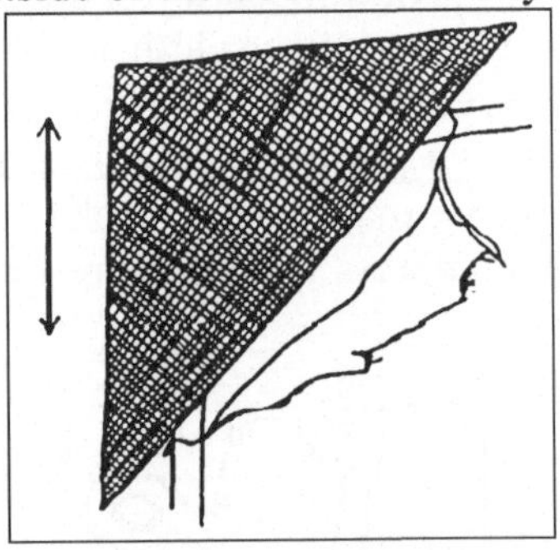

Fold the point of the new book cloth comer over the book board so it forms a 45 degree angle. Use a needle-in-a-stick to mark the position where the book cloth covers the comer. This mark should be as close to the edge of the comer as possible

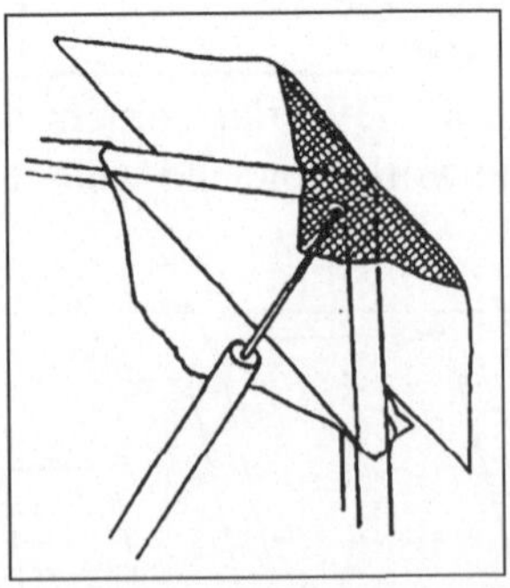

Unfold the new book cloth comer and draw a line through the needle point, along the 45 degree fold. Cut the book cloth along this line.

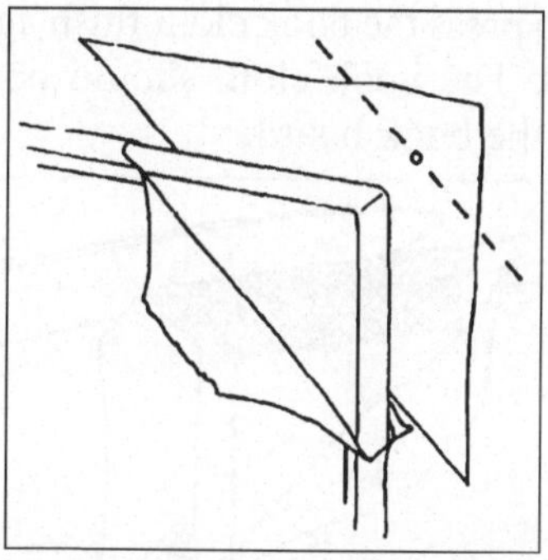

The new book cloth patch has two edges. Regardless of which corner is being repaired, the top or bottom edge of the book will be designated as the top. The other edge will be the fore edge of new book cloth patch.

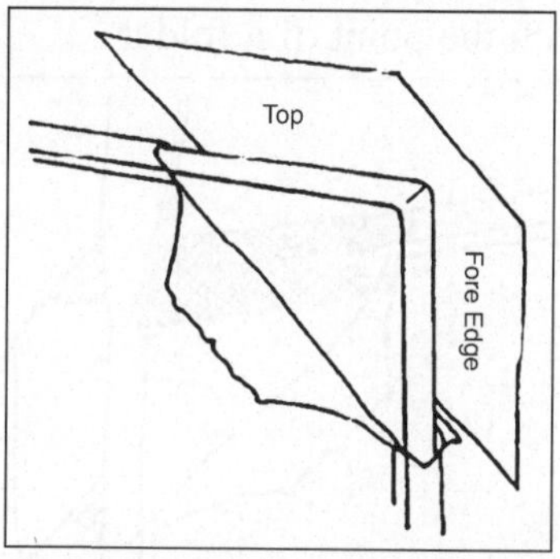

Apply PVA along the top edge of the new book cloth then fold the edge over the book board.

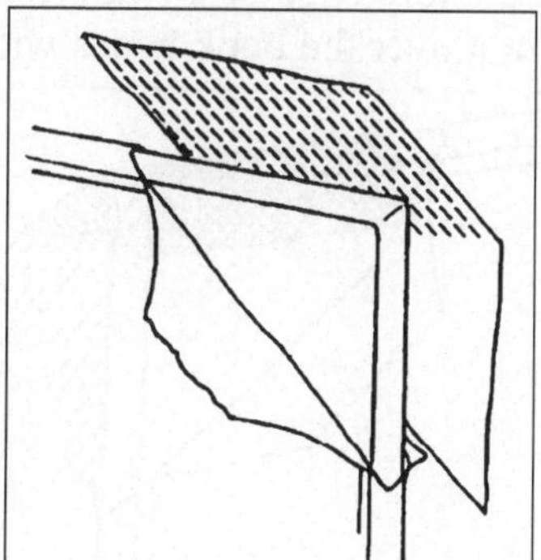

Use a folder to press the book cloth flush against the thickness of the book board. The book cloth should be glued completely flat to all sides of the book board.

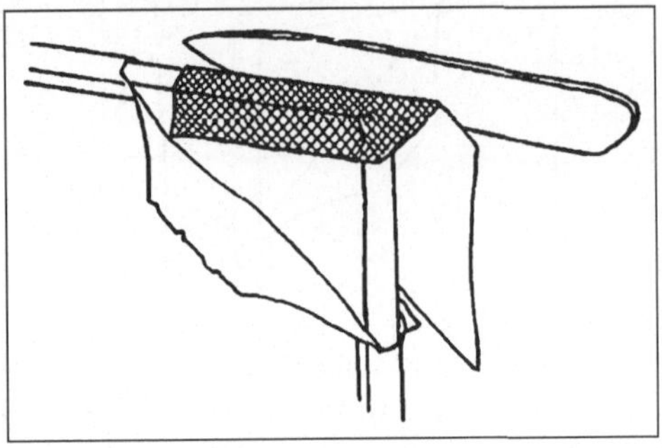

The new book cloth has a tendency to bulge out at the corner so push the new book cloth downward against the front edge of the book board with the point of a folder.

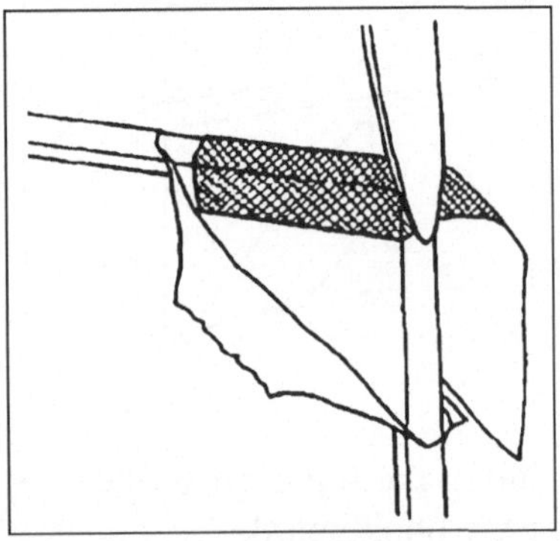

Apply glue to the fore edge of the new book cloth and work the cloth into position over the book board with a folder.

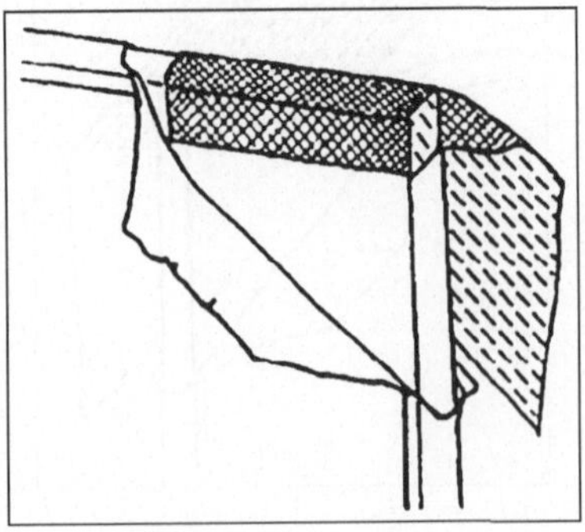

Use a folder to work the new book cloth flat against the book board and slightly round the corner.

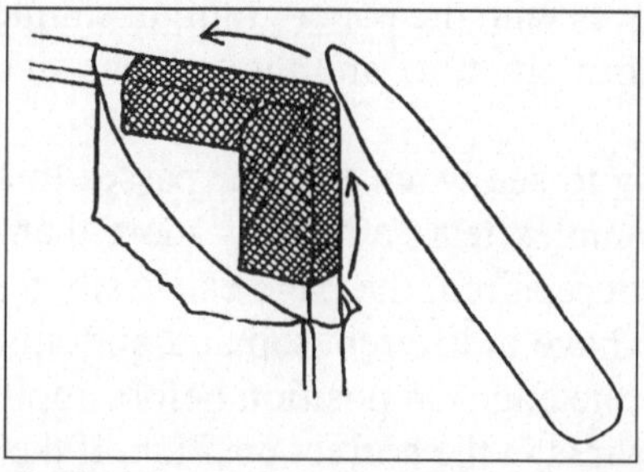

The original cloth can be trimmed to eliminate the ragged edges and glued down or the ragged edge can be glued as is. Gluing the loose threads down can sometimes help camouflage the new book cloth if it is not a good colour match. Dry the repair under weight using paper covered bricks or between pieces of book board with Bulldog clips.

Some older books may look more 'natural' with rounded corners, especially if only one comer is being repaired. For rounded comers, mold the corners into position while the glue is wet; dry without weight or pressure.

PAPER TEARS, CUTS AND LOSSES

Illustrations in this part show each repair completed in a bound book. The same techniques are used for a single sheet of paper not bound in a book.. Paper tears are a simple repair often handled incorrectly with clear plastic tape. Clear plastic tape covers up the problem but it does not repair it and it can cause additional damage to the paper over time.

Repairing Simple or Complex Tear

Paper tends to tear at an angle so most tears will have a top and a bottom. If the tear passes through the text or an illustration, it is easy to see which is the top or bottom because the bottom of the tear will show the white paper fibres. If the tear does not pass through text, look at the tear very carefully before pasting it together.

Some tears will go with the grain of the paper while others go against the grain. Tears that go with the grain of the paper will usually be smooth and straight while tears that go against the grain will tend to have more feathered edges and will curve as they try to align themselves with the paper grain. In simple paper tears the page has been torn one time and the tear has an obvious top and bottom.

This is easy to see when the tear passes through the text or illustrations. Complex tears are really more than one tear. When a tom page is not repaired, the page can easily tear again and the second tear can have a different top and bottom. Always look at the tear and lay the edges in position before applying adhesive to make sure the tear is in the correct position. If the edges are not in the correct position, the repair will not lie flat and the text or illustration may be obscured.

There are three ways to repair paper tears in conservation book repair:

- using wheat paste alone
- wheat paste with Japanese repair tissue
- document repair tape.

Repairing Tears with Wheat Paste Alone

When the paper tear has a strong, obvious top and bottom edge, applying wheat paste to the edges of the tear can be enough to bond them together. Use a very fine paint brush, microspatula or needle to apply wheat paste to the top and bottom edges of the tear and press them together.

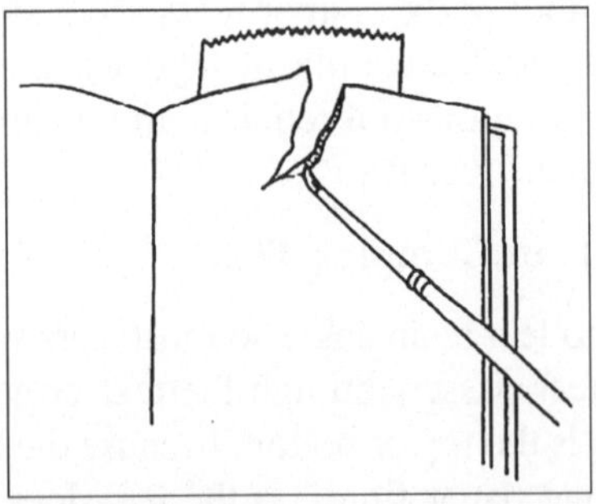

Cover the repair with wax paper or Hollytex and press the edges of the tear together with a folder. Remember to always best to work form the base of the repair towards the edge of the page.

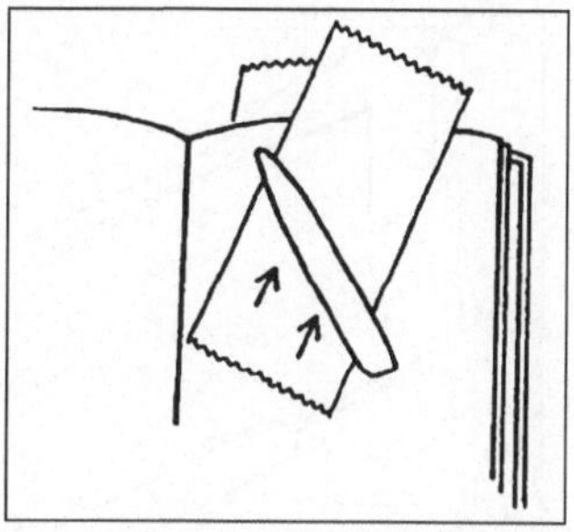

Wipe away any excess paste that is forced out of the edge of the tear. Note how much excess paste was used and try to use less for the next repair. Always aim for enough paste; not too little, not too much.

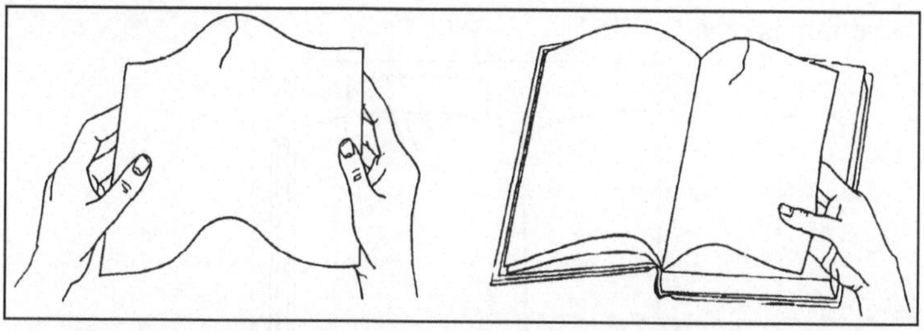

When the repair is dry, curl the paper around all the edges are well adhered. the repaired tear and make sure If there are loose edges, repaste and dry under weight.

If the page creases at the repair, consider applying a Japanese repair tissue patch over the repair. If the tear is not properly aligned, moisten the area with water to release the repair and redo it.

Repairing Tears with Japanese Repair Tissue Patch and Wheat Paste

Japanese repair tissue adds strength to a repair. It is used when the tear does not have wide, overlapping edges and needs reinforcement. Read book repair tools and techniques for instructions on tearing and applying paste to Japanese repair tissue. Choose the best method for tearing and applying paste before beginning the repair. Apply paste on the Japanese repair tissue, then pick up the tissue using a needle, micro spatula or fine tweezers.

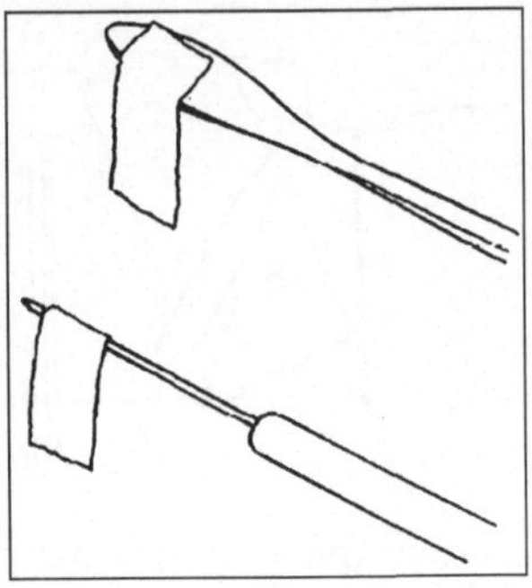

Carefully lay the tissue on the tear. If the tear is at the edge of the page, extend the Japanese tissue 3/8" past the edge of the paper. This extension can be turned under now or trimmed when the repair is dry.

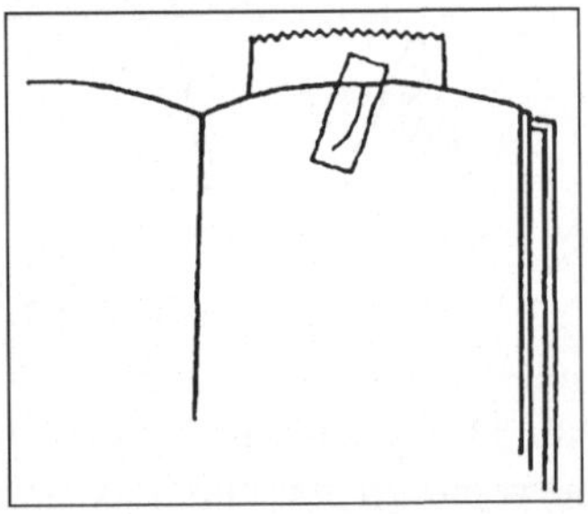

It can be difficult to work with a piece of Japanese repair tissue over 3" so try repairing long tears with several short, overlapping pieces of Japanese tissue. While it may seem inviting to use one long piece of tissue, it is much harder to control, and the finished repair can look clumsy.

Once the pasted Japanese tissue is laid over the tear, cover it with a strip of wax paper and use a folder to gently press the edges of the tear together. Remember to always work from the base of the repair towards the edge of the page.

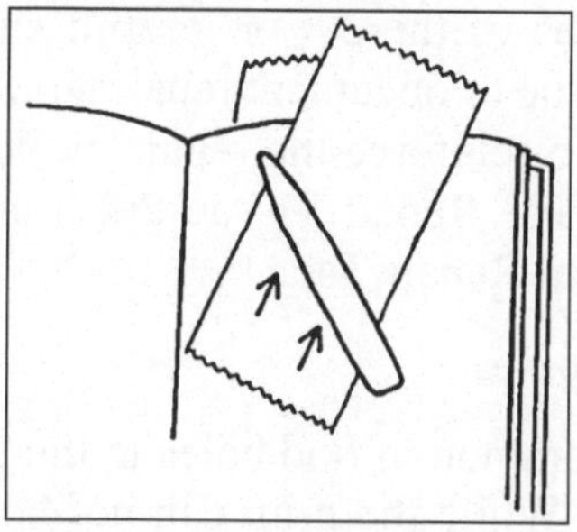

Wipe away any excess paste that is forced out of the edge of the tear. If there is much excess, use less next time. When the entire tear is repaired, cover it with wax paper or non-stick material and blotter paper, then put it under weight. Remember, if the repair does not dry under weight, the paper can buckle and curl After the repair is dry, curl the paper around the tear and make sure all the edges are well adhered. If there are loose edges, repaste and dry under weight. If the page creases at the repair, consider applying a second Japanese repair tissue patch on the opposite side of the original repair.

Repairing Tears with Document Repair Tape

In general, it should only be used on books that are not valuable or part of a library's permanent collection. Make sure the edges of the tear are lined up correctly and apply the tape over the tear. Do not try to repair a long tear with only one piece of tape. If necessary, apply tape on both sides of the paper to attach loose edges but remember that this will add two extra layers of thickness to the book. Archival tapes are usually 5/8 to 1" wide. Tape that wide can often be cut in half or thirds so as to lessen the amount of tape used in each book. In addition to saving money, it will also be better for the book. When tape is applied to both sides of a repair, cut the second piece a little wider than the first so the edges are offset.

Repairing Paper Cuts

Paper cuts slice completely through the paper fibres so they do not have a top or bottom feathered edge. Paper cuts must be repaired with a Japanese repair tissue patch or document repair tape. Since the cut is unsupported, it might be better to put repair tissue on both sides of the cut or wrap a short amount of the Japanese repair tissue or document repair tape around to-the back side of the repair to reinforce the repair. Follow the instructions for applying Japanese Repair Tissue Patch and Wheat Paste or Applying Document Repair Tape.

Repairing Paper Losses

It is not too common to find holes in the middle of the page, but it can happen. While the print can not be restored, the page should be mended to prevent further damage. Choose two layers of Japanese tissue that will be close in thickness to the repaired page. Tear two pieces of Japanese tissue to cover the hole using the techniques covered in Tear A Japanese Tissue Patch Over The Damaged Area. Protect the text block with wax paper on either side of the damaged page. Paste up one piece of Japanese tissue, position it on the page and work the edges into place. Paste up the second piece of repair tissue and lay it in place, working edges down with a folder. Cover with wax paper or non-stick material and blotter. dry under weight. After the repair is dry, curl the paper around the tear to ensure all the edges are well adhered. If the edges are loose, re-paste and dry under weight, then test again.

Repairing Missing Page Corners

Choose two layers of Japanese tissue that together will be close in thickness to the repaired page. Protect the pages behind the repair with wax paper. Use a piece of black mat board to highlight the edge of the repair. Fold a piece of Japanese tissue in half and place over the missing comer. The edges of the patch should extend past the edges of the page.

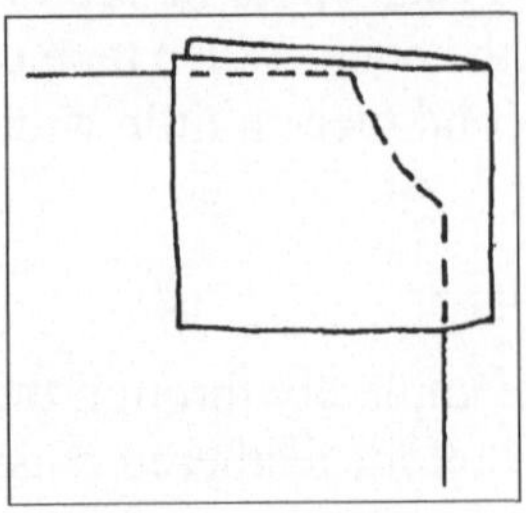

Needle or water tear the two layers of tissue. The patch should be about 1/16" wider than the loss.

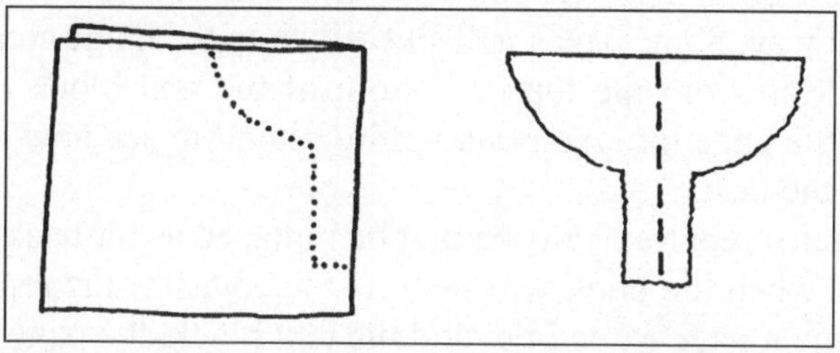

Apply paste to the repair patch and position the repair patch on one side of the missing comer. Work the edge of the patch into place. Fold the patch over and work the edges of the patch into the page. Dry under weight and trim any excess margin. After the repair is dry, curl the paper around the tear to ensure all the edges are well adhered. If the edges are loose, repaste and dry under weight, then test again.

INTERMEDIATE BOOK REPAIRS

Intermediate repairs can be handled easily in a library and will keep books circulating and available to patrons. Read through the directions for each repair before starting and be sure to have all the materials needed on hand.

TIPPING-IN DETACHED PAGES

Tipping-in is one way to reattach a detached page or plate, errata sheet or replacement page. Tipping-in is not used to put a entire book back together. If too many pages are loose from the binding, the book should be re-sewn, sent to the bindery, or replaced.

'Too many pages' can vary from book to book, but generally more than 3-5 pages is too many. Tipping-in is generally used on text blocks that are adhesive bound with tightly glued spines. The tight spine keeps the book from opening flat and will help to hold the tipped-in page in place. While the general rule is to use paste when repairing paper, glue is used when tipping in a page. Paste can be a better bond between paper, but it is not as flexible as glue. Since the tipped-in pages need to flex and bend, flexible adhesive is very important.

Tipping-in a Single Text Page

Each book will accept a repaired or replaced page in a different way. Some pages will sit easily into the hinge area, others will slide in from the top or bottom of the text block. Practice putting the page into the book before gluing to see how the page goes in the best.

Often a repaired page cannot be replaced as far back into the spine as when the book was new. If the edges of the repaired or replacement page extend beyond the text block, the page can tear and need future repair. If the page does not fit correctly in the text block, especially in the case of replacement pages, trim the height of the page so that the top and bottom edges will be flush with the edges of the text block. Use a sharp X-acto knife and straight edge to trim the margins as scissors will not give a straight edge. Leave an oversized margin at the fore edge of the page which can be trimmed to the correct size after the page is tipped-in the book.

Applying Glue to a Page to be Tipped-in

Several methods can be used to apply glue to a page; practice each one and see which works best. Often, different techniques will work in different situations. Using a very small paint brush apply glue to the edge of the page. Do not attempt to use a large brush to apply a small amount of glue. It is very difficult to control a large brush in such a small area and the glue could wind up in all the wrong places.

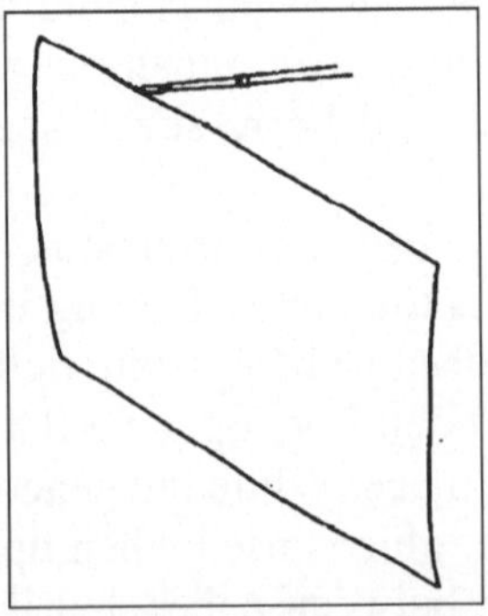

Use a piece of waste paper to mask the inner margin of the page. Leave approximately 1/16" exposed of the page exposed.

Apply glue across the waste paper towards the edge of the page. Remove the waste paper before placing the page in the book.

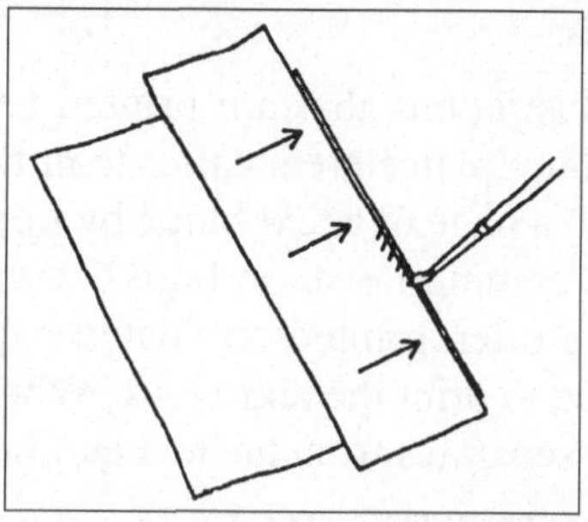

Apply a 1/8" line of glue on a discarded shelf list card or a piece of stiff card stock. Draw the inner edge of the paper along the line of glue making sure the paper edge is covered in a thin, even bead of glue. If the page needs more glue, draw it through the glue again. If there are some areas that have too much glue and others that are not covered, draw the page over a dry piece of card stock to even out the adhesive.

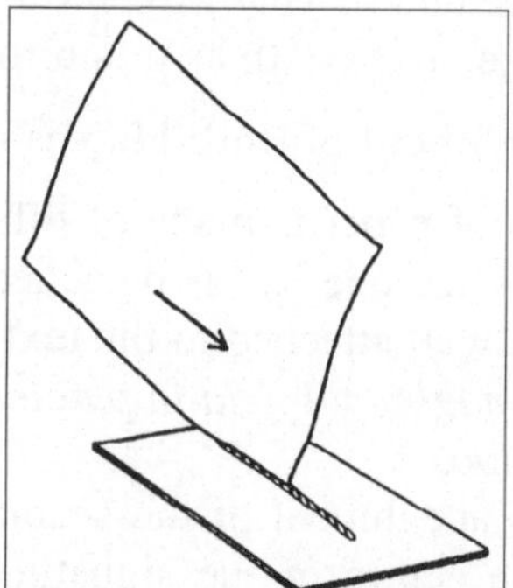

Once the glue is applied to the page, carefully maneuver the page into the book. Use the technique that worked best when the page was positioned in the book before the glue was applied. Put wax paper directly in front and behind the tipped-m page. Besides keeping moisture from traveling throughout the book it also protects the pages from excess glue that can adhere the pages to each other.

Put the repaired book under weight and let dry overnight. When the repair is dry, carefully remove the wax paper and make sure the page is securely attached in the book, then return it to the shelf.

Tipping-in Plates

Plates are illustrations that are printed separately from the text of a book. Many plates are smaller than the text block page and are attached to a page of a text block by tipping them in along one edge. This is common even in books with sewn text blocks because plates are often printed on coated paper that is heavier than the paper used to print the text block. When the original glue dries up, the plate separates from the text and falls out of the book.

HINGING-IN DETACHED PAGES

Hinging-in is generally used when the text block is sewn and the pages open flat, or when reattaching a plate that was originally tipped onto a page in the text block. A detached page can be hinged to the page in front or in back of it. While each mend should be evaluated individually, the strongest mend is usually accomplished by hinging from the back of the detached page to the front of the page irnrnediately behind it. That way, the Japanese repair tissue will support the page underneath as it is turned.

Checking the Attachment of Both Halves of a Folio

Each signature of paper is made of folios and each folio is made of 2 leaves. When one leaf is detached, always check that its other half is still well attached to the text block.

The other half might still held in place by the original glue, or it might also be loose:

- Check the attachment of the second half of a folio by finding the centre of the signature with the detached page. Look for the sewing threads at the centre of the signature and mark the centre with a slip of paper.
- Count from that centre towards the detached page, then go back to the marker at the centre of the signature and count the same number of pages in the opposite direction. That should be the other half of the folio.
- If the other half of the detached page is still firmly attached to the text block, hinge in the detached page using the technique outlined in the Hinging In A Single Page.

- If the other half of the detached page is also detached or loosely attached, both halves must be reattached. Options to reattach the pages are covered in Repairing And Reattaching Damaged Or Separated Leaves, Folios Or Signatures.
- If the spine of the text block is accessible, use the instructions in reattaching a separated signature page to reattach both pages.

Hinging-in A Single Text Page

Tear a strip of Japanese repair tissue approximately 1/2" wide and as long as the height of the page. Japanese tissue tends to stretch a little lengthwise when wet so it can be trimmed a little shorter than the page. Lay the page to be hinged on a piece of wax paper or non-stick material. Lay a strip of Japanese repair tissue on a piece of waste paper and mask one half of the width of the tissue. Brush wheat paste on to the exposed side, remembering to brush across the waste paper towards the edge of the Japanese tissue.

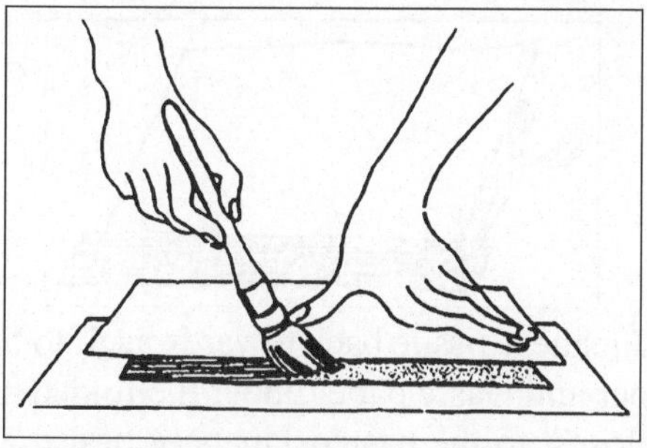

Remove the waste paper from the Japanese repair tissue and carefully lay the repair tissue on the inner margin of the page to be hinged. The pasted half of the Japanese tissue strip should be laid on the page while the half that is not pasted hangs off the page.

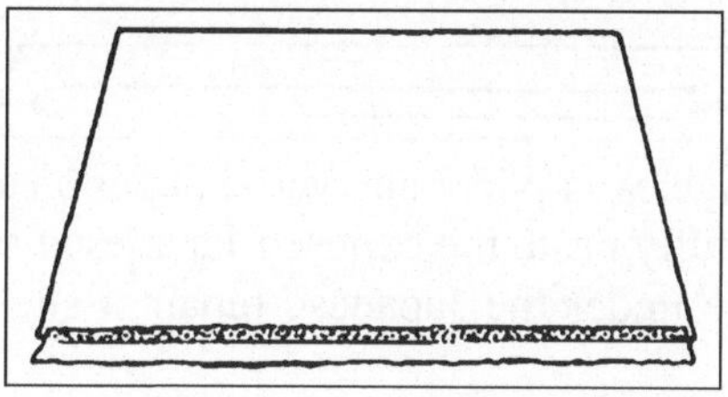

Use a folder to gently smooth the feathered edge of the repair tissue into the repaired page working from the middle of the Japanese tissue strip towards the edge. Take note of any excess paste. Try to use just enough paste to adhere the tissue to the paper and not so much that it is forced out the edge of the repair.

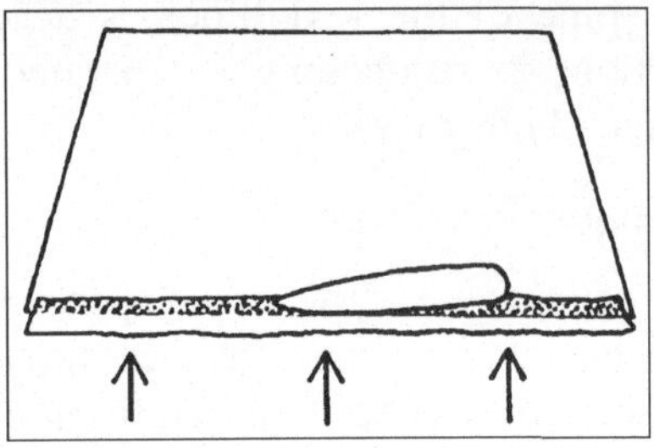

Cover the repair with wax paper or non-stick material and blotter paper then dry under weight. If blotter paper is used, changing it every 10-15 minutes will speed the drying time. When the first half of the repair is dry, trim the top and bottom edges of the Japanese tissue if they extend past the edge of the paper.

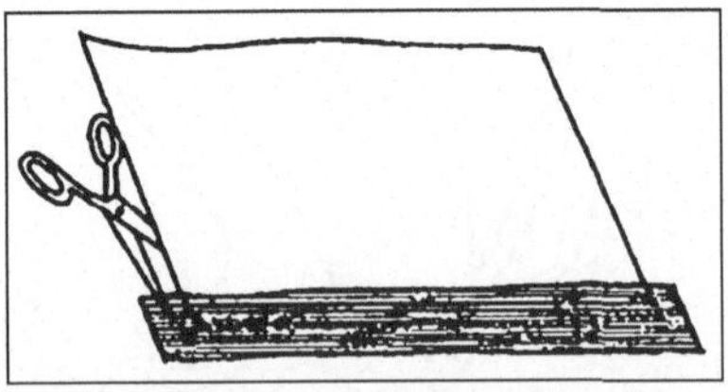

Fold the Japanese tissue back towards itself to form the hinge. Place wax paper and waste paper under the folded hinge, with the waste paper closest to the pasted Japanese tissue.

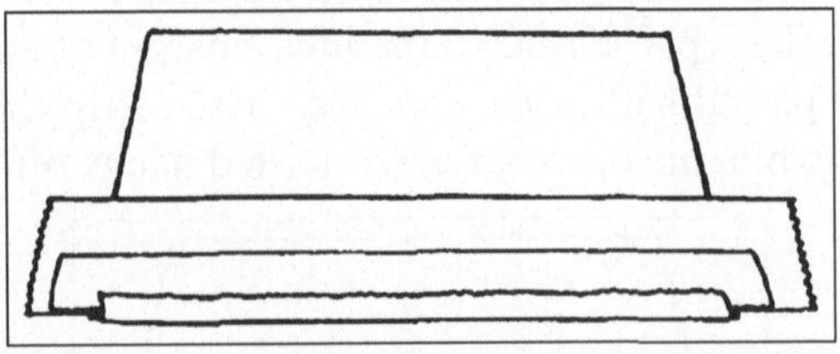

Lay the page, wax paper and waste paper on a sheet of waste paper and carefully paste the exposed Japanese tissue. Be careful not to get paste under the Japanese repair tissue or beneath the printed page.

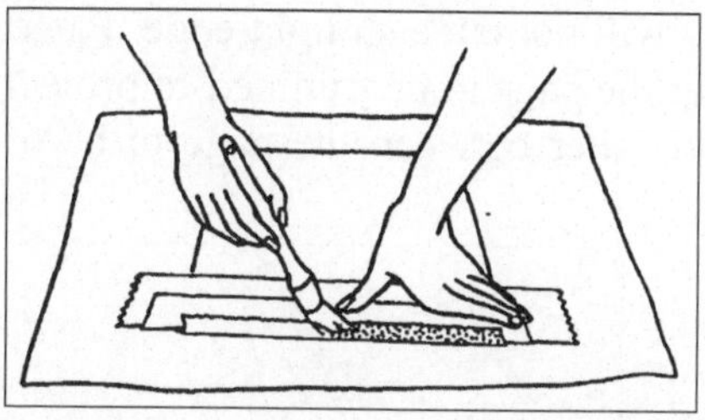

Remove the waste paper and carefully position the hinged page in the book. Use a folder to work the page and repair hinge into the inner hinge.

Double check placement of the page and hinge. Make sure the hinge is smooth and all the way back into the hinge area. Check to see that the edges of the hinged page match the edges of the top and bottom of the text block. Make Sure The Page Is Right Side Up! Place a piece of wax paper on either side of the Japanese tissue repair so the moisture will not travel into the text block. Put the book in a press or rods in the joints and dry under weight Keep the book under pressure until it is completely dry. If the Japanese hinge or the paper feels cool, it is not completely dry. If the edges of the hinge have not adhered to the page, apply a small amount of paste to the edge and gently work it in place with a folder. Replace the wax paper or non-stick material, close the book and dry under weight.

Trimming the Hinged-in Page

The edges of the hinged-in page may not be even with the rest of the text block. If the paper extends beyond the edges of the text block, trim it with an X-acto knife and ruler. Do not use scissors as they will not cut a straight edge. Place a thin piece of cardboard under the page to be trimmed-to protect the text block. Slip a flat metal ruler between the page to be trimmed and the page before it.

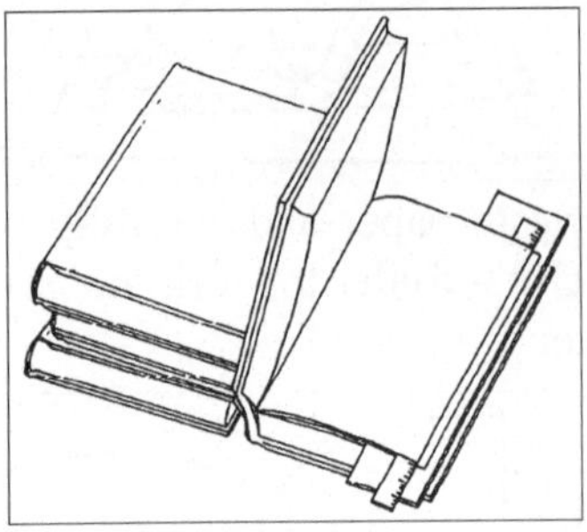

Line up the edge of the ruler so it is even with the edge of the page before it. With a very sharp scalpel or X-acto knife, trim the excess margin from the page beneath the ruler.

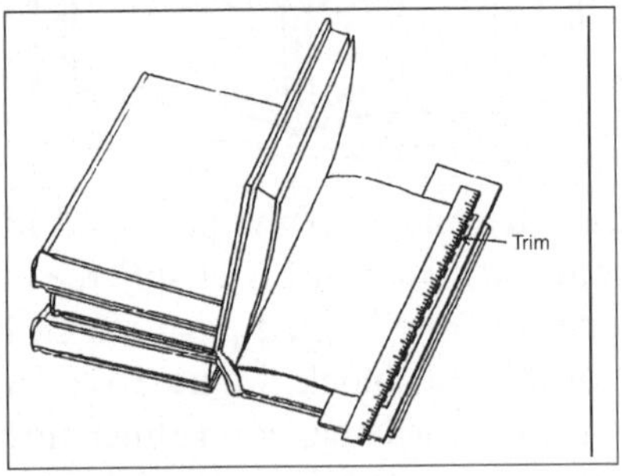

Hinging-in Several Pages

The exact number of pages that can be successfully hinged-in will vary from book to book. Remember, when pages are hinged-in, additional thickness are being added. Do not attempt to replace more pages than the width of the book spine will allow. There are several options to use when hinging in multiple pages.

One choice is to hinge the loose pages to one another as a unit and then hinge the unit into the text block. In another case it is best to hinge each page into the text block one page at a time, especially if only 1 or 2 pages are being hinged-in. The method used will be determined by the individual book.

Hinging-in Plates

Plates can be attached to a text block in several ways. Some plates are printed on folded sheets that are sewn into the text block as part of a signature. Other plates are printed on shiny, stiff paper, then tipped onto the page with glue. As the original glue dries up, the plate can separate from the text and fall out of the book. Plates can be replaced by re-tipping them to the page or reattached by creating a Japanese tissue hinge between the plate and the text block page. Use the Hinging-in A Single Text Page technique to hinge a plate into a book. Check the original placement of the plate on the page as some plates are smaller than the pages of the book and are often centred on the page. If the plate was originally tipped in along the side it can be reattached along that edge or along the top edge of the plate. Hinging from the top edge of the plate gives more support to a heavy plate.

REPLACING DAMAGED OR MISSING PAGES

When a page is damaged beyond repair or has been previously mended with clear plastic tape, it may have to be replaced to keep the book usable. If a page is missing entirely, the only option is to replace the page. Check to see if the library has a second copy of the damaged book to use to photocopy a replacement page. If there is not a second copy, request one through interlibrary loan, noting that the book is being used to photocopy replacement pages to repair a library book. Whenever possible, ask to receive the book, not photocopied pages from the book.

If the requested book does not circulate, ask for photocopies that are actual size, not reduced. The 8 1/2" x 11" photocopy paper will probably be larger than the book so the page will need to be trimmed to fit the book. Replacement pages add thickness to the spine that can cause it to swell or split. Usually only 3 or 4 replacement pages can be safely inserted. All pages should be photocopied front and back to keep the added thickness to a minimum. All photocopied pages need to have a 3/4-1" wide inner margin for tipping or hinging into a book. Replacement pages that fold out of the book, such as maps, should be copied in parts, hinged together, then trimmed to text block height.

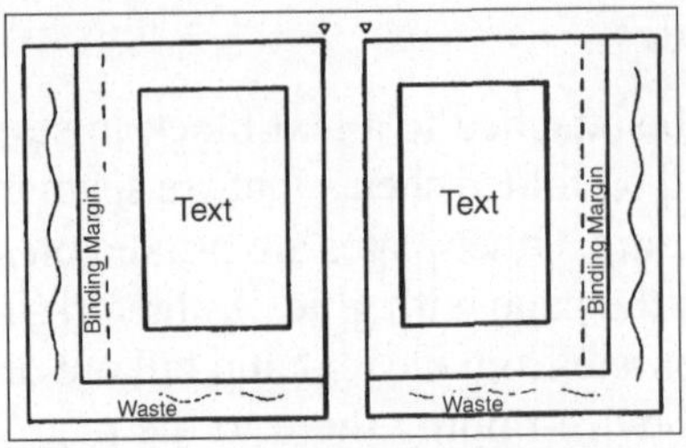

The margins of the copied page should be uniform. The text on both sides should be in alignment. Single-sided copies should be aligned with the upper right hand corner of the paper.

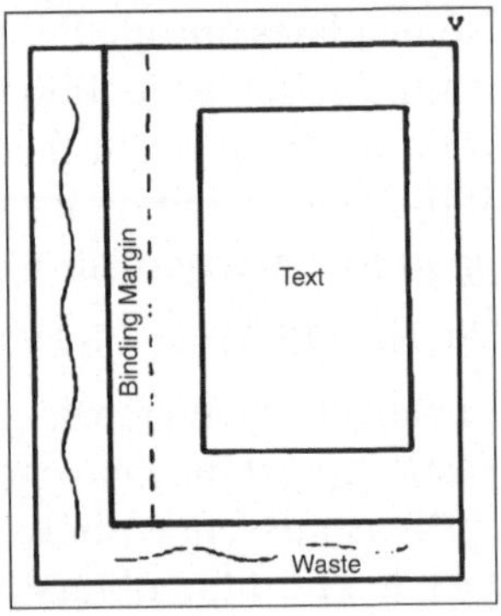

Since most books are not 8 1/2 x 1 1', it will be easiest to photocopy each page, cut and paste them into the correct position on a single sheet of paper, and then photocopy that page front and back. The edge margins can be trimmed to the correct size after the page is copied. Use a light table or work on an outside window to line up the print and margins on the two pages for the correct placement. If the cut and pasted photocopy came directly from the book, the finished replacement page will be a second generation copy. The more generations a copy is from the original, the less clear the print will be. If possible, use acid-free bond paper to make copies for replacement pages.

Regular bond paper is acidic and can cause future damage to the book. Acid-free bond can be more expensive than regular photocopy paper but one package of acid-free paper will last a long time if it is only used for photocopying replacement pages. Acid-free paper is also available in 11 x 14" and 11 x 17". These larger sizes can be useful when replacing end sheets printed with maps or printed information. Some photocopy machines have double-sided copy features, but it is not always best to use this feature. When a photocopy machine has a doublesided copy feature two separate paper trays are used, one outside the machine to load the paper and one inside the machine to store the paper between the first and second printing steps.

Using two different paper trays often means the margins on the two sides of paper do not line up correctly. Each machine is different so experiment to see how a particular machine works. If a photocopy machine does not have a double-sided copy feature or it does not make accurate double-sided copies, double-sided photocopies can still be made by copying the first page and then manually re-inserting the paper into the paper tray to print the second. For proper registration, It is important to use the same leading edge of paper in both procedures. There may still be a difference in the margins but it will be consistent each time and the cut and pasted copy can be readjusted to compensate for it. For instance, the second page of copy might need to be 3/8" lower than the first for the final copy to be even on both pages. Trim the finished copy to the correct height then tip-in or hinge-in the page. Trim the fore edge to the correct width using the instructions in this chapter.

REPLACING MISSING CORNERS ON CASE BOUND BOOKS

It is not uncommon for a corner of a hard cover book to be damaged or destroyed while the rest of the case is in reasonably good condition.

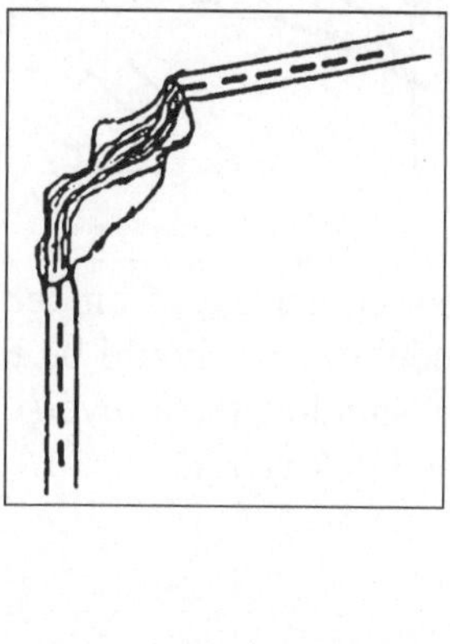

These corners can be replaced, and the book returned to the shelf. Cut through the book cloth along the top and side of the book board, cutting from the undamaged cloth towards the damaged corner. Make sure to cut far enough back so that the ragged edge of the book board is fully exposed.

Fold the book cloth out of the way and make a diagonal cut, trimming off the ragged edge of the damaged corner. Trim only as much board as necessary

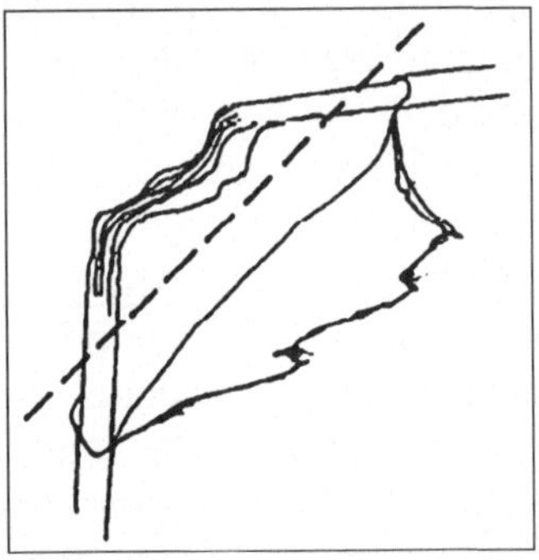

Make a second diagonal cut, about 3/8-1/2" inside the first cut. This cut should only go through half of the thickness of the book board. Use a knife or microspatula to remove half the thickness of the book board to create a step

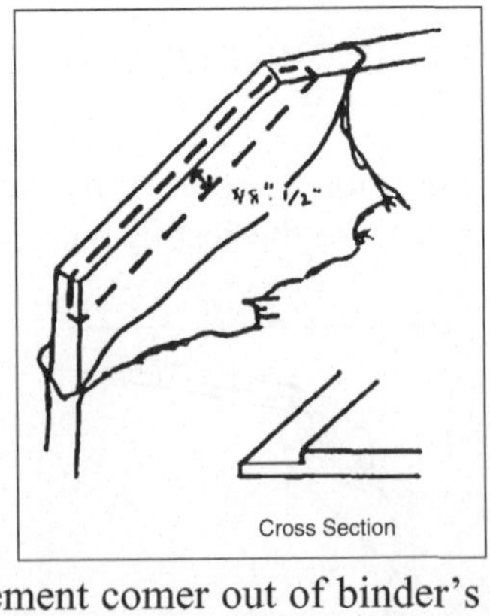

Cross Section

Cut a replacement comer out of binder's book board or mat board. This replacement comer should be the same thickness as the original board and should have a reverse step that will fit into the cut out step on the book cover.

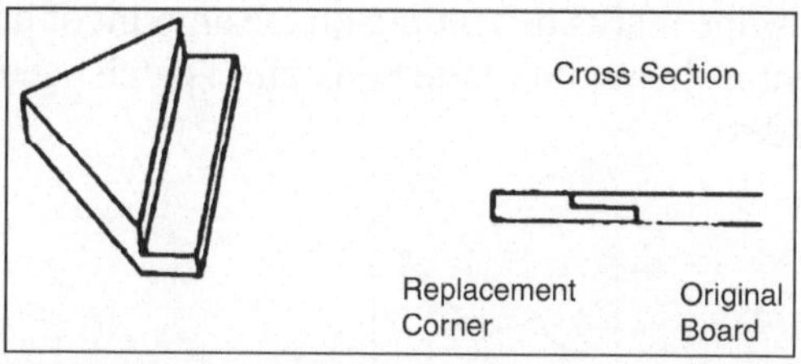

Two or more layers of binder's board or mat board can be glued together to achieve the desired thickness. Board from a discarded book can also be saved and used. If the undamaged comers have become rounded with use, it might be better to round the replacement comer to blend in with the other comers. Fit the replacement comer onto the book and make sure it is the proper fit. Apply glue to the 'step' in the book board and the replacement comer and fit in place. Dry the repair under weight using paper covered bricks. Cut a piece of new book cloth to fit the comer repair. Remember the grain of the comer cloth must run parallel with the spine of the book.

ADVANCED REPAIRS

Serious repair problems take more time and skill to accomplish than any other level of repair. Often, books that need advanced repairs were poorly repaired in the past so a library beginning a conservation book repair programme may have a great many volumes in need of advanced repairs. As the repair programme progresses, there will be fewer and fewer books needing this level of treatment.

REPAIRING THE SPINE HEAD OR TAIL

Often the head or tail area of a book cover spine wears out while the rest of the book is still in good condition. Damage at the head of the spine is often caused by improper handling and shelving techniques, especially pulling a book off the shelf incorrectly. While these problems can be easily repaired, staff and patrons should be educated on safe book handling.

Measuring and Cutting the Repair Patch

Cut a strip of paper 2" wide and 6-10" long. Wrap the paper snugly around the book spine and mark the edges of the spine. Place the marks at the edge of the paper. Add 1-2" to both sides of the book spine marks depending on the amount of damage. This measurement is the width of the book cloth patch needed to repair the tom header.

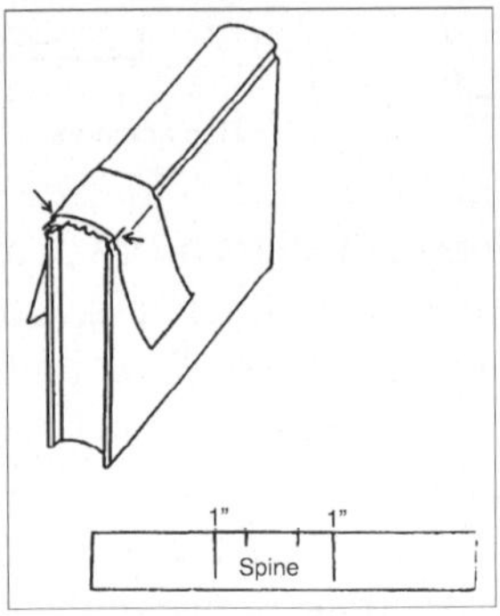

Cut a piece of book cloth the width of the total measurement and the length of the spine damage plus 1 1/2". The comers of the repair patch tend to curl when the patch is inserted, so trim them off diagonally. Cut only the very tip of the comer.

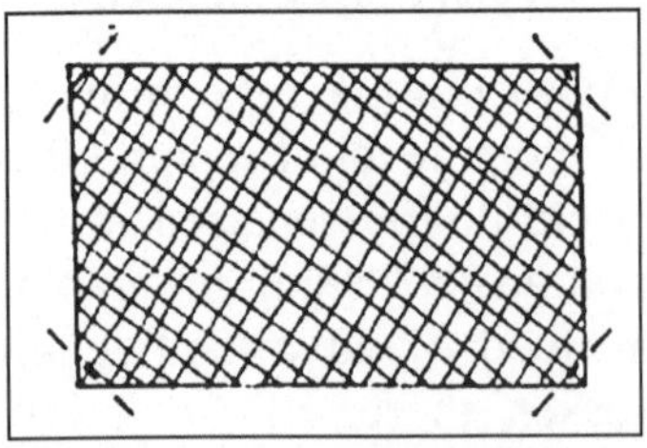

Fit the repair patch on the outside of the book and check to see that the fit is correct. The patch should extend at least 5/8" above the book board and 1/2" below the bottom of the spine damage.

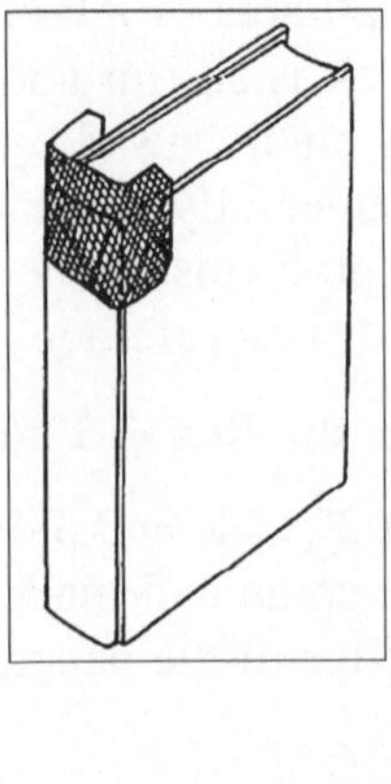

Preparing the Book for Repair

Support the book with another book or a stack of boards. Use an X-acto knife and ruler to cut through the book cloth turn-in along the edge of the endpapers at the head of the book. The cut should be 1-2" long.

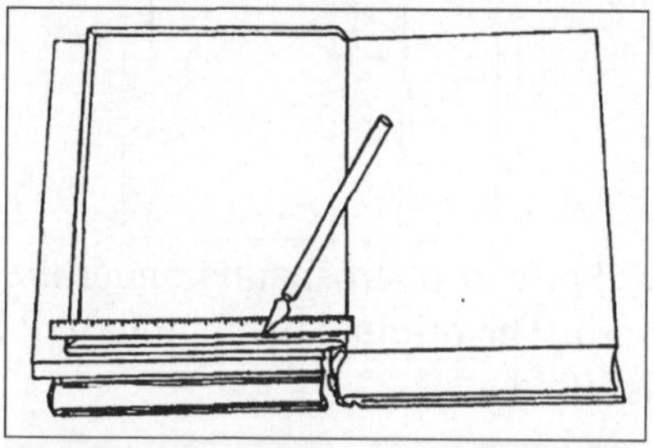

At the outer edge of the first cut, make a 90 degree cut across the book cloth from the edge of the endpaper to the top of the book board.

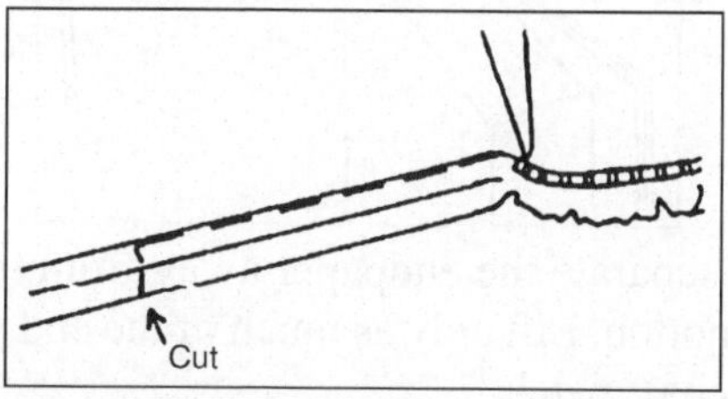

Use a knife or microspatula to lift the book cloth away from the book board. If necessary, clip through the original book cloth turn-in at the hinge to allow the cloth to lift up. DO NOT clip through the endpaper or the crash. Repeat these two cuts on the opposite book board. If the original spine turn-in is completely loose, remove it.

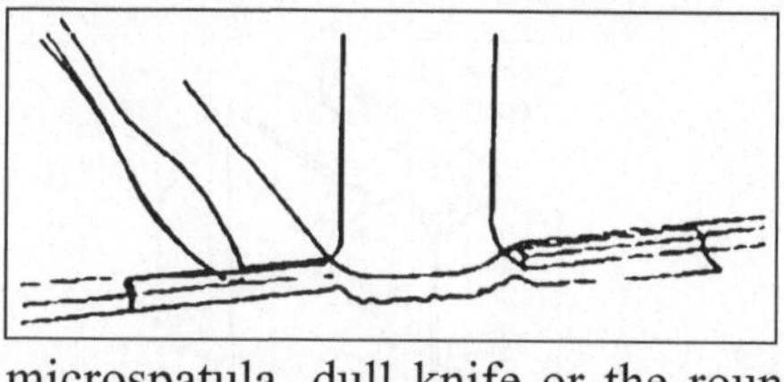

Using a microspatula, dull knife or the rounded end of a folder, lift the book cloth loose from the cover boards. Loosen only as much book cloth as necessary to slip in the repair patch. Work slowly and carefully as the book cloth can stretch or tear.

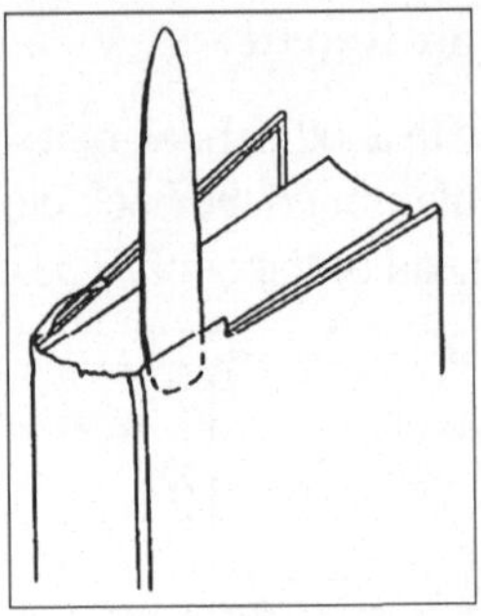

Insert a dull knife or microspatula under the original turn-in and the book board. The original book cloth will help support the endpaper as it is lifted.

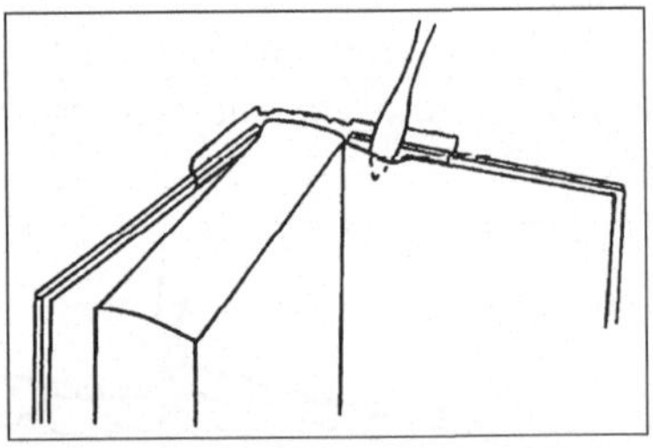

Carefully separate the endpaper away from the board with a gentle prying motion. Lift only as much of the end paper as needed to slip in the repair patch.

Fitting the Repair Patch to the Book

Slip the repair patch in place between the original book cloth and the book board. Make sure the patch is long enough and wide enough to cover the damaged area.

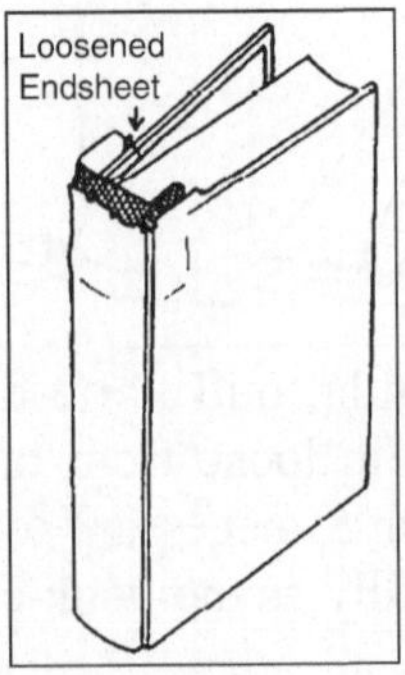

Use the long edge of a folder to work the patch into both cover joints.

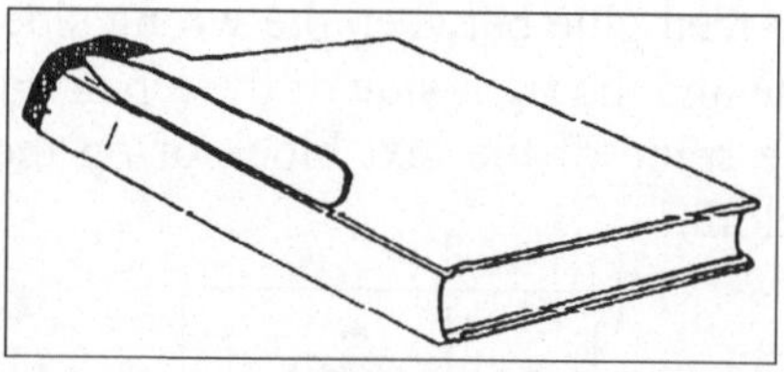

Take a moment to check the position of the patch. The new book cloth patch should lie flat against the book boards and spine of the text block. There should not be any wrinkles or buckles in the patch or the book cloth shine.

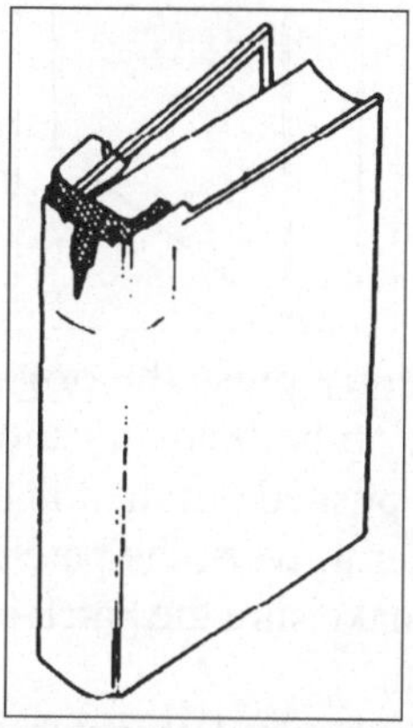

The patch should extend about 5/8" above the top of the book board and should extend at least l/2" below the bottom of the spine damage. It should also extend past both hinges towards the fore edge of the book. If the repair patch does not fit correctly, trim it down or cut a new one.

Gluing the Repair Patch in Place

In modem book case construction, the spine of the book cloth and the spine of the text block must move independently of one another in order for the book to open properly. DO NOT glue the repair patch to the spine of the text block. There are many older book structures that function differently from a case bound book. If a book looks or operates in an unusual way, carefully research the book structure or consult a trained book conservator before attempting a repair. With the repair patch in place, use a knife or microspatula to feed glue between the wrong side of the original book cloth spine and the right side of the repair patch. Do not put any glue on the spine of the text block or on the cut and lifted flaps of book cloth.

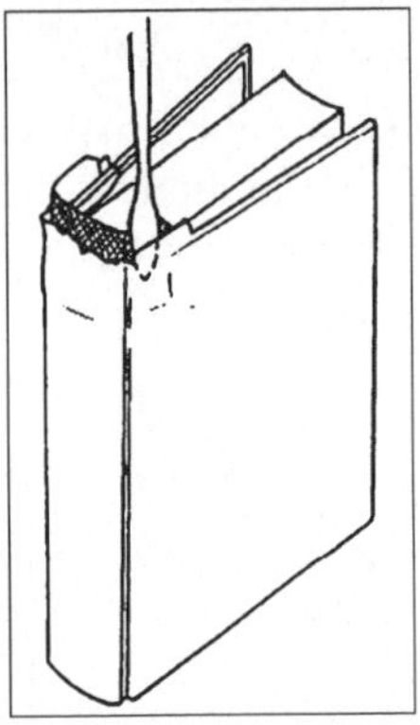

Use a folder to gently press the original book cloth against the repair patch. Work on both covers and the spine. Wipe away any excess glue that is pushed out the top of the repair patch. Use the long edge of a folder to work the patch into both cover joints. work this area well to make sure the patch is in the proper position. Double check the repair.

Make sure the new book cloth patch lies flat against the text block and the original book cloth lies flat against the patch. There should not be any wrinkles or buckles in the patch or the book cloth spine. If it is not a good fit, readjust it or replace it before the glue dries. Put the book in a book press or insert rods in the hinge areas and press under weight for about 10 minutes to allow the glue to set.

Tucking-in the Repair Patch Turn-in under the End Paper

Before applying any glue to the repair patch turn-in, fold it in position to make sure the patch is placed correctly. Starting on either edge of the repair patch, carefully begin to tuck the tumin into the space between the end paper and the board. As one side is tucked in, the rest of the turn-in will follow.

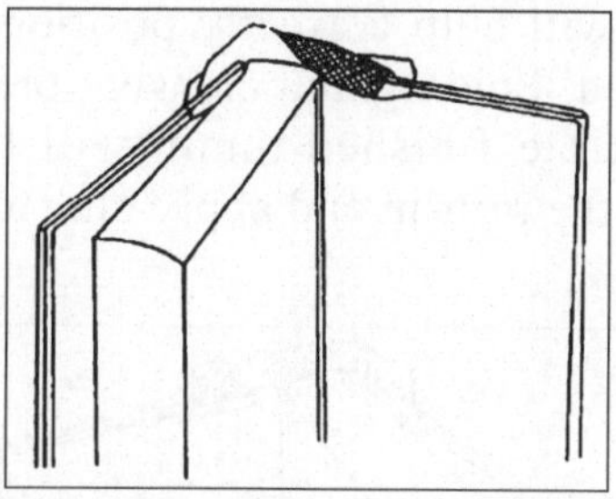

With the entire patch tucked in place, gently crease the top edge of the patch along the boards and in the spine area with your fingers. Set the book on the work table with the repaired end of the spine resting on the table. The edge of the new spine book cloth should be level with the original boards so it rests flat and even against the table.

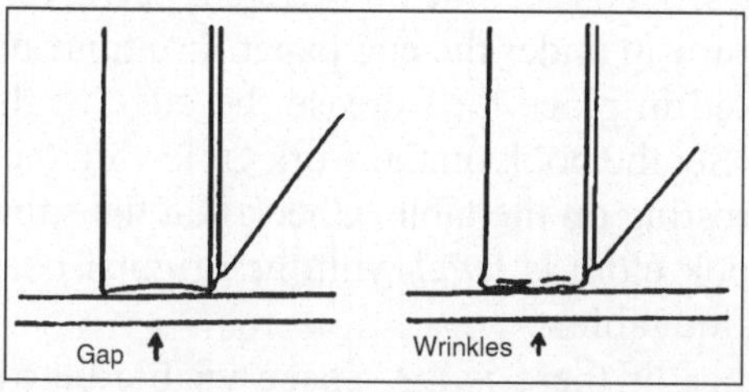

If there is space between the table and repair patch or if the book cloth wrinkles against the table, the position of the turn-in is not correct. Readjust the turn-in and check it again. When the turn-in is positioned correctly, lay the book on the table so that the spine is flat against the table: Use the pointed end of a folder to crease the folded repair patch along the top of the book boards and the spine turn-in.

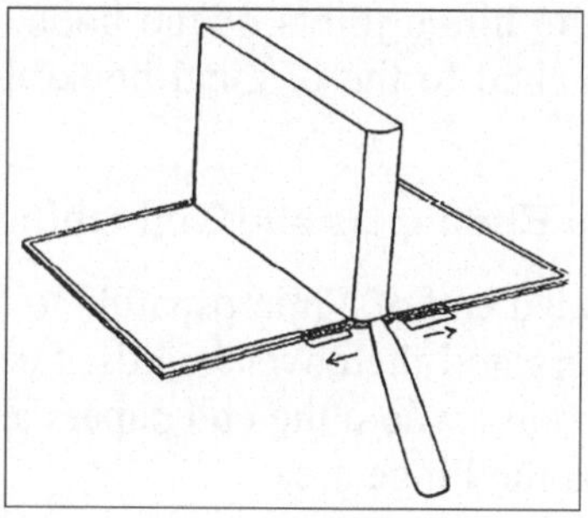

This crease will help correctly position the turn-in after the glue is applied. Folding and creasing the turn-in before it is glued assures the finished tumin will be in the correct position. Unfold the turn-in and apply glue to the inside of the patch turn-in.

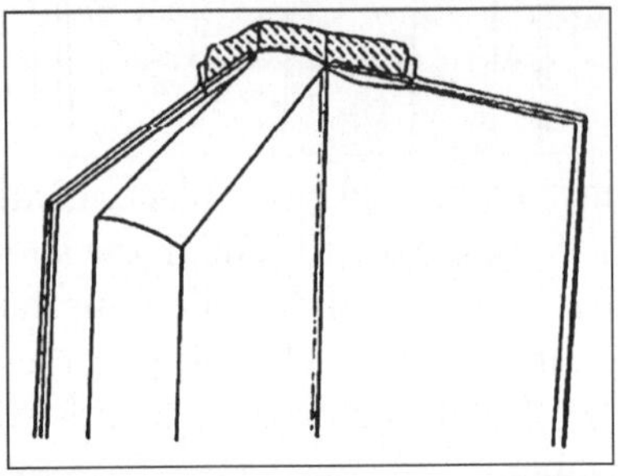

Working from either side of the repair patch, refold the glued repair patch turn-in under the end paper. Continue until the entire patch is tucked in place then crease the edge of the patch with your fingers. Set the book on the work table with the repaired end of the spine resting on the table. Check that the spine edge of the new spine book cloth is level with the original boards and rests even against the table.

Remember, if there is any space visible between the table and the repair patch or if the book cloth wrinkles against the table, the position of the tumin is not correct. Readjust the turn-in and check it again Position the book on the table so that the length of the spine is resting on the table.

Use a pointed end of a folder to crease the folded and glued repair patch along the top of the book boards and the spine turn-in. Use the long edge of a folder to work the repair patch and book cloth into the hinge joints of the book. At this point the patch will be attached to the original book cloth and the book boards.

Gluing Down the Endpapers and Tightening the Hinges

Use the rounded end of a microspatula to feed glue between the lifted endpapers and the cover boards. Feed the glue all the way down to the point where the end papers are still attached to the board and into the hinge area.

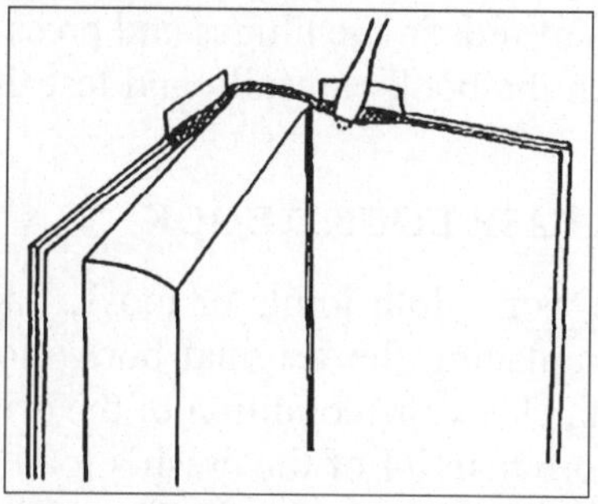

Use a folder to work the end papers into position, working from the centre of the end paper towards the edge of the book board. Wipe away any excess glue that is worked out.

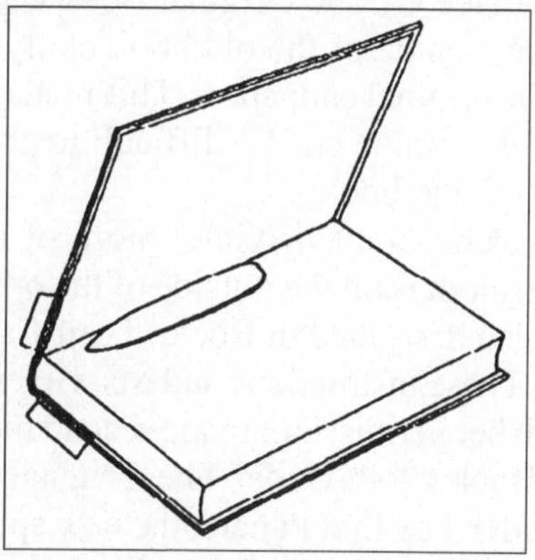

Apply glue to the cut flaps and press them into position. There may be a thin gap between the flap and the edge of the endpaper.

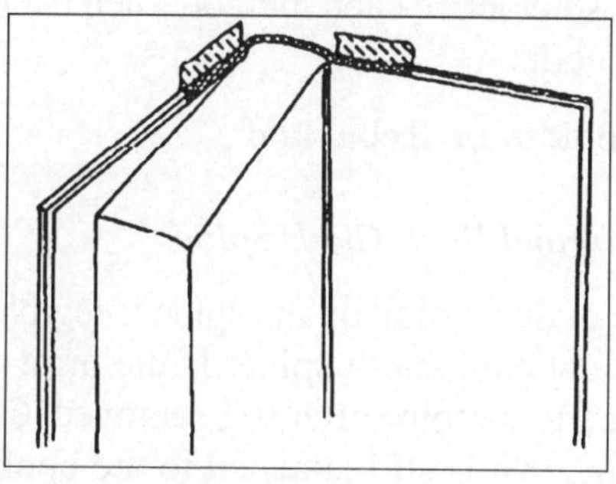

Lay a strip of wax paper in the joint areas. Put the book in a book press or insert rods in the hinges and press under weight for 10 minutes. Open the book carefully and test the front and back hinges.

REBACKING A CASE BOUND BOOK

Books with worn cloth joints or loose, flapping spines can be repaired by replacing the original book cloth spine. Before rebacking a book, check the condition of the original crash in the hinge area. If more than 1/4 of the crash's total height is broken, replace it before rebacking the book. That procedure is covered in Recasing A Case Bound Book. Two methods of rebacking are illustrated in this part. The first method, Rebacking With Book Cloth On The Outside Of The Original Book Cloth, puts the new book cloth on the outside of the old book cloth with the turn-ins glued on top of the original endpapers. This method can sometimes be faster but the new spine can be difficult to position well since it is constructed off the book.

From a cosmetic point of view, more of the repair shows because the book cloth is on the outside of the original book cloth. This method is also described in Books Their Care and Repair by Jane Greenfield, These instructions and Ms. Greenfield's drawings are reprinted with her permission. In the second method, Rebacking With The New Book Cloth Under The Original Book Cloth And The Turn-ins Under The End Papers, the new spine is constructed on the book with the tumins glued under the end papers. When the original spine is replaced, the new book cloth shows in only a small portion of the joint area. Often different methods work for different books so practice each method, then decide which to use on a particular book.

Preparing a Book to be Rebacked

Remove the Original Book Cloth Spine

If the print or decoration on the spine is legible, save the spine to glue to the new book cloth spine. If the print or decoration is not legible, discard the spine after it is removed. Carefully remove the original spine if it is still attached to the book. If the cloth in the joint is broken or terribly frayed, gently pull it loose. If the original spine is more firmly attached to the case, lay a straight edge 1/16-1/8" from the spine edge of the front board and use a knife to cut through the cover cloth. Be careful not to cut through the crash or the end paper and try not to trim away any print or decoration on the cover.

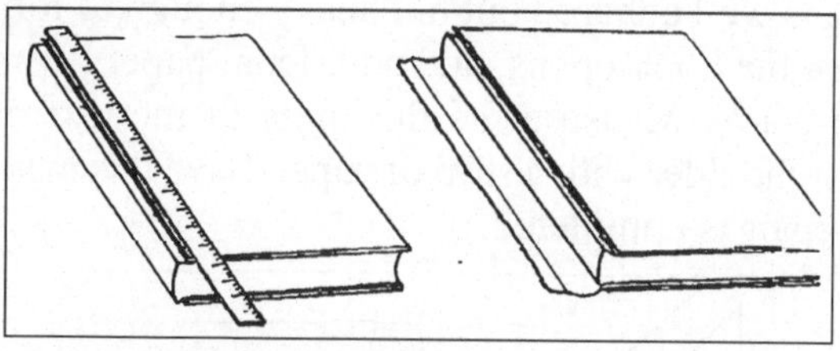

Turn the book over and repeat on the other side.

Check the Original Crash

If more than 1/4 of the total height of the original crash is tom or broken, it should be replaced before the book is rebacked.

Lining the Text Block Spine

When the book cloth spine is removed, examine the paper spine liner attached to the text block. This paper spine liner consolidates the signatures of the text block and helps evenly distribute the stress of opening the book. Many modem book manufacturers do use enough paper liners or a good quality of paper to line the spine. In many instances, the paper spine liner is not even completely glued down. Many libraries do not replace the paper spine liner when rebacking books. Taking the time to replace the spine liner ensures the book will function better and last longer.

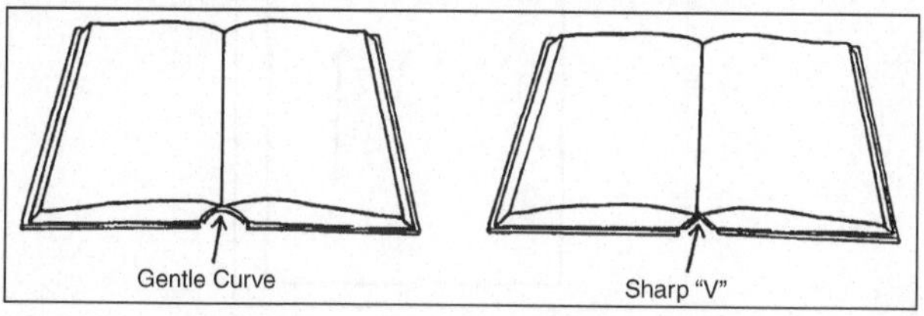

Open the text block to the centre of the book and see how the spine arches. Does it form a gentle curve or a sharp 'V'? When a book opens with a sharp 'V', all the stress of opening the book is concentrated in one place. A gentle curve evens out the stress of opening the book. If the original paper liner is not adhered to the spine of the text block, remove it by gently pulling it away or scraping it away with a dull knife.

Be careful not to damage the crash or the sewing threads. It is not essential that all the paper be removed. If the original paper spine liner is well adhered but not heavy enough to form a gentle curve when the book opens, add additional paper liners to create the gentle curve. Measure the thickness of the text block from shoulder to shoulder with a strip of paper. Save this measurements until the repair is completed.

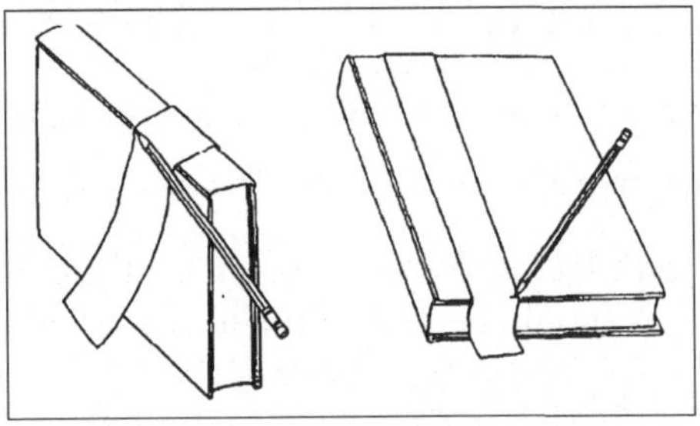

Transfer measurement A to the spine liner paper and cut a strip of spine liner paper. The cut strip should be longer than the height of the book boards. Remember the grain of the spine liner should run up and down the spine of the book.

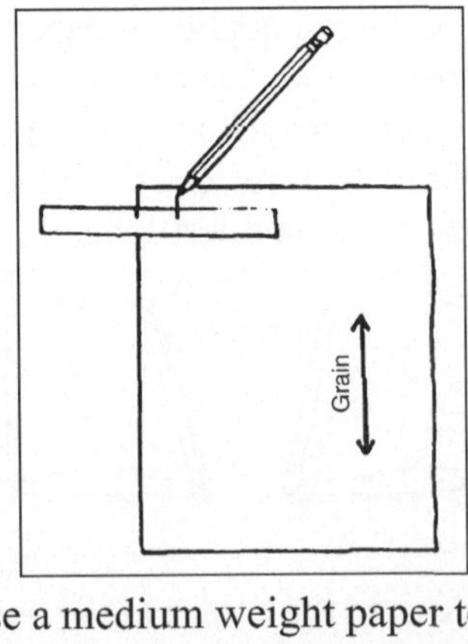

It is best to use a medium weight paper to line the text block spine; two or three layers of thin paper is better than one thick layer. Acid-free papers such as Permalife, Mohawk Superfine or Japanese repair tissue can be used. The paper spine liner must have the grain running from the head to the tail of the book and should be the exact height and width of the text block spine. Lay the spine liner against the spine of the text block, mark the height and then trim the spine liner to the exact height of the text block.

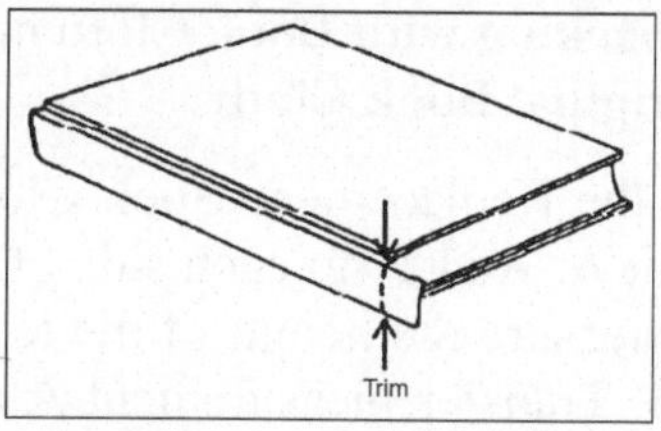

Apply adhesive to the spine liner paper in a star burst pattern and position on the text block spine. Firmly attach the paper spine liner to the text block spine using one or both of the methods below. Use a folder to rub the paper spine liner to the text block spine. Make sure the paper liner is well adhered to the text block; pay special attention that the edges are firmly attached.

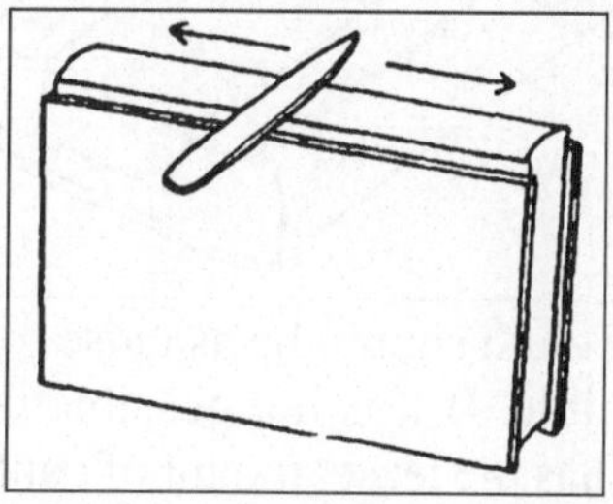

OR,

A 1" stencil brush makes a good tool to firmly attach the spine liner to the text block. Use an up and down tapping motion to work the spine liner into the text block. Pay special attention that the edges are firmly attached.

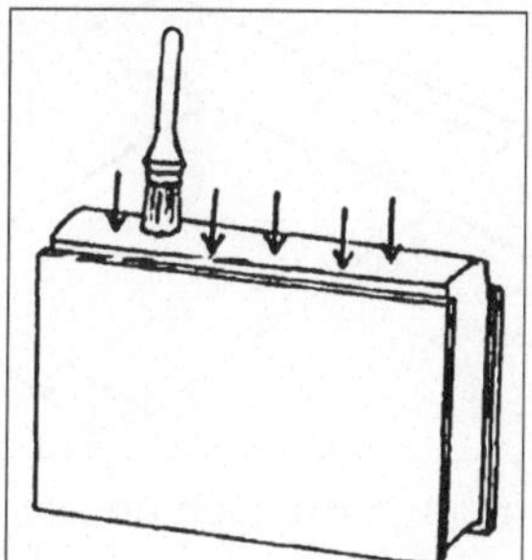

Let the paper liner dry then open the book. If the open text block forms a 'V' instead of a gentle curve, repeat the procedure. Many books need more than one layer of paper liner, especially if they are large or heavy.

Method One: Rebacking with Book Cloth on the Outside of the Original Book Cloth

Constructing the Replacement Book Cloth Spine Make or reuse Measurement A. Add 1" to each side of the spine width in measurement A. Measure the height of the text block and 1 1/2" to measurement B. Transfer measurement A and B to the book cloth. Be sure the-grain of the book cloth runs up and down the spine of the book then cut the book cloth.

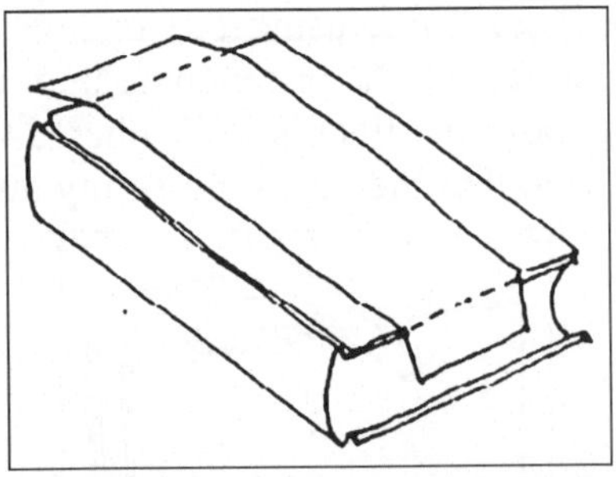

The new book cloth should be as close to the original colour and texture as possible. If it is not possible to match the colour, select a colour that has the least amount of contrast, *i.e.*, new black book cloth on a dark blue book. Centre the new book cloth on the front book board so the same amount hangs over the top and bottom. Crease the top and bottom of the book cloth to mark the height of the finished spine.

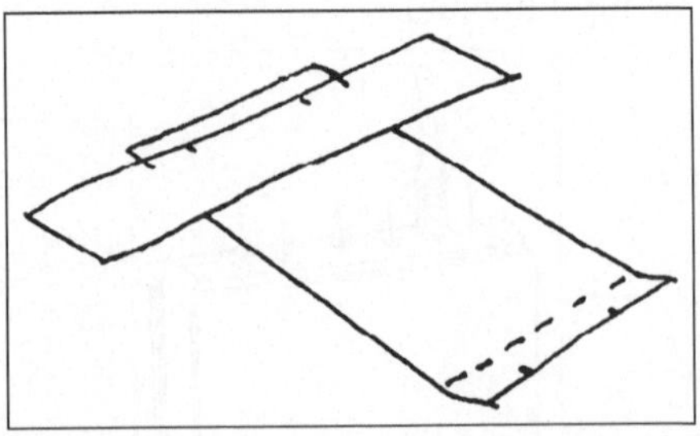

Centre measurement A on each crease and mark.

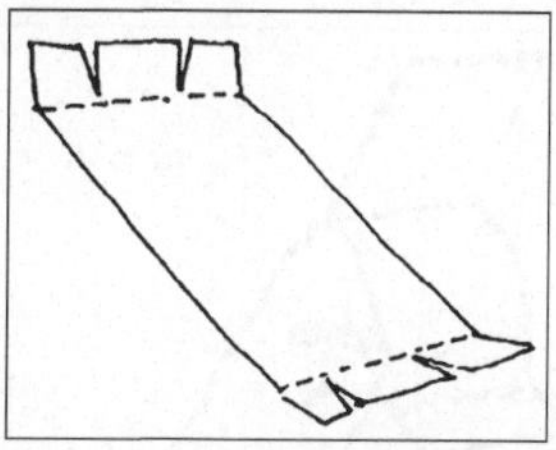

Cut V-slits at the crease line marks that correspond to the text block spine Measurements Cut a piece of acid-free paper to line and stiffen the book cloth spine. This liner is called the spine inlay. Sometimes two or more layers of acid-free bond are used for the spine liner. Mohawk Superfine or Daniel Smith Archival Paper has also been used with good results.

The Book Binding Supply Sources lists sources for purchasing acid-free paper. Always make sure the grain of the spine inlay runs in the same direction as the spine of the text block. If it does not, the book will not open easily. Place the spine inlay on a sheet of waste paper. Apply glue to the wrong side in the star burst pattern. Using the text block measurement marks and top and bottom creases, centre the spine inlay on the wrong side of the new spine cloth. Apply glue to the centre part of the spine turn-in at the top and bottom of the spine cloth; fold them over, and rub them down with a folder.

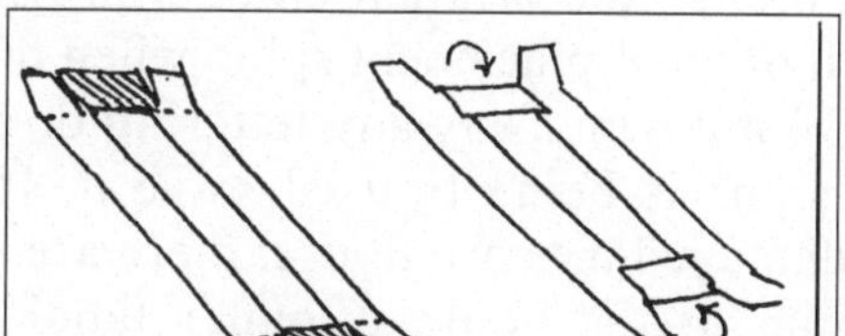

Protect the spine cloth with a piece of wax paper and place under weight to dry. If the original spine can be reused, lift up the turn-ins and peel the paper inlay away from the book cloth spine. If the paper is well attached to the spine, use a microspatula or dull knife to scrape it off. Dampening the inlay can release the adhesive. It is not essential to remove every bit of the paper inlay if it doesn't come off easily. The spine can be easily distorted or damaged so handle it carefully.

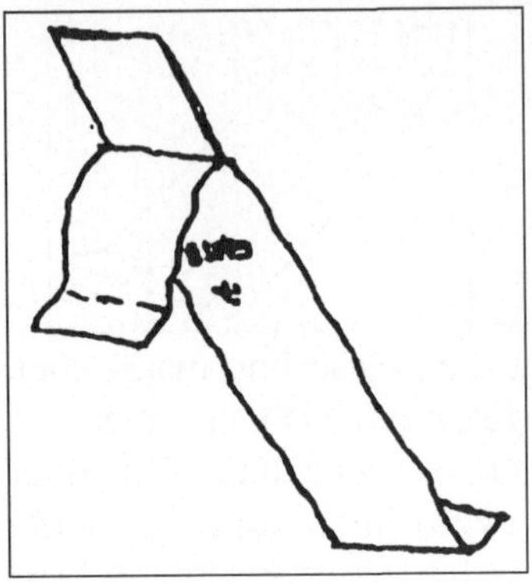

Using an X-acto knife or scalpel and ruler, trim away the ragged edges of the original spine.

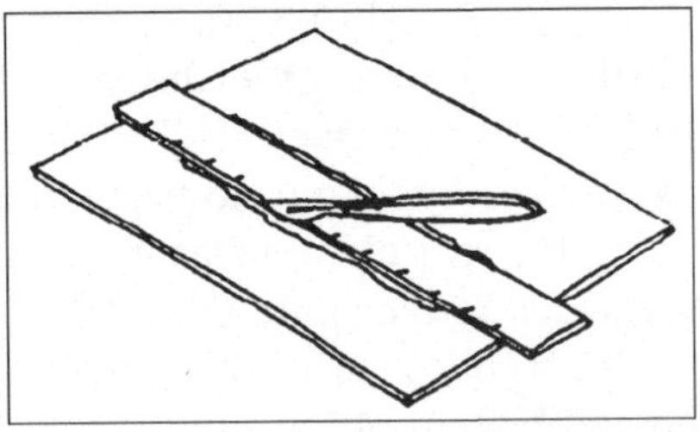

The original spine should be slightly narrower than the text block spine, so the original cloth won't interfere with the joint cloth of the replacement spine when the book opens and closes. Do not trim away any lettering or decoration. If the original spine is being re-used, save it. If the original spine is too damaged or worn to use, there are other ways to label the spine of the book. A paper label can be hand written, typed or typeset on a computer, then glued to the new spine cloth.

Another option is to write directly on the new book cloth with a permanent marker, such as those used to label quilts. Practice on a scrap of book cloth to make sure the label will be legible and attractive. If the option is an unsightly label, consider leaving the title off the spine. Lay the original spine or new label on a piece of waste paper wrong side up. Apply glue in a star burst pattern working from the centre towards the edges.

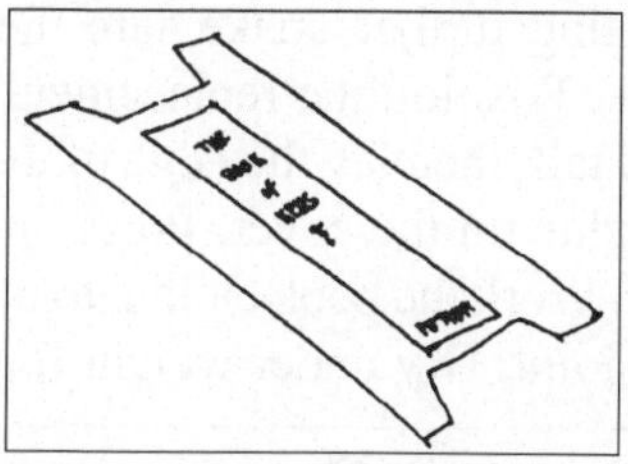

Centre the original spine or new label on the right side-of the replacement spine. Cover it with a piece of waste paper, and rub it down with a folder. All the edges should be well adhered. Protect the spine cloth with a piece of wax paper, and place under weight to dry.

Attaching the New Spine Cloth to the Text Block

Position the spine so the glued-down part of the turn-ins are centred on the text block spine, even with the top and bottom of the book boards. Mark the edges of the replacement spine cloth on the cover board.

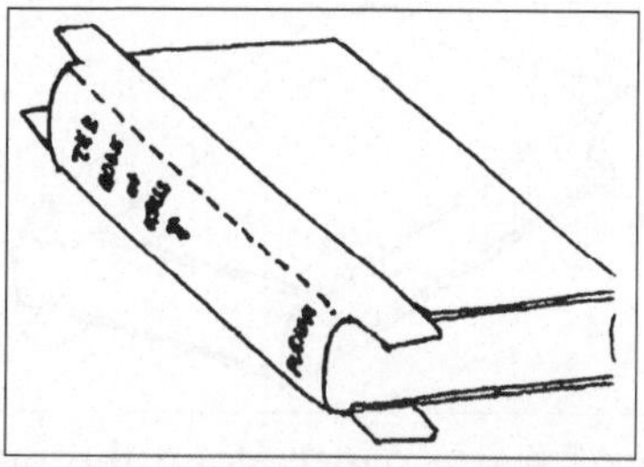

Put a strip of waste paper on the cover, lined up with the marks and glue from the waste paper towards the spine of the text block. Be careful not to get glue on the spine of the text block.

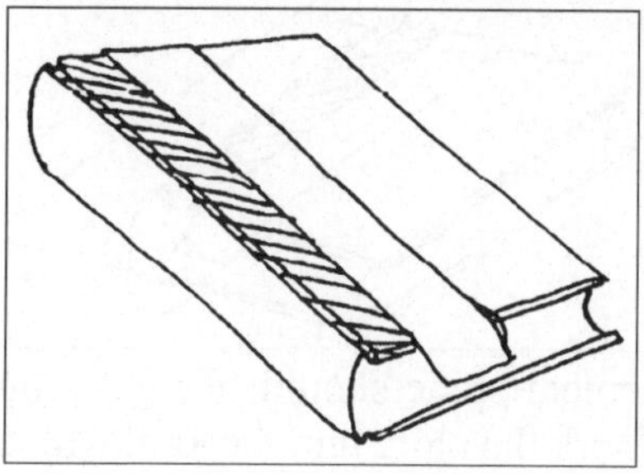

Before proceeding further, make sure the spine is right-side up on the text block. Position the replacement spine on the book. Centre the head and tail; then lay the edge of the replacement spine against the line of glue on the cover. Press the replacement spine onto the book board. Work the book cloth into the joint with a folder. Insert rods into the joint. Dry under weight for a few minutes.

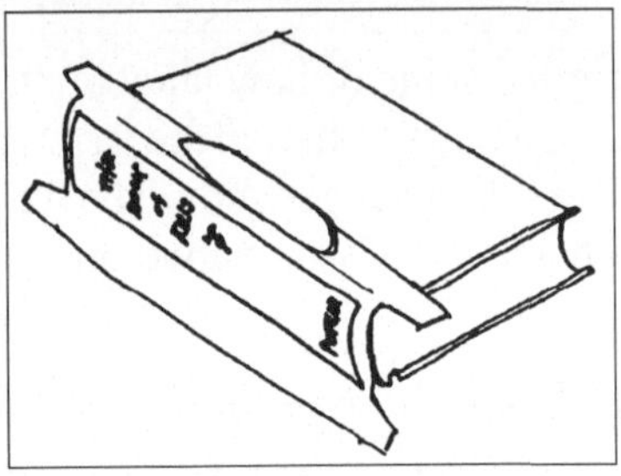

Turn the book. Wrap the replacement spine tightly around the book. Mark the position of the replacement spine on the book cover.

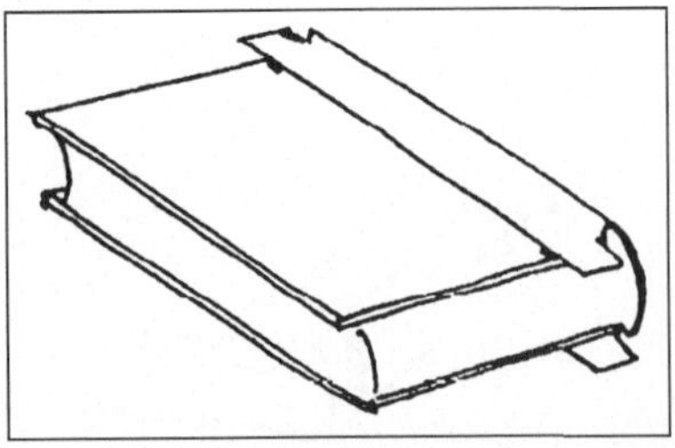

Lay a piece of waste paper along the marks. Apply glue working from the waste paper towards the joint. Be careful not to get glue on the spine of the text block.

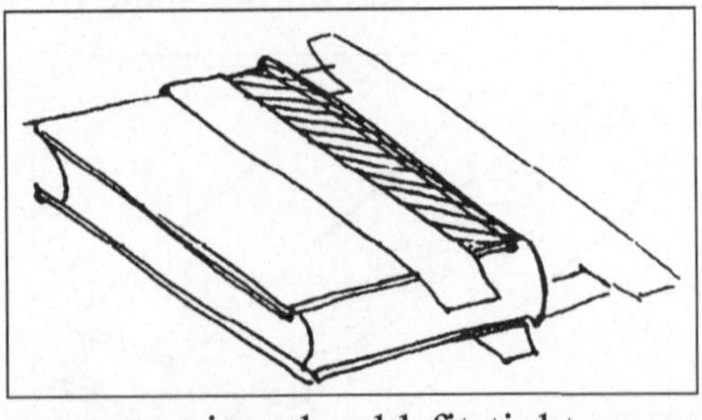

The replacement spine should fit tight around the spine of the text block. Work the cloth into the joint with a folder. Support the cover with book boards or other books. Apply glue to the extending tabs and fold them onto the endpapers. Rub them down with a folder.

Put rods in the joints. Dry the book overnight in a press or under weight.

Rebacking with Book Cloth under the Original Book Cloth

Lifting the Endpapers

Support the book with another book or a stack of boards.

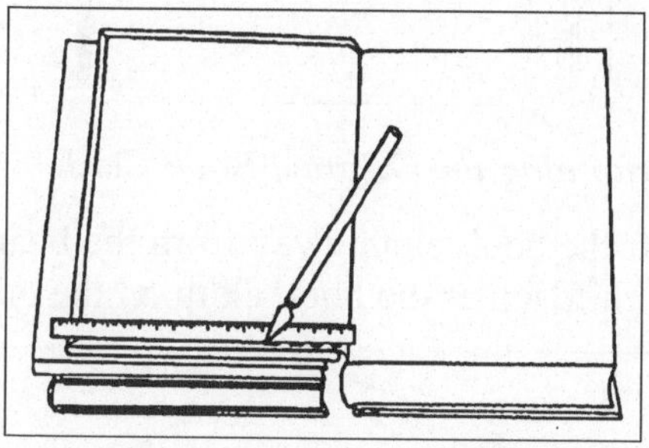

Use an X-acto knife or scalpel and ruler to cut through the book cloth along the edge of the endpapers at the head and tail. The cut should be about 1-2" long. At the outer edge of the first cut make a second, go-degree cut across the book cloth from the edge of the endpaper to the top of the book board.

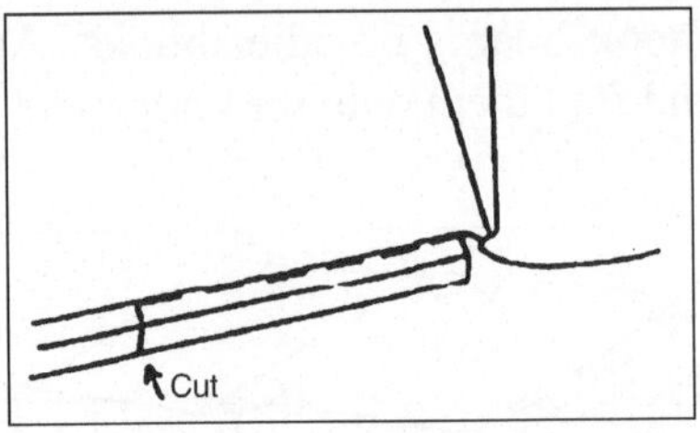

Use a knife or microspatula to lift the book cloth away from the book board. If necessary, clip through the original book cloth turn-in at the hinge to allow the cloth to lift up. DO NOT clip through the endpaper or the crash. Repeat this cut at the other end of the cover and on the opposite book board. If the turn-in in the spine area is completely loose, remove it. Insert a microspatula or dull knife between the original turn-in under the endpapers. The original book cloth turn-in will support the endpaper as it is lifted. Loosen only a small amount of the endpaper as more can be separated later if needed.

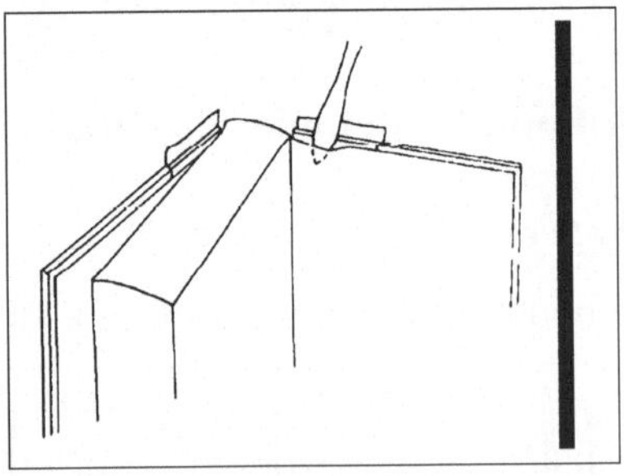

Lifting and Trimming the Original Book Cloth

Gently lift the book cloth away from the board by sliding a folder or dull knife under the book cloth on the outer cover.

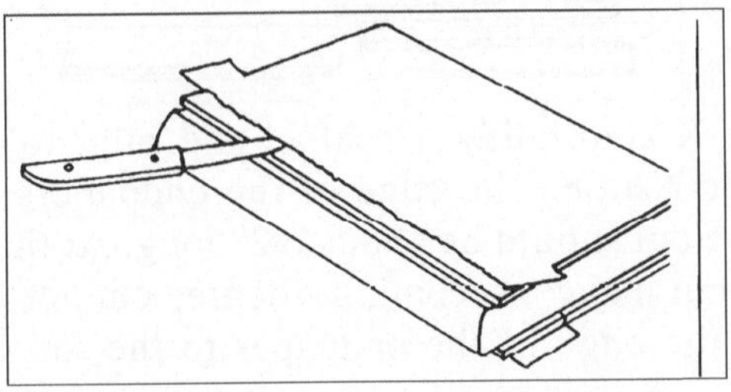

Lift the book cloth only as far as the cut at the top of the endpaper will allow, lifting a thin layer of book board with the cloth if necessary

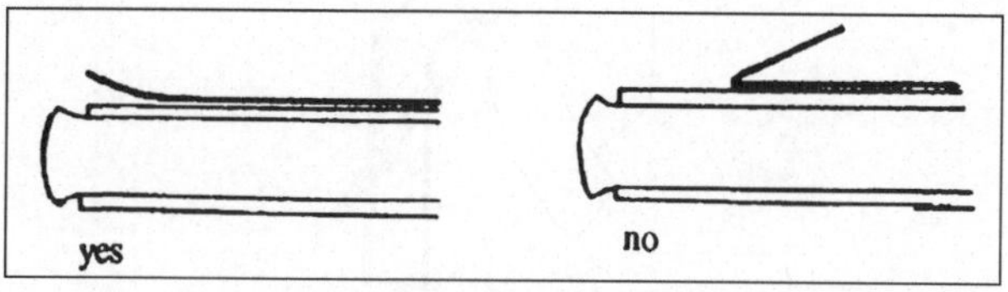

Try not to crease the book cloth as it is lifted or the crease line will show when the cloth is glued back in position.

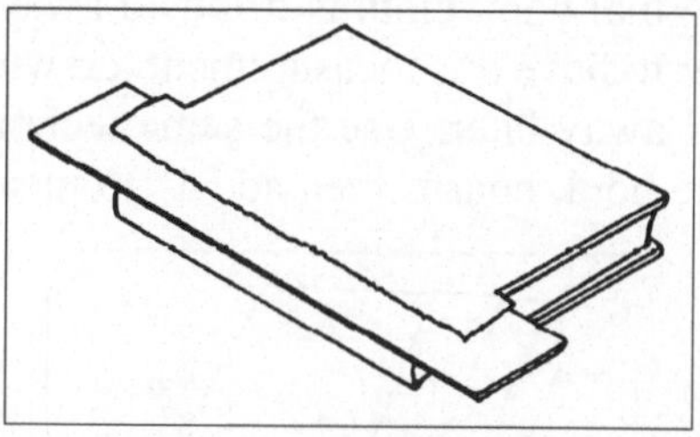

Insert a piece of thin cardboard between the original book cloth and the book board to use as a cutting surface.

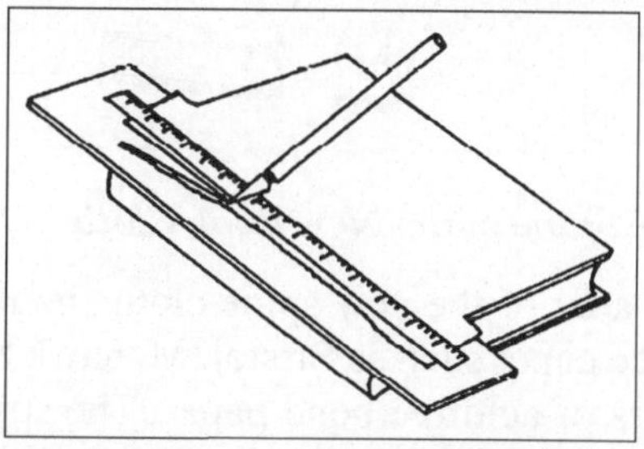

Place a straight edge along the ragged edge of the book cloth and use an X-acto knife or scalpel to trim the book cloth away from the hinge area. Try not to trim away any print or decoration on the cover. Turn the book over and repeat on the other side.

Measuring the Text Block Spine

Use a strip of paper to measure the width of the text block spine, then add 1-2" to each side of the spine measurement marks.

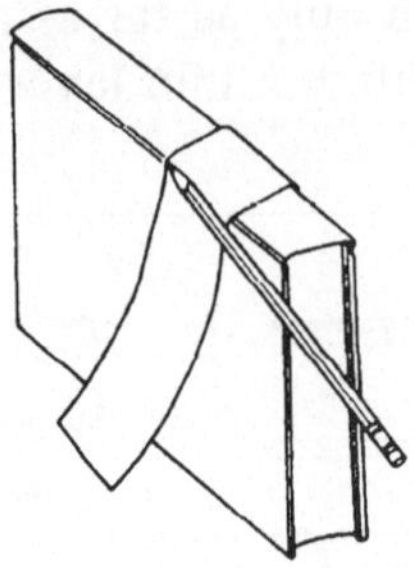

The exact amount added to measurement A depends on how much of the original book cloth is trimmed away from the cover board. It's better to have this measurement too wide as any excess can be trimmed away later. Use the same technique to measure the height of the book boards then add 1" to measurement B.

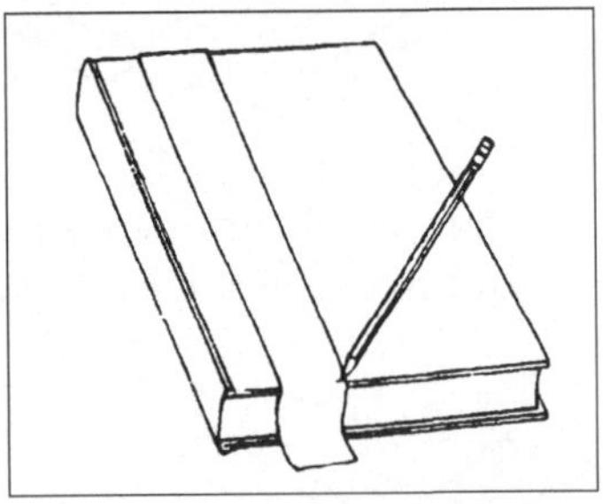

Reinforcing the Spine of the New Book Cloth

The spine area of the new spine cloth should be reinforced with an acid-free paper such as Bristol, Mohawk Superfine paper, or several layers of acidfree bond paper. The spine inlay should be the same width as the text block spine and the height of the book boards, not the text block. It is a common mistake to cut the spine inlay the same height as the text block, which is shorter than the book boards. Cut a spine inlay the width of the text block spine and longer than the height of the book boards. It will be trimmed later. The grain of the spine liner must be parallel to the spine of the text block.

Double check the width of the spine inlay paper by laying it against the text block spine. It should fit the spine from shoulder to shoulder without curving into the joint area. Trim the spine inlay to the correct height. Remember it should be the height of the cover boards, not the text block.

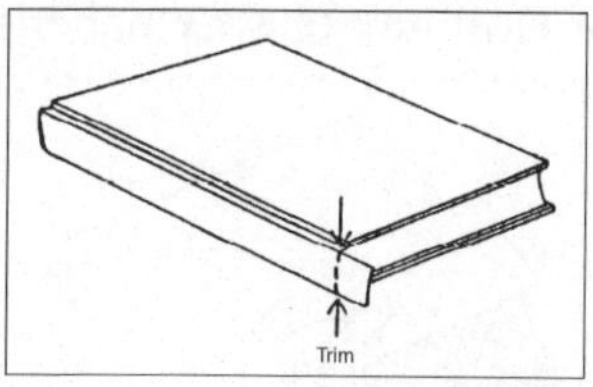

Choosing and Attaching One Side of the New Book Cloth Spine

Choose a piece of book cloth that is a close colour match to the original book cloth. If a close colour match isn't possible, select a colour that has the least amount of contrast, *i.e.*, black book cloth on a dark blue book would be less noticeable than light blue book cloth. Transfer measurement A and B to the book cloth. Be sure the grain of the book cloth is parallel to the spine of the book. Cut the new spine piece. Turn back the original book cloth on one cover. Brush PVA glue on the exposed board. Work the glue all the way back into the area where the original book cloth and book board are still attached.

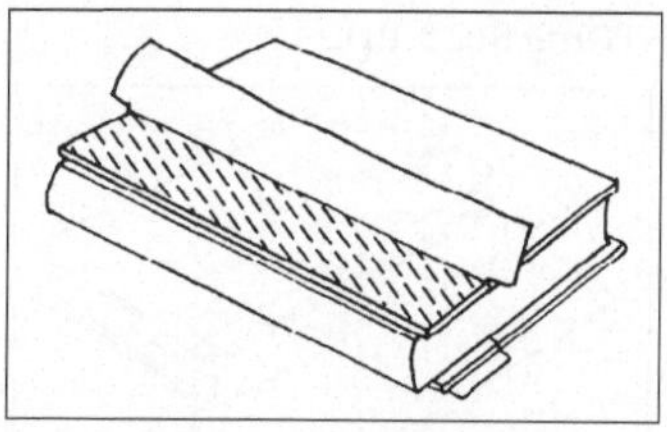

DO NOT put glue in the joint area.

Lay the new book cloth on the glued book board, with the right side up. Use a folder to press the new book cloth onto the board.

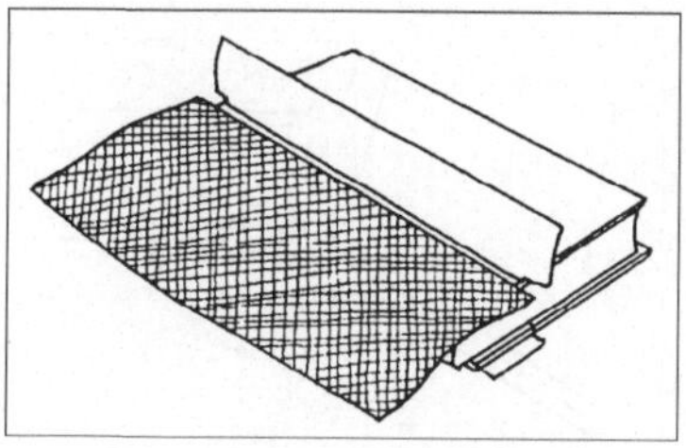

DO NOT glue down the original book cloth. Work the cloth into the joint with the long edge of a folder. Protect the new book cloth with a piece of Hollytex or wax paper if necessary.

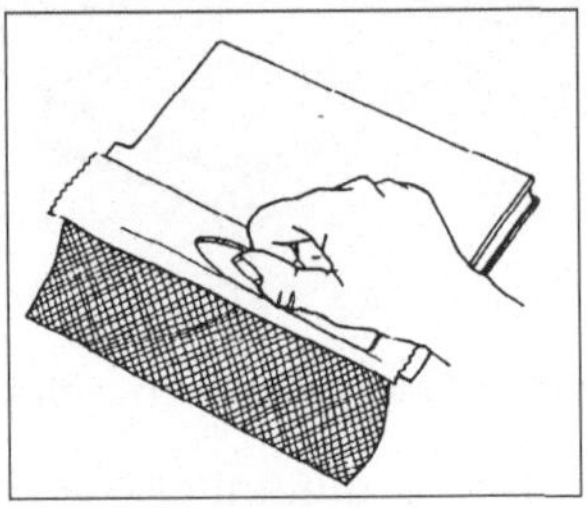

Insert rods in the joints and put under weight. Let the book dry for at least 10 minutes, so the glue will set.

Measuring the Width of the Joint

After the glue has set, use one of the following methods to mark the width of the joint. This gives the position of the spine inlay on the new spine cloth.

Method 1

Lay the book on the work surface-with the new spine cloth against the table, wrong side up.

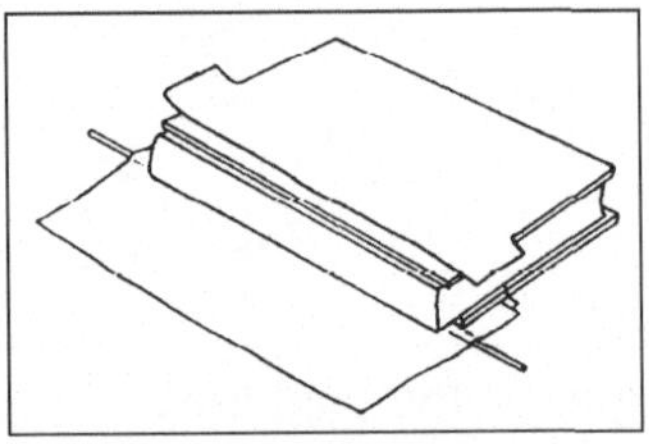

Slip a rod into the joint against the table, press down gently on the joint area. Mark the position where the shoulder of the text block spine meets the new book cloth.

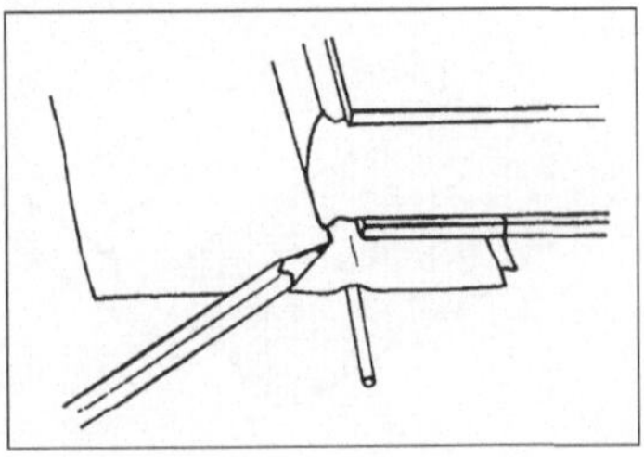

Repeat this measurement on the other end of the book.

Method 2

The joint width can also be measured with the book upright. Protect the new book cloth by supporting the text block on the edge of the work table or a pile of books.

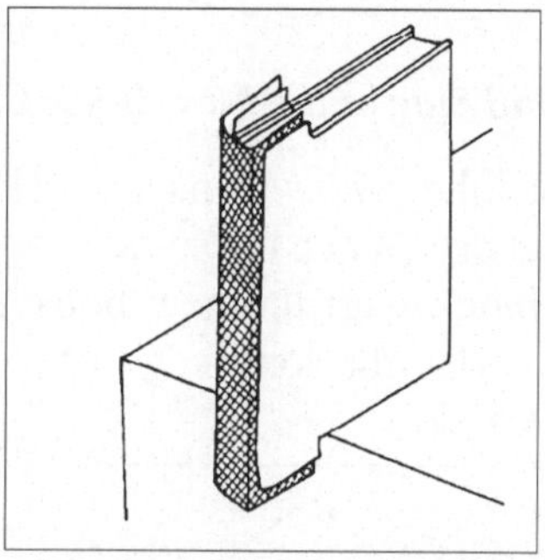

Wrap the new book cloth around the spine and press the new cloth into the joint with your fingers. Mark the position of shoulder on the new book cloth. Repeat on the other end of the book.

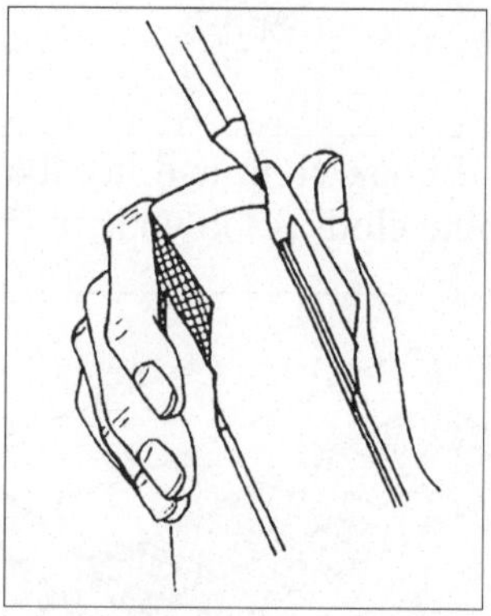

Lay the paper spine inlay on a piece of waste paper and apply glue in a star burst pattern. Use the pencil marks to position the glued spine inlay onto the wrong side of the new book cloth spine making sure the inlay is even with the top and bottom edges of the cover boards.

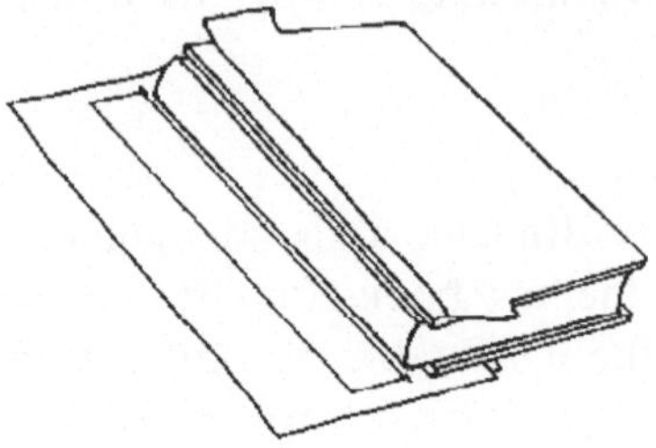

Attaching the Second Side of the New Book Cloth Spine

Cover the spine inlay with wax paper or Hollytex and blotters. Apply weight and let dry. When the spine inlay is dry, gently wrap it around the text block with the new book cloth on top of the original book cloth. Use the long edge of a folder to work the cloth into the hinge area.

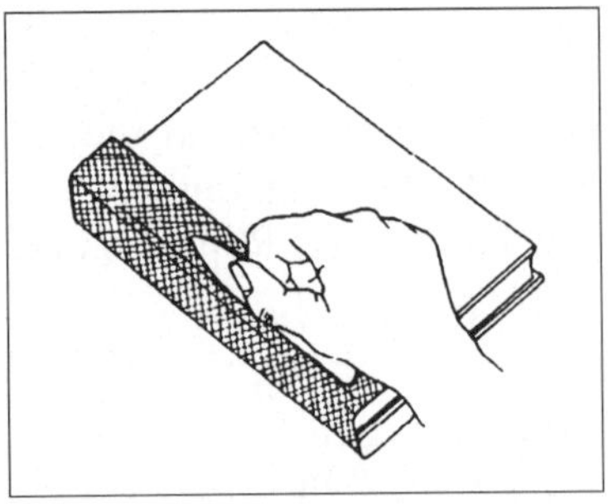

Lift the original book cloth and lay the new spine cloth in place. If the new spine cloth is too wide to fit, trim it down.

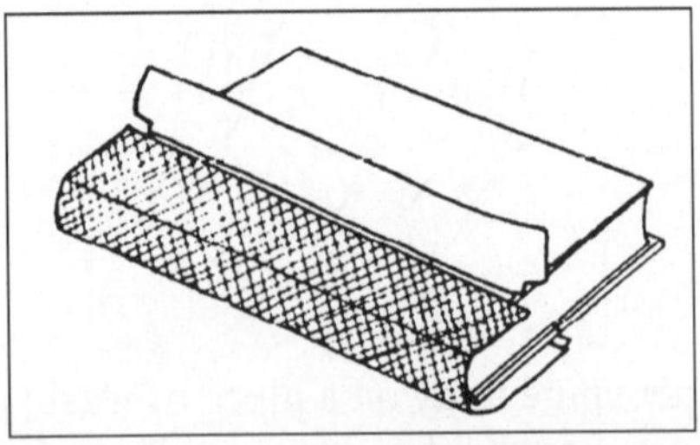

Lift up the new book cloth and apply PVA glue to the book board. Work the glue all the way back into the area where the original book cloth and book board are still attached. DO NOT put glue in the joint area or glue down the original book cloth.

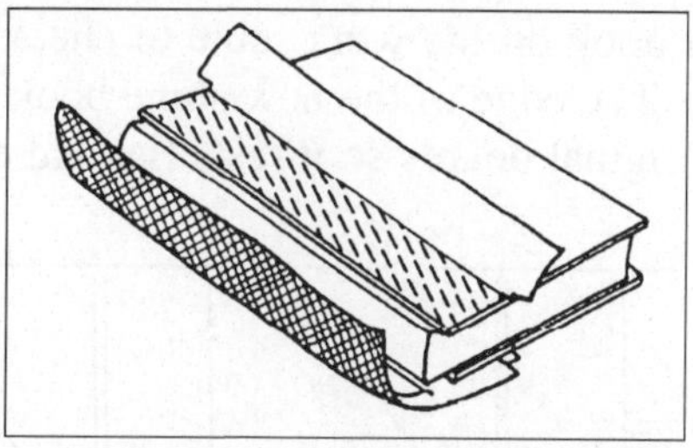

Lay the new book cloth back in place. Work the cloth into the hinge area with the long edge of a folder. Protect the cloth with wax paper or Hollytex if necessary. Put the book under weight to dry for at least 10 minutes so the glue will set. If the new spine cloth extends past the top or bottom of the book more than 5/8", trim it down. Clip the points off the comers for ease in turning-in.

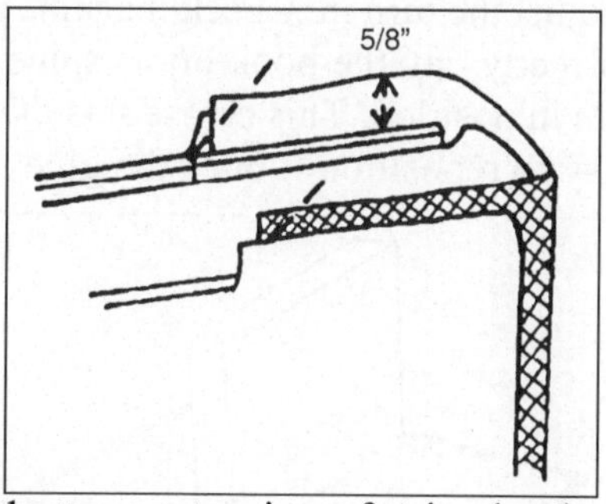

Protect the bottom extension of spine book cloth by placing the book on another stack of boards or another book. Carefully tuck in the right side of the turn-in, then the spine area, and finally the left side of the turn-in.

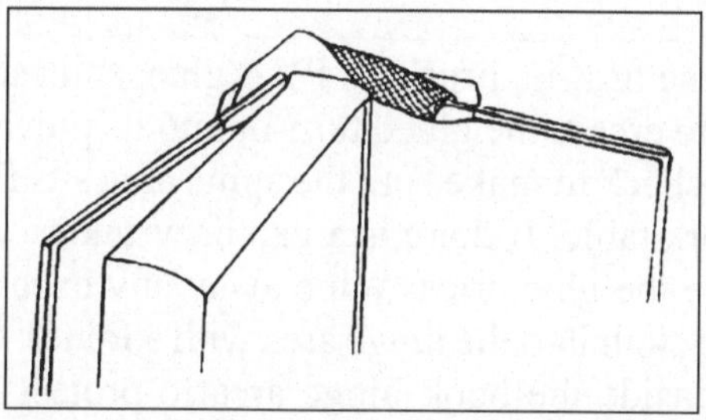

With the entire patch tucked in place, gently crease the top edge of the patch along the boards and in the spine area with your fingers. Set the book on the work table to check the position of the turn-in area. The edge of the new spine book cloth should be level with the original boards so it rests flat and even against the table.

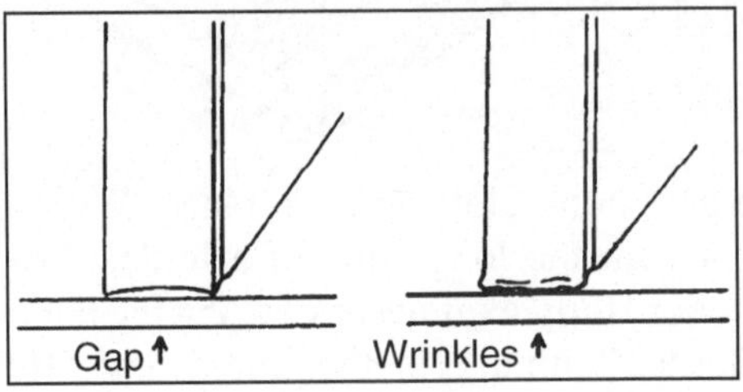

If there is space between the table and the new spine book cloth or if the book cloth wrinkles against the table, the turn-in is not correct. Readjust the turn in. Check it again. When the turn-in is positioned correctly, lay the book on its spine. Use a folder to crease the turn-in in position. This crease sets the turn-in position and makes it easy to reposition it once the glue is applied.

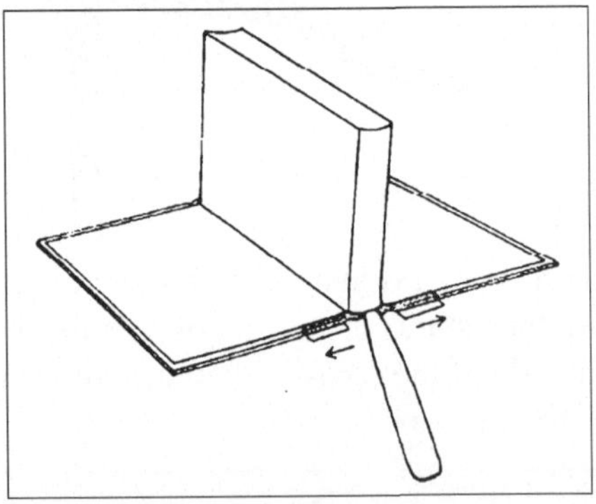

Unfold the turn-in, brush on PVA glue, and carefully refold. Use a folder to crease the glued turn-in into its previously creased position. Re-check to make sure the spine area sits flat against the edge of a work table. If there is a gap or wrinkles, reposition the turn-in before the glue dries. Wipe away any excess glue. Work the new book cloth into the hinge area with a folder. Put wax paper or Hollytex inside the book hinge area to protect the end sheet from excess glue. Insert rods or knitting needles in the joint and dry under weight. Let dry for at least ten minutes and repeat the procedure on the other end of the book. Apply glue to the raised flaps, and lay them into position, pressing them onto the new book cloth. There may be a slight gap between the flap and the edge of the endpaper

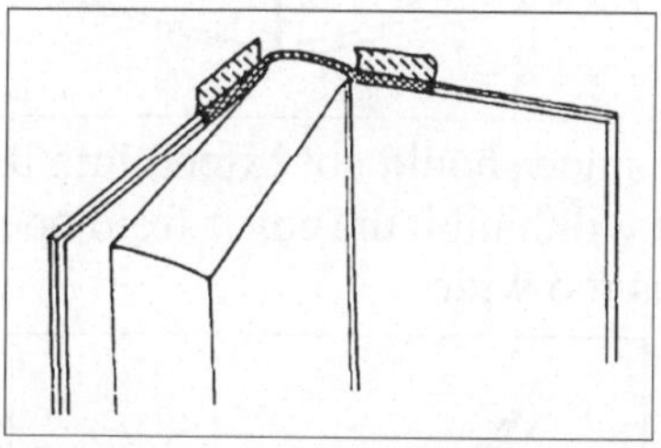

Lay a strip of wax paper in the joint areas, insert rods or knitting needles and dry overnight under weight.

Mounting the Original Spine onto the New Book Cloth Spine

Peel as much of the original paper spine inlay from the original spine cloth as possible. If the paper is well adhered to the cloth, don't force it off the spine cloth.

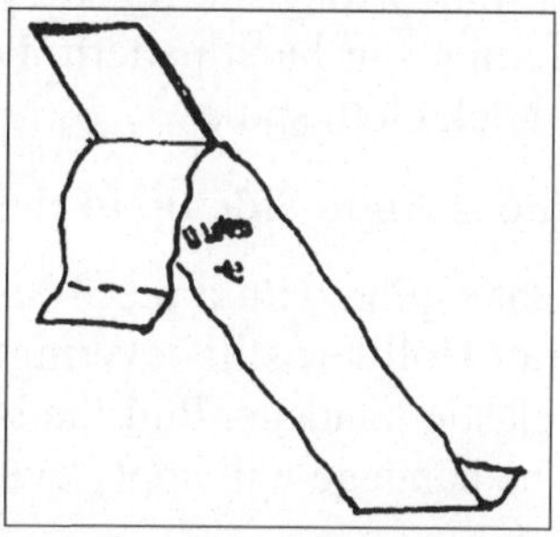

Trim the frayed edges with a straight edge and X-acto knife, taking care not to remove any of the letters or design.

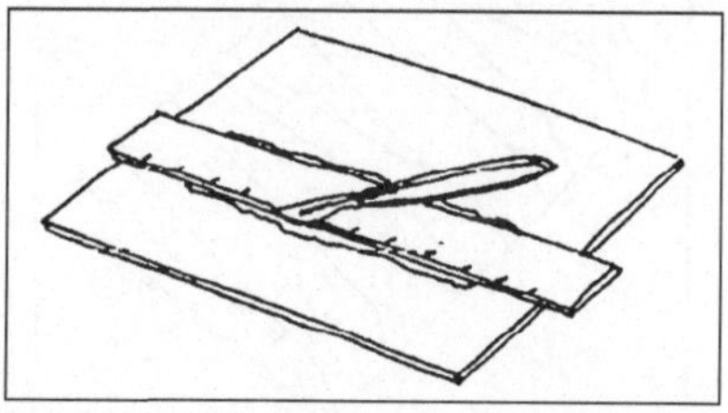

Lay the original spine against the new book cloth spine to check for a proper fit.

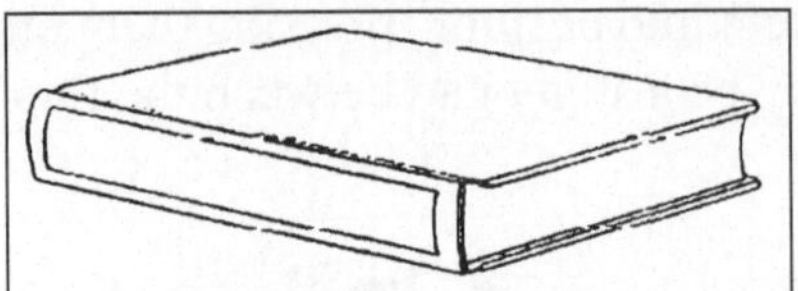

Yes

The original spine should not extend into the hinge area as it will add bulk that will inhibit the cover from opening freely. Trim the original if it is too wide.

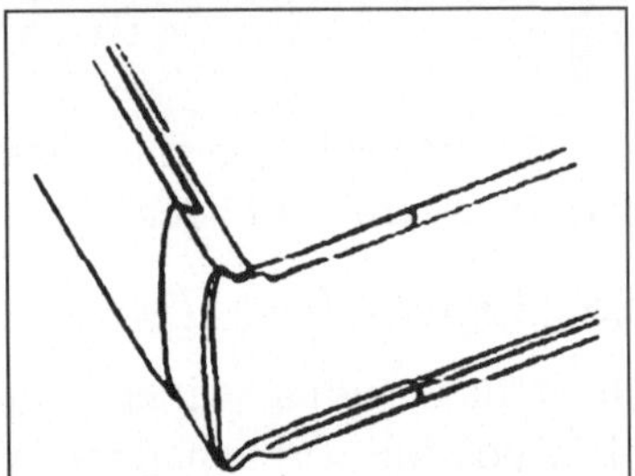

No

Lay the original spine wrong side up on a piece of waste paper and apply PVA glue in a star burst pattern. Position the original spine over the new book cloth spine.

Make Sure the Spine is Right Side up to the Text Block

Cover the original spine with a piece of wax with a folder. With the wax paper or Hollytex still covering the spine, wrap the book snugly in an elastic bandage. Pull the bandage tight as the book is wrapped. The bandage will apply even pressure over the entire curved spine.

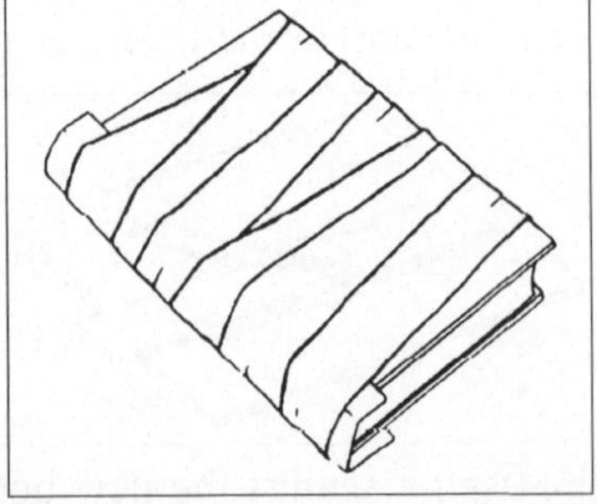

When the spine is dry, double check that all the edges are adhered.

RECASING A TEXT BLOCK INTO THE COVER

The hinge is the weakest part of a case bound book. As explained in book case construction, the text block is constructed in one operation while the case is constructed in another operation. The spine of the text block is covered with crash, and the crash is attached to the book board. The crash is covered by the pasted down endpaper. Over time, gravity pulls the text block away from the cover, or the crash can be damaged which allows the text block to separate from the cover. If the cover is in good condition, the text block can be recased into the original cover.

Some text blocks are so large and heavy that they will always be prone to falling out of their cases. In such a circumstance, it is be wise to recase with text block so it is flush with the bottom of the case. That way the shelf can support the entire text block. The book case joints must be in excellent condition to reuse the case as is. If the joint area is worn, repair the cover using the techniques outlined in *rebacking a text block* as a guideline. The repair will differ slightly from the instructions if the text block is not be attached to the cover boards but the basic principles are the same. When the rebacking is complete, recase the text block. Check the endpapers carefully and determine whether they can be reused or if they need to be replaced or repaired. Detailed information for removing or replacing endpapers is covered in ENDPAPER TREATMENT.

Recasing—One Damaged Hinge

Examine both hinges very carefully to be sure only one hinge needs repair. If more than 1/4 if the crash on either hinge is damaged, that hinge must be replaced. Cut through any crash that is still intact in the damaged hinge area so the cover falls away from the text block.

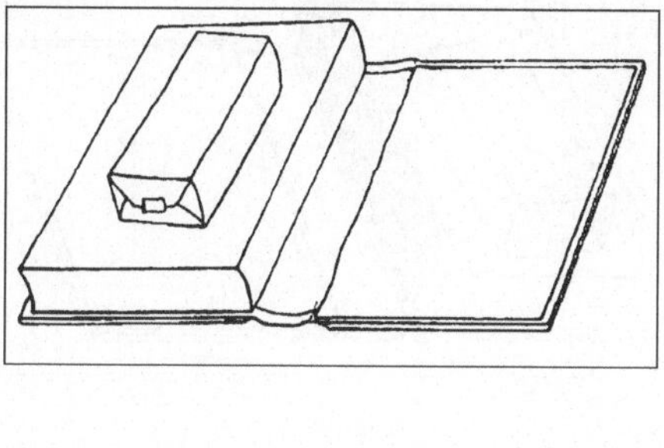

Check the original spine liners. It they are not glued down, carefully feed PVA or PVA/mixture between the spine liner and the spine of the text block. Use a folder or 1" stencil brush to work the liner in place. If the spine liners are damaged or if they are not heavy enough, reline the spine using the directions in Lining the Text Block Spine after the new crash is mounted on the spine.

Examine the endpapers. If either is missing or damaged, replace or repair it before going further. Support the loose cover with a book or stack of boards; then slide a dull knife or a folder between the pastedown and the book board. Work carefully so as not tear the pastedown and lift only enough of the pastedown to slip in the new crash

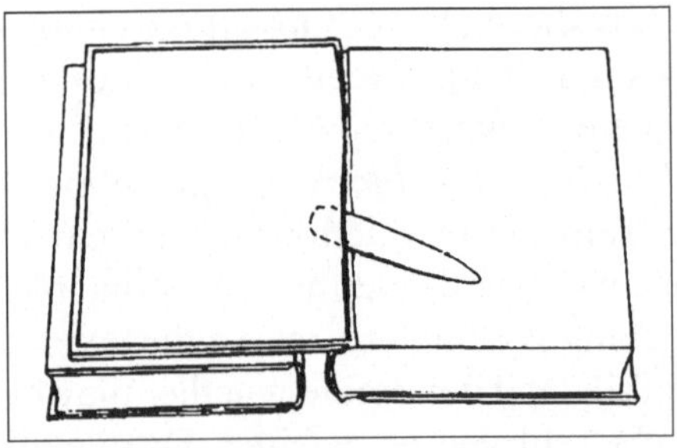

The pastedown can tear easily so try to work the folder or knife under the old crash to support the pastedown as it is lifted up. Cut a new piece of crash 1/2" shorter than the height of the text block and the width of the text block plus about 2". Put a weight on top of the test block then apply PVA or PVA/mixture to the spine of the text block. Place the new crash onto the spine. The crash should cover the entire width of the spine and extend at least 1 1/2" past the shoulder of the text block.

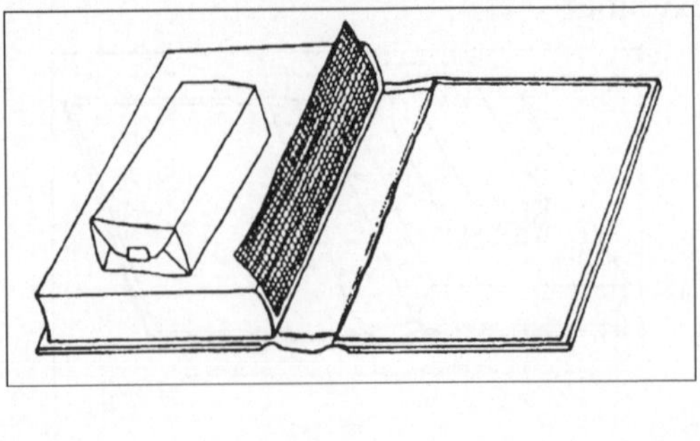

Use a folder or stencil brush to work the crash onto the spine. Let dry thoroughly. When the crash is dry, check the spine lining paper. If the spine liners are damaged or if they are not heavy enough, reline the spine using the directions in Lining the Text Block Spine. The number and kind of spine liners depend on the volume. Even if the spine does not need lining, it is still a good idea to put one thin layer of paper or Japanese repair tissue over the crash to anchor it to the text block. Let it dry before proceeding. Slide the loose edge of the crash under the lifted pastedown to check for fit If the loose flap of the crash is too wide, trim it to fit.

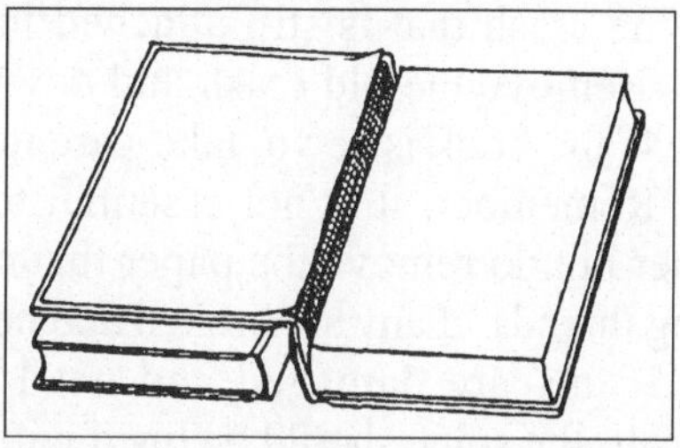

Lift the crash out from under the pastedown and diagonally clip the ends of the comers. They tend to fold under as the crash is inserted under the lifted pastedown. Apply glue to the book board. Do not glue the lifted pastedown. Slide the loose flap of crash back under the lifted pastedown. Work it into place, making sure there are no lumps or folds in the crash. Place a piece of wax paper or Hollytex in the hinge area and close the cover. Use the long edge of a folder to work the joint into place. Open the book and support the cover on another book or a stack of boards. Lift the pastedown and apply glue between the pastedown and the crash/board. Use the flat edge of a folder to press the pastedown into position, working from the fore edge towards the hinge area. Wipe away any excess glue.

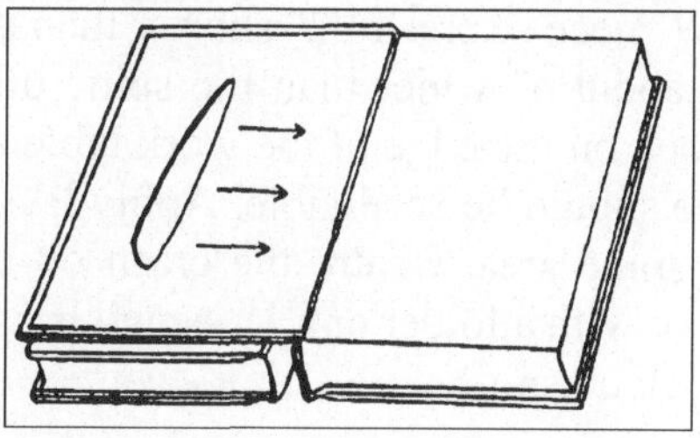

Put a piece of wax paper or Hollytex in the hinge area and close the cover. Use the long edge of a folder to work the joint into place. Insert rods in both joints, and dry under pressure. Open the cover. Inspect the repair. Use the techniques in Repairing Torn Endpapers And Tightening Case Hinges to finish or camouflage the repair.

Recasing the Text Block

When both hinges are damaged or broken, the crash must be replaced before the text block reattached to the case. Cut or tear through any of the crash that is still attached in the hinge area. Clean the spine. Remove the old crash and any paper liners that come off easily. If the book is sewn, take-care not to damage the sewing threads. Remember, it is not essential to remove all the spine lining paper but do remove the paper that comes off easily. Check the sewing threads. If any are broken and need repair. Check the signatures. If any are damaged and need repair. In strict conservation repair, the spine should be lined with Japanese repair tissue before a text block is recased. Since this layer is applied with wheat paste, it is reversible in water and acts as a liner for the other layers of spine materials. The spines of books that are considered valuable or that will be in the collection for a long, long time should be lined with Japanese repair tissue.

Otherwise, proceed to attaching the crash:

- *Japanese Tissue Lining:* Cut a piece of Japanese repair tissue the height and width of the text block spine, with the grain running parallel to the spine of the text block. Apply paste to the tissue in a starburst pattern and attach it to the text block spine. Use a folder or 1" stencil brush to tap the tissue onto the spine. Let dry thoroughly before proceeding.

Cut a NEW-piece of crash 1/2" shorter than the height of the text block and about 4" wider than the spine of the text block. Lay the text block on the edge of the work table and add weight. The entire spine should be accessible. Apply PVA or PVA/paste mixture to the spine area. Centre the crash on the glued spine, and work it down with a folder or a 1" stencil brush. Let the crash dry on the text block spine.

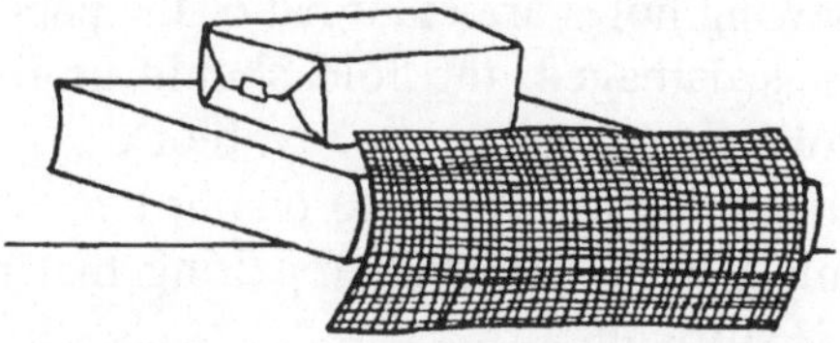

Line the spine. The number and type of spine liners depends on the size of the book. When the pastedown is still attached to the board, use Method 1 for recasing the book. If the original pastedown has been lifted off the cover boards or if the endsheets have been replaced, use Method 2 below to attach the text block into the case.

If the original pastedown is being reused, gently slide a dull knife or a folder under the spine edge of each pastedown to carefully lift the pastedown away from the board. Work the knife or folder under the original crash to support the paper. Lift only enough pastedown to slip in the new crash. Place the text block into the case.

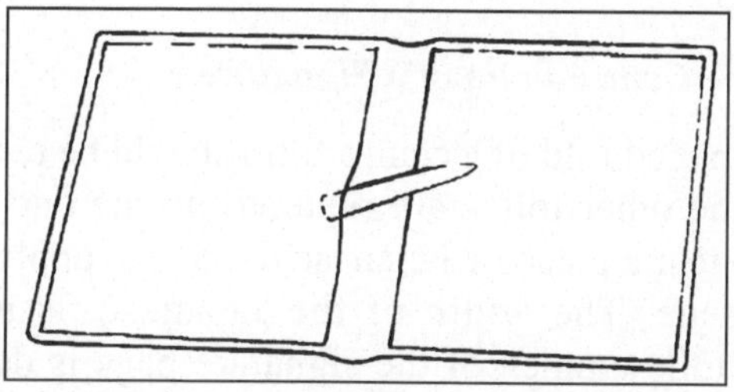

REPAIRING AND REATTACHING DAMAGED OR SEPARATED LEAVES, FOLIOS OR SIGNATURES

Leaves, folios and signatures can all separate from the text block. Each can be repaired in several ways. Read through each of the options below and select the one that will work best for a specific book.

Repairing Signatures

All paper tears should be mended before reattaching a signature to the text block:

- Examine the sewing holes on the fold of each folio. If

the sewing holes are enlarged or the paper between the holes is damaged, the fold should be repaired before the folio is reattach to the text block.

- If the damage is limited to one or two sewing holes or to only part of the fold, repairing that portion of the fold is sufficient.
- It is not always necessary to repair each folio of a signature. The centre and outside folios often sustain the most damage. Repairing only those two folios is faster and decreases the thickness of repair tissue in the repaired signature.
- When most or all of the folios in a signature are badly damaged, each folio should be repaired.
- Repair the folds of the folios in the folded position. Paper repaired flat then folded tends to have a very sharp crease while the original signature folds tend to be rounded. Repairing the folios in the folded position helps retain the proper shape and placement of the fold.

Repairing the Centre Folio of a Signature

The damaged fold of a centre folio should be repaired on the inside. All the other folios are repaired on the outside. Use the technique to tear a piece of Japanese tissue and apply paste to the Japanese tissue. The width of the Japanese tissue will vary depending on how much of the signature page is damaged. Lay the centre folio of the signature on a piece of non-stick material with centre facing up.

Lay the pasted repair tissue down the centre of the folio:

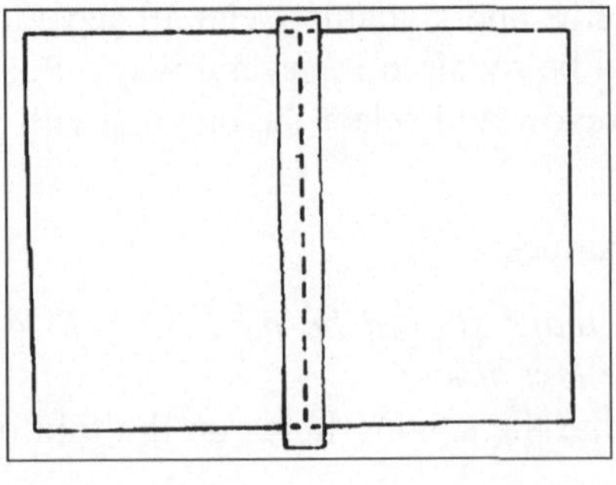

Lay a strip of wax paper or Hollytex along the fold:

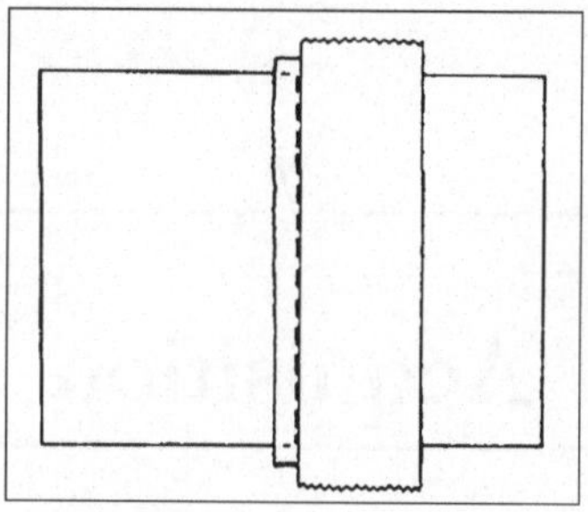

Carefully close the page:

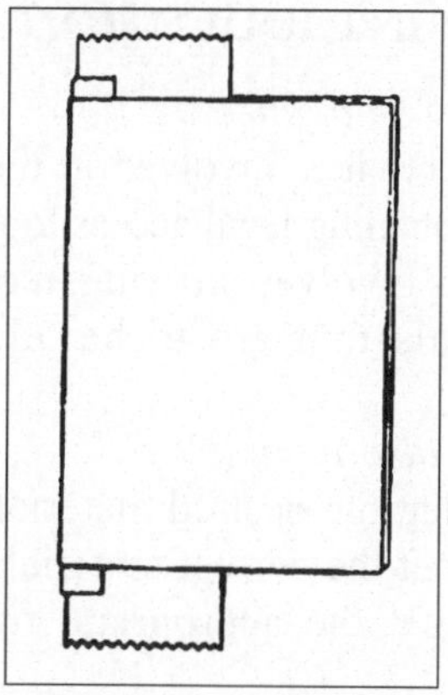

Place the folded page between blotters. Put under weight to dry. If the other folios in the signature do not need repair, place them in the correct position around the centre folio then reattach the signature to the text block following the instructions in 3. Reattaching Partially or Fully Detached Signatures. If all or some of the other folios need repair, continue with these instructions.

7

Acquisition

INTRODUCTION

Acquisitions may be defined as:

- All library activities involved in the purchase, leasing or otherwise obtaining legal access to information sources.

Traditionally this involves ordering, receiving and paying for information materials that are to be added to the library's collection.

These functions also include:

- Verifying that the desired materials actually exist;
- Verifying that the correct materials have been received;
- Verifying that the appropriate funds are used to pay for them.

The types of materials to be acquired have been broadened from print, microforms and audiovisuals to encompass printed or online books, subscriptions to print and electronic journals, CD-ROM products and online databases. Moreover, materials need no longer to reside in the library's collection to meet users' information needs, as they may be stored remotely in digital form and be accessible to the users on demand.

The acquisitions process comes after formulating the collection development policy statement and adopting selection procedures. But there are some functions intertwined with acquisitions, though different therefrom. Upon automation using integrated systems, as the basic record of the item is now created at the acquisitions rather than the cataloguing stage as used to be traditionally the case. The acquisitions process is fundamentally the same in any library setting, irrespective of size of budget and staff, or the type of users served. The differences that emerge stem from: the special characteristics of health sciences collection, on whether and what automated system is used, and other specifics of institutional operations.

The last includes: which library department verifies requests before ordering, whether order records are visible to the public or not, and whether the library is allowed to issue its own cheques. On the other hand, health sciences libraries accord extraordinary importance to journal literature as a primary means of publication. Medical books and journals are very expensive, and books have a limited lifespan.

ACQUISITIONS WITHIN THE LIBRARY ORGANISATION

The placement of acquisitions operation in the library's organisational structure depends upon the type of the parent organisation, the size of the library, the space configuration, the automated system used, and the budget allocations. This may result in a separate department, division or part, or none of them. The important factor is maximizing functional interactions. Another issue is whether serials and book acquisitions are combined or separate, and whether acquisitions of the various formats be consolidated or not. There is no standard for library organisation yet.

Moreover, there are strong links between acquisitions and other library departments:

- Acquisitions with cataloguing;
- Acquisitions with reference using acquisitions information;
- Acquisitions with interlibrary loan and document delivery;
- Acquisitions with library's systems.

ACQUISITIONS AND THE PARENT ORGANISATION

There are entities within the parent organisation to which acquisitions connect more closely than do other library departments:

PURCHASING DEPARTMENTS

Libraries are rarely in a position to conduct financial transactions directly with their suppliers. Usually they must work through the parent organisation's purchasing and payment bureaucracy. Maintaining smooth relations demands understanding of each other's way, and, on the library's part, an understanding of the parent organisation's rules of doing business and a willingness to follow them.

The librarian should seek to:

- Be allowed to order from publishers, vendors or bookstore directly, and to be able to issue official purchase orders that do not require prior approval from the purchasing department;
- Seek authority for making payments directly to the supplier without going through the financial department;
- Win the right not to go through a periodic bidding process;
- Not to be forced to break purchases into separate small units so as not to exceed a single-purchase ceiling imposed by the parent organisation;
- Demand a renewal of blanket requisitions at the beginning of each year for major vendors.

ACCOUNTING DEPARTMENTS

The library needs to pay its suppliers as quickly as possible, which sometimes entitles them to earn a discount. If this is not met, apart from losing the discounts, the librarian is the one to whom suppliers complain. The problem may lie with the size and practices of the parent organisation which interject delays of excessive verification between approval of payment and sending the cheque, or because of work overload. The delays may arise from the automated systems which do not interface between departments.

To ensure successful interaction involves the internal auditors before buying or designing the library automated system without any compromise, and ensure efficient linkage between systems. Data consistency is imperative for a successful interface between automated systems. The librarian has also to be aware of the audit trail: orders must be authorized, allocation and transfer of funds must be authorized, and invoices are as well. Now, the usual practice is to accept as sufficient the financial information recorded on the item's machine-readable record in the library system. This demands not only that specific fields be available for audit-related information, but that records be maintained for as long as the parent organisation's accounting practices require.

Applicable control mechanisms for keeping data safe may include segregating various functions and using different passwords to access each function, requiring authorization for transactions, and maintaining a log of all record updating activities. Libraries may want a way to double-check the accuracy of the financial reports, they protect themselves by running their own funding system whether automated or manual ledger entries.

COMPUTING FACILITIES

Some libraries have their own systems. The acquisitions demands for interconnectivity and interfacing with outside computer systems. Since acquisitions deals in commercial transactions, it needs convenient access to the commercial world's systems.

CAMPUS BOOK STORES

Such stores usually supply titles for the individual needs of the population of parent organisation on the campus. The library may use them for urgently needed replacements. Such stores in hospitals do not store materials of interest to the library.

FUNCTIONS OF ACQUISITIONS

The basic responsibilities of a typical acquisitions unit are as follows:

OBTAINING INFORMATION ABOUT MATERIALS

This function involves the following:

- Securing from selectors a record of the basic bibliographic information for materials to be acquired, often recorded on a request form;

- Completing and verifying the bibliographic information provided by comparing the request form with the listings of materials in national, international and other bibliographies, both those printed and those in online databases;
- Determining that the library does not already hold or has not ordered the requested item; the checker may also record the presence of related works such as previous editions;
- Identifying the expected price and possible sources of supply for each item.

INITIATING THE PURCHASING PROCESS

This involves:

- Selecting the appropriate vendor with whom to place the order;
- Committing the funds needed to pay for the item when it is supplied;
- Preparing the order, whether printed or electronic;
- Despatching the order.

MAINTAINING RECORDS OF MATERIALS ORDERED

This involves:

- Maintaining files, either manually or electronically, which show the status of each firm order, usually accessible by title, author, series, or international standard number;
- Maintaining long-term records on continuations, which are items issued in parts over a definite period of time, and other serials.

RECEIVING AND CHECKING MATERIALS

This involves:

- Opening packages of materials shipped to the library, making sure that the items are undamaged, and preserving enclosed records such as invoices and packing slips;
- Verifying that the items are the ones ordered by comparing

their bibliographic information with the order record;
- Checking the items against enclosed or separately shipped invoices;
- Determining that each item appears to be physically complete and in acceptable condition;
- For items that have no order record because they have been obtained through approval or blanket order plan, or as a gift or exchange, the order forms must be created.

AUTHORIZING PAYMENT

This involves:
- Recording the actual price of each item on its order record;
- Releasing the financial commitment and entering the actual price of an item in the financial records;
- Preparing payment or creating authorization required to release payment for the materials.

CLEARING ORDER RECORDS

This involves:
- Recording the fact that an item has been received, usually by entering the receipt date in its order record;
- Preparing an appropriate transmittal record to accompany the material to the next stage of preparation, which usually is the cataloguing unit;
- Either at this point or at the end of cataloguing and processing stages, changing the status of the order record from 'on order' to 'received' or 'completed'.

CLAIMING AND CANCELLING ORDERS

This involves:
- Monitoring the files to detect if an order has been outstanding for so long a time that it should be claimed from the vendor;
- Informing the vendor that an order of an item has been cancelled;
- Updating the order record to reflect these claims and cancellations.

HANDLING MATERIALS THAT NEED SPECIAL TREATMENT

This involves:

- Developing a programme for soliciting, maintaining records for, and acknowledging gift materials, depository collections, and items received through exchange programmes;
- Developing the routines needed to handle materials supplied through standing orders, blanket orders, or approval plans.

DEALING WITH SPECIAL SITUATIONS

This involves:

- Negotiating credits or refunds for items not wanted or received in unacceptable condition;
- Notifying requesters that their materials have arrived;
- Arranging for the rush purchase and receipt of items required immediately;
- Solving dilemmas related to poor vendor performance;
- Making adjustments in the budget as the fiscal year nears its end.

DEVELOPING AND ANALYSING PERFORMANCE STATISTICS

This involves collecting a variety of statistical information on:

- Number of orders placed, received, cancelled, etc.
- Length of time required by vendors to fill orders
- Time spent by staff in establishing bibliographic information for ordering purposes
- Number of unwanted duplicates and items ordered by mistake
- Accuracy of price estimates compared with final price
- Rate of utilization of budget
- Ratio of current materials costs to costs in previous years
- Number of volumes and titles received by gifts or exchange
- Number of serials issues checked in

Many of these statistics can be routinely collected, analysed and reported by the computer in automated systems.

OTHER FUNCTIONS

- *Withdrawals*: This is not basically an acquisitions function, but the processing tasks are frequently handled by acquisitions unit. For serials, for instance, records of holdings must be adjusted. All types of materials require 'withdrawn marking', before they are removed from the library.
- *Replacement*: This is the replacement of lost, stolen or damaged books. The major problem rests with serial replacements, and the librarian should be aware of possible sources. Replacement of print materials by microforms is acceptable. The availability of lost, stolen or damaged materials in CD-ROM or full text online database should be considered.
- *Binding and Preservation*: Acquisitions units may be involved in preparing materials, particularly serials for binding. Moreover, acquisitions may be involved in preservation when the means is replacement.

MEANS OF ACQUISITIONS

The following means are the ways in which materials are acquired by a library:

PURCHASE

The following are the ways in which purchase is performed, a combination of which may be used:

- *Approval Plan*: The supplier selects and supplies materials according to the library's profile of interest, which may set limits by subject matter, country of publication, publisher, cost, level of material, format, or any combination thereof. It is agreed that the library has the right to return materials that do not meet its profile or unwanted for other reasons. But an approval plan is not really successful if too high a percentage of return occurs. Serials are normally excluded from approval plans. Vendors offer a discount on most publishers' titles.

- *Blanket Order*: It usually covers all publications within broad subject areas and specified formats from a country or specific region. It may focus on all publications of one publisher. It does not permit return of unwanted items.
- *Standing Order*: This concerns publications that are issued irregularly and are not paid for in advance, but rather billed at the time that they are actually supplied to the library. Libraries enter a standing order with the publisher or a vendor to receive new volumes as they are published.
- *Firm Order*: It is a specific order for a specific title sent to publisher, agent or vendor. It is the most common method for ordering serials, media formats and, in small libraries, for books. The availability of online ordering services through book vendors is transforming this method to a more viable option even for large libraries.

DEPOSIT

Deposit has three concepts:

- Materials can be placed on deposit in the library by group, organisation, or publisher as a means of making items more readily available to users. The library usually retains the materials permanently in its collection. In return, the library is responsible for providing free access to such materials to the public, irrespective of other access restrictions it may enforce. Health sciences libraries will have no interest in being a full depository. Partial depository for health-related materials is an ideal arrangement. Institutions that usually deposit their publications are governments, whether national or local, or some agencies of such governments. UN and its specialized agencies have such arrangement collectively and/or individually. WHO publications may be deposited.

- Materials of all types produced by or for the parent organisation and its affiliates are deposited in the library. This type of deposit is often neglected. The least that the library has to do is to be able to locate such materials whenever they are needed by the users.
- *Temporary Deposit:* Here the depositor retains title to his collection. So the library must be certain, before accepting such deposit, that it will be extremely valuable to its users and is unlikely to be withdrawn in the foreseeable future.

EXCHANGE

Exchange can be based on:

- One piece of material for a similar piece
- Title for title
- Value for value
- Page for page
- Everything offered for everything offered

The library is likely to have the following types of materials to offer for exchange:

- Its own publication as well as those of its parent organisation
- Surplus duplicates
- Materials specially purchased to send to the exchange partner

GIFTS

Acquisitions staff may not deal with donors, but they have to bear the processing burden. Materials are acquired as gifts from individuals, groups, other libraries and organisations, and sometimes from publishers. Gifts may be individual items or a collection of materials. The collection development policy statement must define the conditions of accepting gifts.

LICENSING

Electronic formats are frequently acquired through licensing rather than purchase; so the library does not receive unrestricted ownership of the material, as it only assumes the right to use the material or information for a specific period of time under specified conditions. As updates of the product are received, the outdated version must be returned or destroyed. This area of acquisitions is bound to expand rapidly in the next few years, as libraries install *local area networks* (LANs) allowing users online access from multiple locations.

AUTOMATION OF ACQUISITIONS ACTIVITIES

Here, the impact of automation on acquisitions in particular will be discussed. This impact has been explicit in three areas:

- *Creation and Updating of Bibliographic Record*: The bibliographic record connects the various divisions of the library and its users. As soon as the manual files disappear, and a single machine-readable record takes their place, a record will be equally accessible to all staff and users. A complete, accurate record will not cause unwanted duplication, and will state which items have been ordered and received, and will stand as a reliable base on which to add further information. Public services and users will know what is on the shelf, what is on order, and what is waiting for processing.
- *Creation and Updating of the Financial Record:* A good book fund accounting system provides built-in verifications and safeguards to prevent many errors. An automated accounting system saves staff time, improves relations with suppliers and enables a wide range of management reports.
- *Data Transmission and Exchange Pertaining to Both*: Electronic data transfer in place of rekeying has the greatest potential for cutting error rates and increasing both speed and efficiency in technical processing. Internal connection will enable the automatic data transfer between the library and the accounting department. External connection to bibliographic utilities and vendor systems can be used to download bibliographic information and send orders, claims, and payments with a minimum investment of human effort.

ACQUISITIONS OF BOOKS AND BOOK-LIKE MATERIALS

A successful book acquisitions operation depends upon a well-structured and wellmaintained record keeping system. This system should allow staff to issue purchase orders and other communications to suppliers and to track the status of all outstanding and recently received orders. Whether manual or automated, the system aims at avoiding redundant data entry by establishing a single unit record for the order, which is updated as the order moves through the various stages of various order entry, claiming, receipt, payment and cataloguing and processing.

In an automated system ordering process is speeded up; bibliographic records can be downloaded from bibliographic utilities as order records; can provide information needed for management decisions; and can assist in vendor performance. Manual records are still used in small libraries. It involves typing individual orders onto preprinted multipart order forms. These forms are then separated, with one copy sent to the supplier, and the rest kept in one or more files arranged to provide different access points-title, author, budget fund, supplier, number, date, or even card catalogue. Carbonless multipart order forms are available in the market both in standard and customized formats. The format of a basic form may look like figure.

THE ACQUISITION PROCESS

There are three types of purchasing agents for ordering

Book Order

Author ____________________

Title ____________________

Place _____ Publisher _____ Date _____

Edition _____ Volume _____ Series _____

ISBN _____ Price _____ No. of Copies _____

Special Instructions ____________________

Order No. _____ Date Ordered _____ Date Received _____

Fund _____ Price _____

From : __________ To : __________

Fig 7.1 Book Order

- *Jobber:* He is a wholesaler who anticipates what his customers are going to buy, and stocks those items in advance. By buying large stocks from publishers, the jobber obtains a maximum discount. Part of this discount can be passed on to his customers. Many factors are considered when selecting a jobber:
  - — Discount
  - — Handling rush orders, telephone, fax, electronic orders
  - — Stocking of titles
  - — Publishers handled
  - — Reporting
  - — Payment method
- *Dealer*: The dealer can handle a wider range of materials than the jobber. They have variant specialties. Discount offered is usually lower than that of the jobber. So acquisitions staff should know the discount and fee policies of the various dealers, as well as their reputation for good service. Many medical libraries rely on dealers to solve the problem of hard currency in their respective countries.
- *Publisher*: There are sometimes compelling reasons to order directly from the publisher. This may be because of:
  - — The book is only available from the publisher and orders through vendors or dealers are not accepted;
  - — It is sometimes quicker to receive a book directly from the publisher;
  - — Ordering from the publisher keeps the library on his mailing list.

Some libraries arrange approval plans with a jobber or publisher as previously mentioned. Having selected the purchasing agent, the following processes are performed.

Bibliographic Searching

This process is sometimes called 'preorder searching' or 'preorder verification'. It aims at preventing the ordering of something that the library has already ordered or received, and at verifying that the item actually exists by confirming its bibliographic description in an authoritative source.

A third aim has been added: obtaining reliable cataloguing information to initiate a bibliographic record with complete and accurate information. This searching may be manual, if the library is not yet automated or if it has no access to automated sources. otherwise the relevant databases whether in-house or external have to be searched. Although requestors are encouraged to use request forms, selection may be from dealers' lists, photocopies of bibliographies, publishers' catalogues and similar materials.

The process goes as follows:

- *Sort the Request Forms*: This may be by age of materials, country, language, form, or completeness of the citation.
- *Check the Libraries Records*: The catalogue, on-order file and in-process file. If the system is automated, one check of the bibliographic database will be required.
- *Check Bibliographic Sources:* The sources that may be used for this checking are:
  - *Publishers' Catalogues:* These must be the most up-to-date versions. But be careful some mistakes may be present, such as misspelling of author's name, ISBN, date, and price. Some publishers have their catalogues on Internet.
  - *Books in Print and Related Tools*: This is authoritative in the bibliographic information it contains. Its updating is done through: Books in Print Supplement and bimonthly Forthcoming Books. PIB Plus is a CD-ROM of Books in print. In addition Bowker publishes: Medical and health care books and serials in print. The British parallel of books in print is Whitaker's Books in Print.
  - *Vendors' Lists and Databases*: These may be print or electronic. Normally the library which is customer is allowed free access online.
  - *Bibliographic Networks*: Most academic libraries use the major bibliographic utilities, such as OCLC, RLIN, BLCMP, for cataloguing purposes,

but they can be used for verification purposes as well. Downloading from them is enabled in most of them. When CIP records are used, the information may be incomplete or inaccurate.

— *NLM CATLINE:* The medical libraries that have no access to other bibliographic utilities, may use this online catalogue of NLM.

Assigning Internal Ordering Information

Additional elements are required for the order record. They provide necessary or useful information for payment, processing and statistics:

- *Purchase Order Number:* This is required unless the size of acquisitions is so small. Assigning this number may be:
  - — Through the purchasing department of the parent organisation
  - — Assigned automatically by the automated system
  - — By obtaining order forms with sequential number preprinted on them
  - — By using a sequential numbering stamper
  - — By assigning sequential numbers manually
- *Budget Account*: The correct account name or code should be given in the order form, if there is more than one budget account.
- *Subject Code*: Some libraries assign a broad subject heading or code to each order. This breakdown may be useful for collection development and budget preparation. An automated system allows the library to maintain a list of controlled subject terms that can be assigned to orders.
- *Type of Order*: This is used when the library likes to know cases when there is a need for additional copies or replacements of lost or damaged items to be ordered.
- *Name of Requester*: When the item is requested by a library user, there may be a need for notifying him of the availability of the requested item in the library, or that it has been received and ready for him to use. His

name, address and telephone number are recorded in the order form.

- *Information for Cataloguing*: During the verification process some information that cataloguers may require is added. This information should be passed to the cataloguing unit. Such data includes:
  - — Previous editions of the item in the collection
  - — Other copies of the item in the collection
  - — Whether the item is a replacement or added copy
  - — Shelving location of item
  - — Circulation restrictions of the item
  - — Name of requester to be notified
  - — Special funding source or name of donor

This information has fields in the order form in an automated system, which can be produced after the book has been received; otherwise this production is done manually.

Returning Requests

If a request for acquisition is submitted without a supporting citation, the acquisitions staff proceeds according to the policies of the library. In some instances, incomplete requests may be returned to their initiator with a form requesting the needed information. If this is the case, the staff member should not return a request merely because it lacks a technical detail not likely to be available to the initiator, as he is not skilled in identifying or using the sources that provide it.

Sending Orders

Orders may be sent through the following means:

- *By Mail*: Large libraries may batch their orders to consolidate processing time and reduce mailing expenses. Small libraries may send an order out as soon as it has been completed. Rush orders have to be taken care of,
- *By Telephone*: This can be used for rush orders. Telephone orders should be documented for future reference. The problem here is that orders have to be prepayed with a credit card, which is not possible in many libraries.

- *By Computer*: EDIFACT Standard. Many libraries with automated systems still send their orders by mail. With the progress in electronic communications it is now possible to transmit orders from computer to computer, particularly when a standard for *electronic data interchange* (EDI) has been created by the UN *Economic Commission for Europe* (ECE). This standard will allow the library to send its address to any vendor, dealer or publisher electronically. All operations required will be dealt with without human intervention.
- *By Vendor System*: Many vendors have already automated their internal systems for ordering, invoicing and inventory. They provide access to them for their customers, to browse the inventory, enter new orders and enquire about outstanding orders. Some vendors may even allow downloading their online records, and the table of contents of individuals books if provided. For libraries with manual systems, many vendors offer dial-in service and confirm orders on multipart forms by mail. Acquisition staff have to learn each vendor's system when they deal with more than one.
- *By Fax and E-Mail*: Using fax speeds up ordering, and guarantees accurate records to be transmitted. Many book vendors have also set up Internet electronic mail accounts, which is relatively inexpensive to use, and the order records are accurate. Anyhow, some libraries may request a confirmation of receiving the order, as they do not consider faxed or e-mailed documents as legal documents.

Receiving Materials

When receiving materials ordered, the following actions must be performed:

- Boxes are unpacked
- Books are sorted
- Items are matched to the original order and to the invoice or packing slip
- Each book should be examined briefly and checked for blank or damaged pages, broken binding or any other imperfection

- The status of the item must be changed in the on-order file, whether manually or electronically. Date of receipt is recorded.
- The invoice is approved for payment. If the library is authorized to make payments, this payment is done. If not, an internal document called a payment voucher is filled out and sent to the department concerned of the parent organisation. This voucher contains, as a minimum, the supplier's name and address, invoice number and its date, the amount to be paid, and the fund to be used. It should be accompanied with the original invoice. It must also have an authorized signature. A copy of the voucher and invoice is retained by the library. The library should make every effort to pay the supplier promptly.
- If any problem is found in the invoice, it has to be solved before authorizing payment. This may be handled as follows, provided it is agreed upon.
  - — Credit memo issued by the supplier that can be deducted from the invoice if not yet paid; otherwise it can be deducted from a later invoice.
  - — Striking from the invoice, by cancelling the items concerned and subtracting the amount from the total.
  - — Requesting a new corrected invoice. This may be preferr-ed by the parent organisation.
  - — Returning the invoice with the item. This can be done if the invoice is for a single item.
- Recording the payment for each item in the individual order record. The completed record will have:
  - — All of the original order information
  - — The date the item was received
  - — Invoice number and date
  - — The amount paid
  - — The payment voucher number
  - — The date the payment was processed

In a manual system, this information is recorded on purchase order form which is then placed in the completed orders file. In automated system, it is in recorded the order record.

The amount committed for each item is automatically zeroed and the amount paid is deducted from the account charged:

- The library has better to keep the order records after the item is received and its payment sent. Some libraries do this until the books are shelved and the catalogue records are made available to the public. Others may retain them to enable staff to compile information required for various reportings; while others may never destroy their order records.
- Once the order record is cleared from the current file some libraries alert a staff member or library user that the item has arrived and is available for use.
- If a library uses an acquisitions/cataloguing form, this form is inserted into the book before it is sent forward to cataloguing. Automated systems that produce such processing forms may allow batch printing of the forms for books received that day, or can print out forms for each book as soon as its status changes from ' on-order " to ' received ".
- Acquisitions may be responsible for adding property stamps, book plates, security strips, etc. or sending paper backs for binding.
- The library has to report its purchase to other libraries or bibliographic agencies for cooperative purposes. This reporting may be in the form of a paper record sent by mail or messenger, or as an electronic message to a centralized, computerized database.
- Receiving materials in an approval shipment requires slightly different procedures, since they arrive with no preorder searching or records preceding them. Most libraries follow procedures similar to the following for receiving:
  - — Verify the package contents against the invoice or packing list.
  - — Check the approval items against the catalogue and on-order file to detect duplicates.
  - — If previous editions of a book exist, check as to whether the library owns any.
  - — Assign purchase order number, budget account, subject code and type of order.

Returns

Vendors and publishers sometimes send the wrong item, or send two copies of a book when only one was ordered. The book sent may be defective or damaged during transit. Such books must be returned. Most vendors allow returns with a note explaining the problem.

Publishers may:

- Require returned items to be sent to a special address;
- Require returned items to be identified with a special shipping label which they supply;
- Require postal insurance.

Claims

Orders that remain outstanding too long, require the library to send claims. Timing of claims is essential, as they are made when the waiting periods exceeded the time schedule agreed upon. In a manual system the order file has to be examined for possible claim. An extra copy of the order form may be used for this purpose, or a claim form is sent to the supplier. A typical claim form looks like figure.

Sometimes, there is a need for sending more than one claim, in which case the claim number should be mentioned on the form. Automated systems can produce claim forms on demand. When EDI is operational, it will enable sending claims electronically to which suppliers will respond electronically too. Moreover fax and e-mail are already used for speeding up claims.

Claim Form

Form : ________ To : ________

Claim Number : ________ Date : ________

The Following Order is Overdue. Please update its Order Status.

Author : ________ Title : ________

Publisher : ________ Edition : ________ Year : ________

ISBN : ________ Price : ________ No. ot Copies : ________

Order Number : ________ Order Date : ________

Fig 7.2 Claim Form

In addition to responding to specific claims, suppliers send out periodic reports indicating the status of all outstanding orders. The information provided in such reports is entered into the order records, so that the library does not claim for a book that has been reported as delayed.

Most suppliers use standard abbreviations or phrases for their claims responses and status, among which are:

- NYR-Not yet received, the order remains active
- OS-Out-of-stock, the order remains active
- OSI-Out-of stock indefinitely, the order is cancelled
- NYP-Not yet published, the order is mostly cancelled Claiming-Claiming from the publisher, the order is active
- OP-Out-of-print, the order is cancelled
- NOP-Not our publication, the order is cancelled Cannot Supply-the supplier cannot supply the item, the order is cancelled. It has to be ordered from another source.

Many libraries cancel an order if it has been outstanding for too long, say over one year, with no predicted delivery date. Others cancel all outstanding orders at the end of a fiscal year in compliance with the requirements of the parent organisation. Libraries usually use a cancellation form to identify the items being cancelled.

Direct Orders

Direct ordering is ordering directly from the publisher.

This may be for one or more of the following reasons:

- Publications are not available through book vendors. Publishers may not have business relations with book vendors because they demand prepayment, do not offer attractive discounts, or because the publisher feels the need for a direct relationship with the library customers.
- The library may find it preferrable to deal with the publisher directly: the publisher may offer a special sale or the library needs the item.

Direct ordering includes ordering from professional societies and associations. This requires prepayment as well.

But there are two unique aspects for this ordering:

- *Deposit Accounts:* This is done when the library places

a standing order of the society's publications. In return the society will offer a discount and exemption of shipping and handling expenses.

- *Membership Pricing:* Many associations offer special discounted pricing for their members.

ACQUISITION OF SPECIAL BOOK-LIKE MATERIALS

Microforms

Microforms are included here because they are always reproductions of books and booklike materials. They range in format, size, reduction and storage media. This means that microforms require different types of readers and copiers. Microforms are usually acquired directly from publishers. Micropublishing is often on demand publishing process. The types of materials covered include: out-of-print books, current serial subscriptions, backfiles of journals, working copies of rare books and manuscripts, government or international organisation documents and dissertations. Among the best guide to microforms is: Guide to microforms in print, published annually by K.G. Saur. It has to be noted that libraries are themselves main sources of microforms, as they hold negative films that another library may want copied.

Government Documents

Government documents are either issued by a central government publisher or by government agencies. They are mostly difficult to acquire from book vendors. They are ordered directly either prepaid or charged to a deposit account. Some countries distribute all or some of such documents free or on exchange. Care should be taken in verifying bibliographic information of the ordered items. International organisations documents are normally included here.

The source may be the individual agency which usually publishes its catalogue of publication or provides access to its data base, a local sales agent in the respective country, or the International bibliography published quarterly by UNIPUB, New York. Of special interest to health sciences libraries is WHO, which issues publications from both its headquarters and from regional offices. It also distributes publications of the *International Agency for Research on Cancer* (IARC), the *Council for International Organisations of Medical Sciences* (CIOMS) and the English Language publications of *Pan American Health Organisation* (PAHO).

Out-of-Print Books and Reprints

Health sciences books stay in-print for short periods. This means that unless a book is ordered within a few years of its publication, it is likely to be out-of-print when it is ordered.

The ways to obtain this type of books are:

- Borrowing the title through interlibrary loan service.
- Publishing a list of desiderata or want list, and either publishing in the Library bookseller or Antiquarian bookman's weekly, sending it to OP book dealers, or to search services, individuals or companies who take desiderata from libraries and attempt to find the items using their own contacts.
- Contacting authors or editors directly.
- Obtaining reprints. The library can use Guide to reprints, published annually by Microcard Editions. UMI produces reprints of OP books in hard-cover, paper back, or microfilm. Their ' books on demand " service covers many subjects including the medical subjects. Subject catalogues and an author guide are available upon request from UMI.
- Exchanging OP materials.

Remember the following when handling OP materials:

- It is time consuming
- The desiderata lists should be reviewed periodically
- Acquiring OP books in microform or in a photocopied version should be considered
- Prices should be considered carefully.

Dissertations and Theses

It is rare that a health sciences library has to acquire a dissertation or thesis produced at another institution. If any need arises, the right sources for selection should be used.

Among these are:

- UMI dissertation abstracts international
- UMI master abstracts
- Index to theses
- Some countries include them in their national bibliographies
- In the Arab world the Jordanian University Library is a depository library for dissertations of the universities that are members of the Union of Arab Universities. Some libraries published bibliographies of Arab dissertations as onetime publication.

One negative aspect of this type of material, is that some universities place restrictions on acquiring their dissertations. These may include the time limit preventing even the use of them before, say, five years; some do not allow reproduction completely or provided the author authorizes it.

SPECIAL PROBLEMS

But they are given here as a summing-up:

- *Item Not Supplied*: Unsupplied items should be claimed. Sometimes the vendor may fail to report. Some libraries, to avoid claiming process, specify that orders not supplied within a stated period of time are automatically cancelled.
- *Wrong Item Supplied*: The library may accept the loss, or return the item for credit.
- *Defective Item Supplied*: The item must be returned for replacement. Complications may arise if the vendor does not have access to another copy, or if his staff misunderstand the reasons for an item's return.
- *Incomplete Order*: Some of the items in the invoice were not supplied. This is likely to occasion written or oral communication with the vendor, sometimes over an extended period of time.
- *Missing Order Record*: The order record cannot be located in manual system, a lost record in one file may be found in another. But in automated system, the record is actually lost unless a backup file is maintained.

- *Duplicate Item Ordered or Received*: The library may accept the item and absorb the loss, or return the item for credit. If the item is to be returned, it should not be marked with the ownership stamp. If the item is accepted, it may be used for exchange.
- *Incorrect Item Checked In*: An item is received but incorrectly checked in against a wrong purchase order. When the correct item comes, it appears to be duplicate although in fact it is not. This may result in a mix-up as the item was considered duplicate and returned, or the library may claim it and the vendor reports that it was sent.
- *Unavailable Items*: An item is reported as not available and the order is cancelled. This resulted in many disagreements between libraries and suppliers. Some vendors are not careful in reporting the item as out-of-stock or even out-of-print inaccurately. It may be wise for the library to initiate further checks on the status of the item and confront the supplier with evidence of incorrect reporting. Repeated wrong reports can justify terminating the relationship with the supplier.
- *Unexpected Prices of Items*: An item may be priced far higher than the library expected, and payment either cannot be made or will severely unbalance the budget if it is made. Libraries, to solve this problem, state a limit when the supplier should not send item until agreement is reached. This precaution is vital for libraries with low budgets, and those in which overspending is not permitted.
- *Invoice Errors*: Among these errors are:
  - — The item on the invoice are in disagreement with the item sent;
  - — The discount may be computed erroneously, or omitted;
  - — The invoice total is not in agreement with the sum of the prices listed on it;
  - — The number of copies for which the library is billed is incorrect.

Such mistakes should be corrected before payment is made:

- *Improper Payment Made*: Improper payment may have been made by the library, or the supplier has incorrectly credited a payment. This has to be corrected by the library.
- *Incorrect Accounting Records*: A mistake may be made in keeping the financial records. Among such mistakes are:
  - — Failing to deduct a payment from the budget
  - — Deducting the amount from the general budget rather than the specific fund
  - — Debiting payment against the fund account but not against the general budget
  - — Failing to remove the committed price when the actual cost is entered.

Such errors are substantially reduced when an automated system is used. But it has to be remembered that even the most sophisticated automated system cannot prevent staff from entering figures incorrectly or failing to enter them at all.

ACQUISITION OF SERIALS

The Anglo-American cataloguing rules, second edition defines a serial as:

- A publication in any medium issued in successive parts bearing numeric or chronological designations and intended to be continued indefinitely. Serials include periodicals; newspapers; annuals, the journals, proceedings, memoirs, transactions, etc. of societies; and numbered monographic series. Series is a group of separate items related to one another by the fact that each item bears, in addition to its own title proper, a collective title applying to the group as a whole. The individual items may or may not be numbered.

The indefinite continuation of a serial is important from the acquisitions point of view, as it continues arriving, which necessitates updating its record.

CATEGORIES OF SERIALS

Periodicals

Periodicals are serials characterized by the regularity of

publication and frequency of issue. They are generally paid for in advance.

They include scholarly journals, popular magazines, newsletters and loose-leaf publications with a regular updating service:

- *Journals*: Journals constitute the majority of periodicals in the health sciences library. They are usually distributed unbound, bear a volume and issue number, and mostly have continuous pagination throughout the volume. A volume index and cumulated table of contents are common.
- *Magazines*: They are usually intended for a wider audience. Advertisements are interspersed with articles, each issue is paginated independently, indexes are uncommon, and article content is not generally subject to peer review.
- *Newsletters and Newspapers*: These are typically composed of folded sheets and frequently lack standard journal feature such as table of contents and index. Libraries keep simple records for them, and are most likely discarded when they are outdated. A microform copy may be kept instead. Some of them are now available electronically online or on CD-ROM.
- *Loose-leaf Publications*: These are issued in loose-leaf format, and are updated regularly with additional or replacement pages for an annual fee. Many of them are now offered on CD-ROM.

Annuals and Proceedings

Annuals are titles published on a more or less annual basis. They can provide:

- Updating review of the literature in a specific discipline
- Compilation of standard data
- Directory information, or
- Proceedings of annual professional meetings

Many libraries establish a standing order for acquiring this category, and process items the way books are processed.

Numbered Monographic Series

These include series that are issued with a collective series title and a consecutive volume number, frequently with but not necessarily accompanied by a unique title for each work in the series. Publishing is generally irregular, and mostly processed like books after checking-in as serials. They, thus, have two records, one as serials, and another as books.

Pseudoserials

These are not strictly speaking serials, but are treated as such for acquisitions purposes. They include any publication that appears in separate parts or editions under a consistent title, and continues for more than a year or two years.

Examples of this category include:

- Encylcopaedias or dictionaries issued in parts over a period of several years.
- Successive editions of reference works, such as directories, cumulative bibliographies, biographical lists of 'who's who' type and handbooks for special disciplines.

SOURCES OF SERIALS

Publishers

Most publishers accept subscription orders for their serials, although a few make their publications available only through agents or exclusively through a general purchase arrangement, such as a standing order or a membership in the publisher's parent organisation:

- *Commercial Publishers*: Libraries may place a subscription directly with a publisher. Commercial publishers may provide some services useful to libraries, such as providing sample copies of issues before the library makes a subscription decision, and establishing standard terms for claiming missing or damaged issues and for purchasing backfiles.
- *Society Publishers*: These publishers publish their serials for the membership of the association or society, and for broader distribution to the scientific community. Some publishers will not sell their serials except to

members, while others give discount or provide their publications as part of the membership perquisites. Some do not allow an agent to be involved in subscription.

- *Government Agencies*: Many government agencies publish serials. Procuring such publications present a challenge to the library in identifying and receiving them promptly. They may be obtained directly from the government central publishing house, from the individual issuing agency, or through a specialist vendor.

Gifts, Exchange or Deposits

Exchange or gift arrangement may be effective in the acquisition of serials published in other countries under the auspices of academic institutions or scholarly groups. Sometimes titles may be available only through exchange arrangement or gift. Deposits are much like gifts and exchange, except that they may not be officially the property of the receiving library. A factor that should be considered in accepting arrangements for exchange, gifts or deposits, is whether the library would be willing to pay for a subscription if the agreement were suddenly terminated.

Subscription Agents

At the most basic level, subscription agents accept subscription orders and forward them to the appropriate publishers with payment. The agent, in return, sends the library a consolidated invoice, which the library pays to him. The agent represents the library in communicating with the publisher when claims for skipped or late issues are necessary.

The library usually pays the agent the list price of the subscriptions plus a service fee, usually calculated as a percentage of the subscription costs. Some libraries may employ the services of multiple subscription agents. However, this number should be kept to a minimum in order to realise the full benefits of order and payment consolidation.

The following services provided by subscription agents are customarily covered by the service charge paid by the library:

- Place new orders with publishers

- Notify publishers of renewals
- Pay publishers for orders and renewals
- Notify publishers of cancellations
- Obtain refunds from publishers when due
- Transfer subscriptions from previous agents
- Notify publishers of nonreceipt of issues, *i.e.* claims
- Notify library of publisher response to claims
- Intervene with publishers to resolve unsatisfied claims
- Provide consolidated invoices and account statements
- Provide information on changes of title, frequency, or publishing schedule affecting the library's subscriptions
- Notify publishers of changes in library ship-to address
- Provide standard and financial reports on the library's account.

Moreover, the following additional services may be covered by the service charge or may have to be paid for:

- Place orders for replacement issues and backfiles
- Supply sample issues of journals
- Provide a comprehensive catalogue of published serials, either in print or electronic format
- Provide custom reports on the library's account
- Provide online access to the agent's serials information databases

In addition, some agents may provide specialized services such as:

- Consolidated shipment of foreign publications
- Provision of machine-readable bibliographic records
- Software for automated serials control
- Union list products

A key person in the success of agent-library relationship is the account executive, or the customer representative designated by the agent, to coordinate services for the library's account. This person should be available to the library by telephone, fax and e-mail to respond to the queries of the library.

SERIALS CONTROL SYSTEM

Automated Systems

Automated serials control systems typically accommodate

multiple simultaneous users, and provide rapid access to records by title, keyword and other identifying elements such as the ISSN. They can display current receipt information and summary holdings, both for the public and for staff, and provide automatic prediction of the next expected issue which enables routine claiming of skipped or delayed issues.

They can accept electronic invoice information and create printed listings and online reports in a variety of formats. They can support related functions such as binding, routing and union listing. Library journal regularly publishes a review of the automated systems marketplace that profiles the systems and includes a directory of names and addresses for each. Some agents have developed stand-alone microcomputer-based serials control systems, such as Microlinx of the Faxon Company.

The functions of an automated serials control systems may be summarized as follows:

- Public search and display
- Order entry and payment processing
- Check-in
- Claiming
- Report production

Manual Systems

The most common manual system for serials control is the cardex, where the cards used are formated in a calender-like fashion so that receipts can be recorded in the appropriate chronological block and so that any skipped issues are obvious upon visual inspection of the cards. There should be room for: processing notes, routing instructions, summary statement of the library's holdings and payment information.

SERIALS RECORD KEEPING PROCEDURES

The records required for serials are basically similar to those for books, including copies of purchase orders, commitments records of the general budget and special funds, and accounts of receipts, billings and payments. However, many libraries find it useful to keep books and serials acquisitions responsibilities separate.

Record of the Subscription

New serials order requires instructions that apply to all titles, invoicing requirements, delivery address, starting year, ISSN, number of copies for each title ordered.

Elements of the standard instructions include:

- Ship-to address
- Invoicing requirements including:
  - Bill-to address
  - Required number of copies of invoices and credit memos
  - Batch vs. individual invoices
  - Inclusion of library assigned codes such as order number and department
  - Preferred handling of credit adjustments
- Policy on supplements
- Renewal policy
- Acceptability of multiple-year orders
- Order confirmation requirement

A requisition or purchase order is required to initiate an order which is forwarded to the agent or publisher. Some agents can accommodate on-line entry of orders. Once the new order has been placed, preparation for receiving the issues should be made. This includes check-in records, and payment record.

Check-in Record

Important elements of the check-in record include:

- Title
- Publisher
- ISSN
- Frequency
- Pattern of publication, and anticipated supplements
- Supplier
- Supplier's title number
- Notes for labelling and marking
- Other instructions: binding, special issues expected, retention policy, and volumes or issues that receive monographic cataloguing

- Routing instructions
- Availability of title pages and indexes
- Order reference number, if the check-in record is not otherwise linked to the payment record.

Procedures must emphasize accurate record-keeping and efficient processing of serials as they are received by the library. Check-in begins in the mail room where incoming mail is received, sorted and prepared for distribution. Mailing labels or envelopes are examined to avoid misrouted mail, and to assist in resolving delivery problems in case the issue turns out to be unwanted or duplicate. Backlogs in mail processing and check-in are unaccep-table. Maximum of twenty-four hours is reasonable to get the issue to the shelf.

The correct check-in record in most automated systems can be selected by entering the ISSN or keywords form the title. Some systems can use the bar code printed on the journal to call up the corresponding check-in record. If a manual system is used, it is advisable to sort receipts alphabetically before check-in. When a check-in record cannot be found for a received title, it should be reviewed by a supervisor before it is treated as unwanted or misrouted mail. When the record is located, the issue receipt is recorded. When check-in is completed, routine physical processing is carried in accordance with the instructions set by the library.

This processing includes:

- Stamping receipt date
- Stamping library name
- Placing a mark on the cover identifying the title for purposes of alphabetic filing
- Attaching special labels identifying locations, call numbers or circulation status
- Inserting a security strip
- Attaching a bar code
- Inserting date due slip

It has to be stressed that serials may have various changes that should be addressed. These typically include: title changes, change of publisher, frequency changes, combined issues, issuing supplement and other special issues, and delayed publication schedules.

Reasons for title changes usually include one of the following:

- Change in editorial board, sponsoring organisation, or publisher.
- Response to new concepts or terminology in the field.
- Change in subject scope or targeted audience.
- Change in language, frequency, or peer review status.

Payment Record

Payment records identify funds committed for new tittles not yet invoiced, and provide a retrospective listing of all payments and credit for each continuing title. They ensure not paying twice for the same purpose, and monitor price increases. Whether manual or automated the payment record must be linked to the check-in record so that claiming can be carried out with convenient access to relevant payment information.

The following data is included in a basic payment record of serial:

- Title
- Number of copies on order
- Name and address of the supplier
- Account number of the supplier
- Title number of the supplier
- Fund charged
- Ledger of payments and credits
  - — Invoice number and date
  - — Amount paid
  - — Volume and Year covered

To be effective, the payment record should enable the library to renew or cancel subscription promptly. If the publisher is the direct supplier, it has to be noted that some do not send renewal invoice.

Claiming

Claiming is the process of notifying the publisher directly or through the subscription agent that an issue was not received or was received in unsatisfactory condition.

A notice is typically sent which includes the following essential elements:

- Library name and account number

- Title being claimed
- Enumeration, chronology or edition of the issue being claimed
- Reason for the claim
- Date of the claim
- Claim sequence
- Publisher
- Order reference number
- Alternative identifiers such as ISSN
- Explanatory notes

The most common reasons for a claim are:

- Skipped issue
- Overdue issue
- Issue damaged in transit
- Defective issue
- Incorrect number of copies

Claims forms are usually supplied by the supplier. Some may allow automated systems online claim. EDIFACT will facilitate automated claiming when it is widely adopted. Claims should be made within the time frame specified by the publisher and before the publisher's supplies of the issue are exhausted. In a manual system, the check-in card can be flagged at check-in with a coloured tab to indicate that an issue has been skipped. Claims are based on the flagged cards.

The bigger problem is with overdue issue as this needs reviewing every check-in card. In automated systems, skipped issue can be identified upon check-in of a subsequent issue. But overdue issues are identified based on the frequency of the serial, the number of days since the last issue was received and the title-specific grace period assigned by the library. Titles that are overdue based on this interval are flagged as potential claims by the system.

Such intervals may be as follows:

- Daily 10 days
- Weekly 14 days
- Monthly 60 days
- Quarterly 150 days
- All others 30 days after expected arrival

Premature and unnecessary claims may be caused by the library or by the publisher.

The causes of this may be:

- The system-supplied expected receipt date has gotten off track, or the grace period is too short.
- Delayed publication not reported to the library.
- Combined issues not noticed at check-in.
- Issue checked in as supplement or on wrong title record.
- Frequency change.
- Issue received but not checked in due to human error.
- Title changes.

From the publisher:

- Misnumbering of issues.
- Publishing out of sequence without notifying subscribers.
- Changing frequency without notifying subscribers.

For following up of unresolved claims, subscription agents usually send to the library a monthly claim report. The library has to review this report and return it promptly to the agent. Issues not received should be reclaimed and recorded as such in the library's files. It is important for the library to document that its first claim was sent within the time period acceptable to the publisher.

Renewals

Many publishers send subscribers renewal invoices about three or four months before the end of a subscription term. These invoices need to be paid six to eight weeks before the end of that term to guarantee continuous delivery. Needless to say that special care must be taken not to overlook renewal notices for titles ordered directly from the publisher. Subscription agents offer two methods for renewal, one automatic and the other requires manual reauthorization by the library. The second method is preferred by the library.

Listings are usually sent by agents between July and August. The library reviews the list, makes necessary changes, and returns it to the agent with payment by mid October. The agent must make follow-up later with a supplemental invoice, covering the price increases. Renewal decisions in the library involve one of three options: renew, cancel or hold. They may also involve changing the number of copies. Hold option means that the final decision will be given later, because the library needs more time or when a title is substantially behind schedule and the library does not want to be invoiced for it until it has received what it has already paid for.

Payment by the agent to the publisher should be timely to avoid missing any issue. The future trends in serials acquisitions will deal with both print and electronic formats or a hybrid of both. This means that it may be difficult to separate purchase process from licensing of digital products. On the other hand a number of subscription agents are now offering serials check-in and records maintenance as an addition to their basic subscription services. The developments in electronic publishing is paving the way to the transformation from subscription to journals to article-level acquisitions. Moreover there is an increase in the efforts of creating standards applicable to serials.

Among these efforts the following may be briefly mentioned:

- *CONSER*: Is a cooperative effort which aims at establishing a core database of bibliographic information on serials titles.
- *ISBD*: International Standard Bibliographic Description for Serials, is issued by the *international Federation of Library Association and Institutions* (IFLA).
- *ISSN*: International Standard Serials Number is an eight digit code whose last digit is a check number, issued by ISDS.
- *ISDS*: International Serials Data System has responsibility for assigning ISSN and the key title of serials.
- *CODEN*: It is a unique five character code. The Chemical Abstracts Service is responsible for its maintenance since 1973.

ACQUISITIONS OF AUDIOVISUAL MATERIALS

Since earliest times medical education has relied on illustrative teaching materials in addition to printed materials. They were always visual and then incorporated sound. Being essential as teaching/learning materials, they are expected to form part of library stock.

AUDIOVISUAL SOURCES

General Commercial Publishers

Many commercial publishers of printed materials also produce and distribute media items. These materials are the only types of media materials that can be ordered from book suppliers. They may be included in the same catalogue with the publisher's book and journal publications.

Specialized Commercial Media Publishers

There are many commercial publishers or distributors that deal only with media materials, with some producing a variety of formats, and others limited to one format.

Educational Consortia

National and regional consortia and other membership organisations are also sources of media materials. Membership organisations provides the library with catalogues of available materials, as well as discounted prices. Special acquisitions procedures may be required for such materials to ensure that member discounts are correctly applied.

Non-commercial Materials

Health sciences faculty, their schools and universities are also sources of media materials, as they sometimes develop media materials for use by teaching staff and students and may agree to make them available in the library. Some academic institutions have media centres and close cooperation with them will offer fast acquisition of their products.

Pharmaceutical Companies

Some pharmaceutical companies offer media materials such as slides free of charge to medical schools and hospitals.

Professional Societies and Organisations

Many professional societies and organisations, such as the

Radiological Society of North America and the American Society of Clinical Pathologists, sell educational media materials. Their marketing efforts are most likely to be aimed towards members, so requests for purchases may often originate from health professionals and faculty. The ordering process is straightforward, although prepayment is frequently required.

ACQUISITION PROCESSES

Communication with Selectors

Because media materials are used for a variety of reasons within the library—such as reference information, as educational materials and as office productivity tools—requests for them may originate from various departments of the library, as well as from departments outside the library, such as patient education or continuing education department.

In addition to the standard order entry elements, such as title, date of publication, publisher, price, the media acquisitions request should include:

- Format
- Whether or not a preview copy is required, and who will do the previewing
- Full address of the producer or distributor, if available
- Notes on any special publisher/distributor policies already ascertained or negotiated by the selector
- Notes on special processing requirements

Bibliographic Searching

In addition to the usual preorder check of library files to avoid duplication, some preorder research is frequently required to verify or complete the item identification. An essential element is the publisher address as many titles have to be ordered directly from producers or distributors.

It has to be noted here, that bibliographic verification is often difficult because:

- Comprehensive bibliographies and directories are not available for audiovisuals
- Records in bibliographic utilities, such as OCLC and RLIN, can be unreliable

- Records of the Library of Congress and NLM AVLINE may be slow to appear or unavailable.

For these reasons, the library has to maintain bibliographic resources of its own for audiovisuals. These include commercially published directories, individual producer and distributor catalogues, media listings compiled by vendors and listings of media holdings compiled by other libraries. If all these fail, it is advisable to contact the producer or distributor directly, preferably by telephone, where the responses have to be documented.

Order Entry and Record Keeping

Whether the tracking system of media orders is manual or electronic, consideration should be given to accommodating data elements unique to media items, such as format, version and notes on handling preview copies. The order form itself has to be as clear and explicit as possible. Larger acquisitions operations may want to have a higher level supervisor do a final signoff on all media orders, or at least those with an estimated cost above a specified amount.

Ordering Items on Preview

Many media items are available on a preview or on approval basis. There are many factors in determining the suitability of an item by seeing and using it. A faculty member, for example may want to view a videocassette to determine its appropriateness and quality of the visuals. In health sciences libraries, it is usual to buy one item that most closely matches local needs, rather than a spectrum of viewpoints on a specific topic.

Placing preview orders are similar to entering firm orders, except that the order itself must specify the preview nature of the request. Although a standard form for preview requests simplifies the process, the policies of publishers are different. Once the preview item is received, it must be sufficiently processed, the evaluator contacted, the item reviewed, and a purchase decision made within the specified preview period. If the item is to be returned, it has to be mailed and insured according to the publisher's instructions. When a decision is made to purchase the item on preview, it is better to return the preview copy and enter a new firm order to guarantee obtaining a new copy rather than the one used.

Alternatively, the library keeps the preview copy and requests an invoice. Some previews are charged for, while some publishers may waive the fee if the copy is retained. Some publishers, instead of providing a preview option, do provide 'satisfaction guaranteed' allowing an item to be returned, if it is not satisfying, within a specified period of time.

Receipt and Precataloguing Processing

Items, once received are first checked to determine that the correct title and version have been received and that all the pieces are included. Additional check of completeness may be required by the requesting department. A thorough quality review to ensure that the item is not defective is required.

ACQUISITION OF ELECTRONIC RESOURCES

Procedures for acquiring electronic resources can be based upon procedures and policies for acquisition of other types of materials, as described in the preceding parts. However, particularly as in audiovisuals, some distinct attributes of these resources and of their distribution channels do merit specialized policies and procedures.

Among the factors that affect such materials are those concerning audiovisuals as well, and the following unique to these resources:

- The increased emphasis on licensing arrangements as opposed to outright purchase;
- The availability of the same title in a variety of versions for different hardware, requiring special care in the specification process of the order;
- The frequent presence of parallel formats both print and electronic;
- The presence of two distinct categories of resources, as one is the general purpose software, the other is the files that contain information.

The nature and usage of these resources mean that there are shared responsibilities for their acquisitions among different library departments. Nevertheless record keeping process should provide adequate tracking of the item throughout the acquisitions process. The acquisition of free Internet distributed documents and data files is especially prone to communication gaps, since they can be down-loaded, or simply connected to, by staff members not involved in the acquisitions process.

SOURCES OF ACQUISITIONS

- General Commercial Publishers
- *General-purpose Software Producers*: These may be available through direct order, mail-order wholesalers and retail outlets
- *Non-commercial Software*: The source here may be the faculty, their schools and university
- *Network-distributed Software and Data Files*: These can be downloaded from Internet FTP sites and electronic bulletin boards or by establishing connections to remote sites. Many of them are free of charge, others may require site licensing payments.

ACQUISITION PROCESS

Communication with Selectors

The process is almost identical to the acquisition of audiovisuals, while the following are unique for electronic sources: the acquisitions request should include:

- Computer environment
- Version number
- Whether or not a network version is needed
- Number of copies or number of authorized network users

Special Issues

- *Licensing*: In acquiring software, the library is essentially purchasing a license to use the software in most cases. This licensing requires that the software is not to be altered, reproduced or made available at more than one workstation without the consent of the producer, and, in the case of networked availability, the payment of additional fees. The license-based purchasing of software requires that some procedures to be in place for handling them:

— All licenses should be reviewed by a staff member responsible for ensuring library compliance with licensing restrictions.
— Staff should be cautious in unpacking commercial software as unpacking implies acceptance of licensing restrictions.
— Licensing agreements are generally accompanied by some form of user registration system, which is also used to determine eligibility for free or discounted upgrades and for user support. Registration forms should be completed and returned, and internal records of all currently registered software kept.
— Licensing terms may require that a software be returned if the agreement is allowed to expire.
— Ongoing licensing fees for some products, such as CD-ROM databases, may vary depending on the number of years of indexing the library wants to retain.

- *Multiple-copy Licensing*: Producers differ in multiple use li-censing among libraries. Negotiation of terms require technical knowledge about the network environment and an understanding of the anticipated level of use.
- *Purchasing General-use Software*: Libraries differ in purchasing such software as some have this done by the acquisitions unit, while others consider them under administrative or computer services departments.
- *Ordering Upgrades*: These are generally offered to registered licensees at reduced prices. When an upgrade arrives, registration form is completed and returned to the producer. Acquisitions unit should ensure that upgrades are routed through the cataloguing department to ensure that the required changes are entered in bibliographic and holding records.

- *Maintenance and Customer-support Fees*: A maintenace and support fee is paid annually by the licensee, particularly for complex interactive products based on a large database of information that requires regular updating. Some agreements include these fees, while in other cases the fee pays for all software upgrades and updates.
- *CD-ROM Serials*: The subscription to serially published digital media titles, such as audio and video journals, diskette or CD-ROM-based journals and databases can often be placed through regular subscription agents. But libraries which do this may still need to deal directly with the publisher in matters related to licensing.

Unlike most print serials subscriptions, new issues completely replace some or all of the earlier issues. For such titles new disks should be reviewed by professional staff who are completely familiar with the product.

Subscription to CD-ROM titles involve three different kinds of materials:

- The CDs themselves
- Manuals and other documentation
- Periodic upgrades to the search and display software

Each of these materials may require different types of routing and processing.

So, the person carrying out check-in should have clear instructions on how to identify and route each component:

- *Network-distributed Publications*: A growing number of publications in digital format are being distributed as digital files on the Internet. Many electronic journals and newsletters distribute complete text of each issue to the e-mail addresses of subscribers, others distribute only a table of contents or brief summaries of the article, along with instructions for requesting e-mail or FTP transmission of particular articles. Most of the titles are presently free of charge, and a large portion of them are government documents. The major difference between print and electronic serials is that the issues of the latter arrive at a designated electronic mail-box rather than through the postal service. The following generalized procedures for checking in, routing and storing electronic serial issue are emerging:

— Issues are received at a designated electronic serials mailbox, sometimes to a separate one for each title.
— Serials check-in staff record issue received in the regular check-in system.
— Issues are forwarded electronically to technical staff who strip out extraneous lines from the header of the e-mail message and store the issue as a file on a network-accessible server.
— Pointers to the files are created, typically using the menuing and searching capabilities provided in Gopher, WAIS, WWW or similar software for network navigation.

There are international efforts to standardize the issue title and identification, such as IFLA's attempt to issue the International Standard Bibliographic Description of Electronic Resources which was issued in 1997 to replace ISBD. It is also possible to eliminate the first three steps and simply point the library's WWW server to the publisher's or some other institution's Web site where the rest of the work has already been done. This means that the real 'acquisition' activity made is the creation of an automatic link to the remote site.

This 'acquisition by linkage' is definitely going to change the concept of acquisition altogether:

- *Commercial Journal Publishing in the Digital Era*: The large commercial publishers are experimenting for finding viable electronic parallels of their print titles. Such serials are being developed in a full graphical format to accommodate complex illustrations and sophisticated gradations of font and type size. Of these are the *British medical journal* (BMJ) and the New England journal of medicine, which are acquired in the same way as other CD-ROM serials. But there are others like ADONIS, which entail the licensing of access to established journals in digital format. They have ongoing charges for printing and downloading articles.

Another model of publishing is publishing articles rather than journal issues. Of this model are the Online journal of current Clinical trials, and the *Online Journal of Knowledge Synthesis of Nursing* (OCLC). Some libraries consider this model has more in common with interlibrary loan functions or with other database searching services than with standard serials acquisition procedures. This may lead to the merging of acquisitions and document delivery operations. To summarize, more and more acquisitions will be in electronic formats including multimedia materials. This will require reengineering the present acquisitions procedures, particularly as many will not involve acquiring physical units, but rather legal access rights.

8

Library Stock Verification

INTRODUCTION

Stock verification or physical verification is to periodically check and account for the documents acquired by a library. Stock verification is an insignificant aspect of librarianship as far as teachers, researchers and library experts are concerned. But in practice stock verification is considered as a sensitive, controversial and unwanted evil activity. Practicing librarians are often perturbed and worried over the process of library stock verification and its results and implications.

The spirit and philosophy of librarianship towards books as emotion filled animate beings dissipates when books are subjected to stock verification. As such some consider stock verification as one of the occupational hazards. The other hazards include mutilation of documents and loss in transit of supplies. Stock verification is often done like a ritual without clear identification of aims and objectives and hence a host of confusion surrounds stock verification. If the objectives and procedures of physical verification and responsibilities about loss of documents are clearly enumerated, the process becomes plain and simple.

STOCK VERIFICATION: A RITUAL/POST-MORTEM

Often, the cost of carrying out a stock verification, particularly in a dynamic, comprehensive, well defined and compact collection like that of a special library far exceeds the benefits derived and even the loss discovered. Hence at the outset this post-mortem or futile exercise appears to have no positive benefits except accounting for the stock. On the other hand this may cause inconvenience to users, disturbance to routines of library, health hazard to library staff, loss of man hours, time, money and service in a library.

Whether to take up such an activity or not, if taken up at what frequency and is it for entire collection or for a sample collection, etc. are mostly decided by the parent organisation and the rules governed by it. For example, in case of Government of India organisations complete annual physical verification of books has to be done by a library having not more than 20,000 volumes and not fewer than two library qualified staff.

However, complete physical verification has to be done at intervals of not more than three years in case of libraries having upto 20,000 volumes with only one library qualified staff as well as libraries having more than 20,000 volumes but not more than 50,000 volumes. Further, only a sample physical verification at intervals of not more than five years is needed in case of libraries having more than 50,000 volumes. If such sample verification reveals unusual or unreasonable shortages, complete verification shall be done. What type of documents need to be counted for the above purpose is not enumerated but it can be assumed to be books and bound volumes of journals ignoring the ephemeral and gray literature and microforms.

ADVANTAGES OF STOCK VERIFICATION

A library should also take note of some advantages in carrying out stock verification. *Firstly,* periodic stock verification and write-off of resultant loss helps to reduce unnecessary escalation in book value of assets. *Secondly*, physical verification also helps in replacing relevant, useful and on demand documents with new copies wherever lost or mutilated. *Thirdly*, stock verification is the time to introduce new ways of arrangement of stack, modified or new lending system and other procedures.

Fourthly, if a library calls back all issued out documents for stock verification purpose, it can provide an opportunity for its users to browse the entire collection after verification. This very much counters the otherwise bias of less useful books lying on shelves all through the year. *Fifthly*, stock verification helps to review the precautionary measures already taken in preventing loss and mutilation as well as to identify any deficiencies in the existing procedure of maintenance of library and vigilance.

Stock verification helps as a way of identifying and discarding obsolete volumes. Normally in an active collection of a well organised library, loss of on-demand books are only noticed in day-to-day working. Other incidental benefits of stock verification include identification of damaged and worn-out documents for repair or rebinding, keeping shelf list and other records up-to-date, rearrangement and cleaning of stack, better acquaintance of collection and popular documents by library staff, etc.

METHODS OF STOCK VERIFICATION

As far as methods of carrying out stock verification are concerned the parent organisation may involve or may not involve external persons in the team of stock verification and may decide to exclude certain types of material in the library. The rest of the methodology of verification depends on the provisions already made in the design and organisation of library records. There are a number of methods followed for stock verification. The most crude method is to numerically count the number of documents and it practically does not serve any purpose except to know the number of documents lost.

The old and fairly crude method is to physically check and tally documents on shelves with accession register. This method is not only cumbersome and time consuming but also require the entire register to be kept while checking. It may also lead to spoiling the register with tick marks. However, with the advent of new ways of reproduction of accession register now the original register can still be saved. Another accession number based scheme which also has the disadvantage of keeping the entire register is to have prewriting/typed/printed cards carrying accession numbers in blocks of 100 numbers while physically checking the documents on shelves.

In both these methods the simultaneous working of number of batches depends on availability of number of copies of accession register or its surrogate and if more than one copy of accession register is used the results of checking needs to be consolidated from different copies/batches. All these not only make it cumbersome but also lead to waste of time and efforts. It is also possible now with the proliferation of personal computers to just key-in all accession numbers as and when checked to consolidate the loss in terms of missing accession numbers.

The most economical and fast way of entering accession number is to use a mobile bar code/wand reader to scan accession numbers of books from the bar code stickers in the books. But bar code system is yet to pickup in this country. The most popular and fairly reliable and quick manual method is to verify stock based on shelf list. This method requires an up-to-date shelf list. All these methods presuppose closing library for verification purpose.

Yet another shelf list based method which does not require closing down the library but ensures reasonably economical, quick and dependable stock checking is to have two card systems. In this method two different colour book cards are prepared for each document and one of them is maintained as shelf list card and the other kept in book. At the time of stock verification these two book cards are exchanged. This method allows for simultaneous working of many batches as both shelf list and documents are arranged in the same sequence and also allows for rectifying errors of stock verification at a later date.

PRECAUTIONARY MEASURES AGAINST LOSS

Having carried out stock verification in a library, the very first question to be asked is that 'are the existing precautionary measures against loss of library documents enough? and `is there any scope to take further precautions?'. Here again the preventive and precautionary actions normally cost much more than the value of loss. The usual precautions taken at the time of planning a library is to operate with one exit cum entrance, not allowing personal belongings inside the library and covering all windows of the building with suitable wire mesh or metal grills to avoid passing books through windows.

Additional precautions like a check point at exit gate with a person and/or vigilance manpower including security guard, magnetised document checking/burglar's alarm and other electronic book security system, CCTV, insurance against loss, etc. cost substantially to the organisation in addition to being not fool proof. What additional precautions are to be taken depends on how much additional expenditure the organisation is willing to incur.

Here two things need special mention. Firstly some of the costs like salaries of vigilance/checking staff are often invisible. Secondly, any physical check by a security guard in reputed institution may not only bring resistance from users but also makes an ugly show. Apart from intensifying vigilance, another positive approach propounded is to liberalise services like extended library hours during examination time, liberal or subsidised xerox service and liberal lending of books marked 'not to be issued'.

It is natural to raise a question as to how library books are lost that too in research institutions where majority of the users are from higher strata of society. Mysteriously, it becomes almost impossible to pin point at any individual or set of individuals. Nor it is easy to catch redhandedly such thieves. Where they are caught also, surprisingly the legal process is so fragile that it becomes difficult to establish a theft.

Any way librarian is not a police officer. While discussing various security methods Pierce says "... maintaining the security of library materials has changed from a minor irritant to a major problem. Many libraries have discovered that they are loosing more than one per cent of their collections each year vandalism, arson and wanton destruction have become more common in libraries and will probably continue and even possibly increase".

An analysis of types of books lost and the distribution of value of books lost as against the strength of collection and average cost of books acquired should provide some guidelines about type and nature of books lost the need for vigilance, the need for change in arrangement and organisation of collection. Such analysis with some useful ratios like loss to use/consultation, loss to stock, loss per user per year, etc. would be quite useful. One such analysis of loss of ISRO Satellite Centre (ISAC) Library for the year 1987-88.

It has clearly indicated that text books and other popular books in the area of office rules, electronics, computer science, etc.

costing far less than the average cost of book acquired are lost. Further, for every 1000 documents in stock on an average 3.67 documents are lost. As against Goverment of India guideline of allowing 3 books for every 1000 circulated/consulted, ISAC library has lost only 0.58 document. Lastly the value of loss of ISAC library is just 80% of the incidental revenue earned in the form of nominal overdue charges levied by library.

RESPONSIBILITY AND WRITE-OFF OF LOSS

After accepting and probably implementing wherever possible the additional precautionary measures against loss of library documents the ordeal does not end. No precautionary measure without fully undermining the service function in an open access library can ensure total elimination of loss. A negligible number of perverted, possessive, habituated persons responsible for loss and mutilation are likely to continue inspite of liberalised services and strict vigilance.

Further what has already been lost and what is going to be discovered as lost in the future stock verifications need to be explained to and got write-off by the competent authority. At this stage the question of who is responsible for loss of library documents often surfaces with an indirect hint at librarian or librarian together with his staff though most of special libraries and information centres are directly or indirectly managed by non-librarians either in the form of committees or as officer incharge. In some libraries, the librarian may be directly held responsible for the loss.

Loss of moveable property, stores and consumable is a universal phenomenon. Individuals, insitutions, departments, public and private enterprises incur loss of many types of moveable property, stores and consumables. An individual library user, who looses a book borrowed from the library pays the 'replacement cost' to the library, rightfully and sometimes vengefully feels that what is lost by librarian should be made good by librarian. But he conveniently forgets to distinguish librarian as individual user from librarian as a functional head of the library.

In no other area of loss like that of minor equipment and consumable in any organisation so much of fuss about responsibility of loss arises as it happens in loss of library documents. As such stock verification is covertly viewed as a tool to punish librarians. Librarian in the process of providing service to users antagonises those who loose documents borrowed in their names and earns a psychological dislike or hatred by recovering the 'replacement cost' of documents. It is extremely rare to see a situation in an organisation where recoveries are made for loss of minor equipment and consumables even though they are issued in the names of individuals for keeping in their exclusive possession.

Compared to the magnitude of losses in many types of stores items in an organisation, the loss of library documents is meager. Secondly the stores items including smaller equipments would have been kept under exclusive possession in lock and key and there may not be a need to share them with others. Infact, many times books issued to individual departments are also lost. Further all other types of items are subjected to strict security with gate passes. On the other hand, documents in an open access library are meant for shared use by many.

Library staff is not meant to keep custody of library documents alone. This comparison of the circumstances in which loss of library documents occur with that of stores items clearly shows that loss in libraries are inevitable. For argument sake, an anti-service attitude can be taken by a library and advocate for having security guarded closed access library with gate pass system. But it takes away the essence of library services.

Results of stock verification should not be used to impose restrictions. In any organisation, if librarian and his colleagues have to take the full responsibility for the loss of documents and make good the loss from their salary, it is obvious that he and his colleagues who share the responsibility be given a 'risk allowance' on line with allowances given for jobs like that of cashier in offices in addition to providing freedom in amending the policies and procedures of library to minimise loss.

However, the more reasonable way of clearing the deadlock of responsibility is to treat the loss of library documents like any other loss in the organisation and the competent authority write-off the same unless the situation warrants an enquiry about negligence and dereliction of duty on the part of librarian and library staff. The rules governed by the institution would indicate the financial powers and limits for write-off and the extent of loss allowed.

For example in case of Goverment of India institutions, librarian in the rank not below that of a Deputy Secretary to the Goverment of India or Head of the Department who has financial powers can write-off loss of library documents to the extent of financial powers and monitory limits. A loss of 3 volumes per 1000 volumes issued/consulted in a year is proposed as reasonable limit for loss unless the loss is attributable to dishonesty or negligence on the part of librarian. Loss of a book of the value exceeding ₹200/- and the books of–special nature and rarity shall invariably be investigated and consequential action taken.

Further rare books and books of special nature may be kept under closed access. There is also a provision in the rules that there should not be any objection to the disposing of mutilated/damaged/obsolete volumes to the best interest of the library as long as it is based on recommendations of a three member committee appointed by the Department.

In practice, many authorities have a peculiar way of looking at new policies, procedures, services including write-off of loss. They wish to know what is the situation in Y&Z libraries nearby and how they have acted. Unfortunately the authorities of Y&Z libraries would have desired to know the situation in X&Z and X&Y libraries, respectively. This kind of conservative and risk less attitude prevails in many places. Lastly, there is also a dishonest way of handling this occupational hazard of library stock verification being practiced by some libraries by way of declaring the loss as much less than actual and hence defeating the very purpose and advantages of stock verifications.

CONCLUSION

Library stock verification is not just an unnecessary evil which brings very little benefit to the users and library staff but has some advantages. There are many ways of quickly and effectively completing stock verification depending on the organisation of records, magnitude of work and availability of tools and men. There are an array of precautionary measures against loss of library documents depending on the purse of the institution. But the cost of such measures often far exceed the saving they may provide to the library. The issue of fixing responsibility for loss of library documents has created an occupational hazard for librarianship.

Rationalisation and updation of rules regarding stock verification and the prescribed limits regarding write-off of the loss in service, oriented libraries would go long way to provide better services to users. Particularly, the guidelines should be made more explicit about type of material to be covered for stock verification and rational about fixing the limit on the cost of the book for initiating enquiry and action. It may be reasonable to say that a book costing more than 150 per cent of the average cost of the book acquired during the year only need to be subjected to further enquiry when it is lost. Professional bodies have a vital role to play in this regard.

9

Cooperation

INTRODUCTION

Cooperation is fundamental to the operation of libraries and, among and between libraries, and has taken many forms. Partnerships large and small participate in interlibrary lending and borrowing, purchase materials collectively, offer reciprocal access privileges to users, develop storage facilities, manage joint technical processing systems, and provide reference services.

Libraries face the reality of not always being able to supply needed materials on site to serve their users. They have neither the space nor the materials budgets to do so. To compensate for these factors, libraries turn to cooperative systems which allow the walls of the library to expand to include other libraries known to have what is needed and which are willing to offer access. Such a system is defined as: a group of independent and autonomous libraries bended together by informal or formal agreements or contracts which stipulate the common services to be planned and coordinated by the policy making body of the cooperative system.

Libraries cooperate for three essential reasons:

- They can enhance the quality of services offered, be they online services, shared cataloguing, document delivery or preservation;
- The leadership role of a cooperative in achieving the goals of the group as well as having a forum for problem solving;
- The financial pressure to reduce costs and the belief that sharing with others will help them do that.

Thompson and Carr say that the variety of cooperative activity in university libraries falls into the following main types:

- Interlibrary lending
- National library initiatives
- Interlibrary study facilities
- Cooperative acquisition schemes
- Cooperative storage schemes
- Transfer of materials
- Local and regional cooperation
- Research library groups
- Mechanized cooperatives
- Library research organisation
- Professional associations

NATIONAL LIBRARY INITIATIVES

Many countries have their own national libraries. These should have a leading role in local, regional and national cooperation.

This includes the following:

- Interlibrary loan, particularly serials literature not necessarily of the size of the *British Library Document Supply Centre* (BLDSC).
- *Central Cataloguing*: This is concerned with national publications. This is best served if libraries have direct access to the national bibliography database where downloading is allowed. Another way is make sure that the *Cataloguing-in-Publication* (CiP) data is accurate and standardized. A third way is the construction of union catalogues and union lists.
- *Central Indexing*: Many national libraries in developing countries ignore indexing the serials publications of the country. This vital service can be accomplished on cooperative basis. The work load shared by several libraries either on subject or availability of titles. The output may be routed on regular basis to a central pool—the national library-to be published or added to a database. It is also possible-and preferable—if this is shared among countries speaking the same language,

such as Arabic. A good example of such central service is the EMRO Index Medicus, which is a current contents service of medical journals published in the East Mediterranean Region of WHO and is available on the Internet. MeSH descriptors are used for this service.

- *National Bibliographic Centre*: This centre is not confined to bibliographic information on the publications of the country but the coverage is extended to include bibliographic tools on the country or of interest thereto.

INTERLIBRARY STUDY FACILITIES

This used to be called inter availability of tickets which means the use by members of one library of the resources of other libraries also. This kind of cooperation exists between different types of libraries. It should be a logical extension of the idea of all libraries in the country being regarded as components of what is really a national system. It is restricted to the in-house use of the collection in some libraries while it may include borrowing as well in others.

COOPERATIVE COLLECTION DEVELOPMENT

Cooperative collection development is the coordination of collection building activities in some agreed upon way between two or more libraries.

This includes:

- Mutual notification of purchasing decisions
- Joint purchase
- Assigned subject specialization in acquisitions

There is a good guide for libraries contemplating cooperative collection development.

The activity is looked at to achieve:

- Reduction of unnecessary overlap or duplication between collections, while maintaining or expanding the universe of materials available in the combined collections of participants;
- Ensure that materials currently available to users in a given geographic area are not lost through uncoordinated collection development decisions;

- Coordination of cancellations, storage or preservation decisions in comparable collections;
- Establishment among larger research collections of library of record status or primary collection responsibilities for specific subject and formats;
- Acquisition of collective site licenses for databases of common interest among user groups;
- Distribution among smaller closely neighbouring libraries of certain core or basic subjects in order to reduce unwanted or unsupportable redundancy.

Cooperative collection development, whether on local, regional or national level, assumes a commitment to resource sharing as well. Resource sharing is commonly defined as the sharing of library collections through one or more of the following mechanisms:

- Provision of information on what cooperating libraries own;
- Actual interlibrary lending and borrowing of materials;
- Direct service to the user populations of cooperating libraries.

It has to be emphasized here that cooperative collection development is meaningless without both a commitment among participating libraries to share their collections and an effective mechanism to do so. Cooperative acquisitions form part of cooperative collection development.

This may be organised among participating libraries in different ways:

- *Cooperative Purchasing:* This may be organised along subject lines, by publishers, by countries of publication, by type of publication, or by any other logical division. Another way of cooperative purchasing is to buy multiple copies collectively through an agreement among nearby libraries, so that these libraries get better discounts. This volume purchase may require the vendor to deliver the orders to one receiving point, thus making shipping easier and cheaper to the vendor.
- *Exchange of Publications*: This activity may be carried out in different ways:

— Individual libraries sign exchange agreements. This commonly covers publications of parent organisation, duplicates, withdrawn materials or publications specifically acquired for exchange purposes.

— Exchanges may be organised by professional societies such as the *Medical Library Association* (MLA), by the national library of the country by a non-profit organisation such as US Book Exchange, or by a commercial service such as the Faxon's Company Serials Quest.

- *Retention Agreements*: This is based on membership in a union list of serials holdings. Additions and deletions of titles are sup-plied to a central agency, or an advance notice may be sent to a central listing of new serial titles the library is intending to buy or cancel.

COOPERATIVE STORAGE SCHEMES

The little-used materials identified in this process, may be re-moved from the main collection and stored in more compact manner either in the library building or somewhere else. Cooperative storage may be chosen as a solution. Nevertheless, such arrangement is not very popular among libraries, as storing, transferring or discarding are costly in themselves and they require the alteration of records and the actual removal of the books and serials. For smaller libraries cooperative storage may not sound ideal, and it is more likely for individual libraries to store its little-used materials in its own premises rather than in far-away stores.

Anyhow, if cooperative depositories are to be there, the following recommendations are to be observed:

- The material deposited should be limited to categories which conform to very strict interpretation of the description ' little-used ";
- The material deposited should be easily retrievable;
- Bibliographic control should be of the simplest;
- The provision of reader accommodation in such depositories must be regarded of secondary importance.

LOCAL AND REGIONAL COOPERATION

This type of cooperation is of two kinds:

- Multitype or modular scheme, where all or many types of libraries in a given area cooperate;
- Cooperation among the same type of library, where a number of the same type in a particular geographical area cooperate.

This type of cooperation is not limited to one cooperative activity, but may include activities such as: study facilities, cooperative acquisitions, cooperative storage, regular consultation, staff training, technical facilities such as binderies, setting up of an information services for the assistance of industry and commerce, and interlibrary loan.

MECHANIZED COOPERATIVES

This cooperative activity has resulted in the creation of many bibliographic utilities.

Such utilities have served the following:

- Broadening access to materials.
- *Lowering the Unit Cost of Cataloguing:* This is enabled through co-operative cataloguing and the adoption of MARC format.
- *Document Delivery:* Although it is better to rely on local or regional cooperative document delivery, bibliographic utilities are getting more involved in providing this service as well. They are also contributing to electronic publishing.
- Cooperative acquisitions.

Several bibliographic utilities flourished in many countries of the world with the American utilities leading the way.

Among these are:

- *OCLC (Online Computer Library Centre)*: First started in 1967 as cooperative resource sharing system among Ohio college libraries then changed its name in 1981 to reflect its international scope. Now it has around 16,500 participating libraries, with around 30 million records and about 15 million terminals/workstations online. It is the prime example of cooperation across all types of libraries. It supports a variety of other services such as CON-CER in 1976.

- *Research Libraries Information Network* (*RLIN*): First founded in 1974. Its strength is its large, academic library focus and the unique materials catalogued on the system. Its database grows through online cataloguing, tape loading from the Library of Congress, other utilities, retrospective conversion projects, etc. Its structure enables it to accept and manage a variety of data, including vernacular files for Chinese, Japanese and Korean.
- *Western Library Network* (*WLN*): It is composed of several subsystems which support interrelated modules for cataloguing, authority and holdings data. It offers a wide range of services and data formats for its members such as distributing data on CD-ROM. Its database depends heavily upon the subscription services from LC and other providers. It focuses on its geographic area.
- *UTLAS (Originally University of Toronto Library Automation System):* Started in 1971. It is now international, and is the premier source for Canadian materials.

Other parts of the world have built upon the American experience and developed other cooperatives.

OCLC has extensive international operations:

- *OCLC, Europe Office Serving Europe and the Middle East*: Its latest effort is to include materials in Arabic as it has contacted a number of libraries in the Gulf region for this purpose.
- *OCLC Asia Pacific Services:* Some of the members have online connections with OCLC database while the remaining members use CD-ROM products to obtain cataloguing records. Other cooperatives that need to be noted here are:
  — *Bief*: This is an international database for French-speaking countries, located in Ottaw, Canada. It was developed initially as a bibliographic database

to record documents of interest to the members of the Francophone Summit. Membership includes French-speaking countries in Africa, Asia, Europe, North America and South America. Records are distributed on microform, as catalogue cards, or on magnetic tapes for reuse in the receiving country.

— *REBUS:* It is located in herzogenbuchsee, Switzerland. It is a cooperative of networks in the three countries that use the SIBIL system software, Switzerland, France and Luxembourg. It is concerned with the development of SIBIL software, the free ex-change of catalogue data without the need for conversion, the interconnection of regional networks and increased cooperation within REBUS.

— *BLCMP*: It is located in Brimingham, U.K., and is an international network. External cataloguing data files available to members include:

a. British National Bibliography, complete;

b. LC, 1974;

c. British catalogue of music, complete;

d. Whitakers books in print, complete;

e. British Document Supply Centre, complete.

STAFF TRAINING COOPERATIVES

There are no formal cooperatives that are exclusively devoted to staff training. It is rather one aspect of some existing cooperatives or gatherings.

It may take one or more of the following forms:

- Participating in the various training activities, continuing education programmes, or conferences of other bodies such as professional associations, library schools, other libraries or the various library cooperatives. This participation may be as instructors or trainees.
- Forming and participating in user groups of certain activities, whether these groups are physically, or electronically existing. These groups may be on local,

regional, national or international level. An example of such groups is the user group of a certain computer system software such as MINISIS or CDS/ISIS.

- *Exchange of Staff*: This may be in the same country or abroad as a result of formal arrangement or a cultural agreement. This includes a system of internship between libraries as well as between libraries and library schools.
- *Library Visits:* Library staff should be persuaded to visit other libraries, to be exposed to other people experiences and be able to assess what they are doing in their own library.
- Library staff should be encouraged to serve on professional bodies and associations at all levels.

PROFESSIONAL ASSOCIATIONS

Many professional associations, especially those operating on national or international level, offer a range of services to members, including: publications such as journals, newsletters and directories; annual meetings and conferences; continuing education courses and other training events. Some also offer career and recruitment services, scholarships and research grants, and consultancy services. Membership of professional associations can be personal or institutional. Some of them allow both types of membership but with different rights and benefits. Some restrict their membership. So examples given below will be limited to those allowing international membership or enabling non-members to benefit from the services they provide.

INTERNATIONAL PROFESSIONAL ASSOCIATIONS

There are several important professional associations in health sciences which are open to health librarians.

Europeam Association for Health Information and Libraries (EAHIL)

It aims to improve cooperation among health librarians in Europe, to raise standards of provision and practice, to inform health librarians and information officers, to encourage mobility and to represent the interest of health librarians at the European level, especially at European institutions and WHO. It has about 500 European librarians and members from USA, Canada, China and Australia.

Medical Library Association (MLA)

It was founded in 1898 and is based in USA, but has members from many countries. It has a membership of over 5000 institutions and individuals. It has 14 geographic chapters, 23 parts including one on international cooperation, and 11 special interest groups. In 1989, it established the *Academy of Health Information Professionals* (*AHIP*), which is the only peer-reviewed certification programme for professional development and career achievement in the health library sector. MLA publishes a quarterly bulletin.

Special Libraries Association

It was founded in 1909. It serves more than 14,000 members who work in special libraries. It has 55 chapters including a European chapter, and 27 divisions including a pharmaceutical division. It also offers conferences, continuing education events, self-study programmes, career and employment services, scholarships and research grants.

International Federation of Library Associations and Institutions (IFLA)

It is open to national library associations, institutional members and personal affiliates. It runs an annual conference which is held in a different country every year. This conference usually includes a part in bio-medical information and libraries. IFLA also sponsors the organising committee in the *International Congress on Medical Librarianship* (*ICML*) which is held every five years. The 8th ICML was held in Lon-don in July 2000. IFLA produces the various ISBDs as part of its programme *Universal Bibliographic Control* (*UBC*). It is responsible for Unimarc format.

NATIONAL PROFESSIONAL ASSOCIATIONS AND GROUPS

Some countries have specialist health library associations or groups. The following are examples.

Canadian Health Libraries Association (CHLA)

It aims to improve health and care by promoting excellence in access to information. It produces Bibliotheca medical Canadiana, a quarterly journal committed to assisting the worker in the small and isolated library.

The Library Association

It is the British professional association for the regulation of the profession of librarianship. It has 26,000 members from UK and overseas countries, and has 12 branches and 23 interest groups, including the *Health Libraries Group* (*HLG*), with 2000 members.

The HLG has three sub-groups:

- *Libraries for Nursing* (*LfN*): It provides a communication and education network for all interested in the provision of library and information services to midwives, nurses, health visitors and community nurses, and makes representation to professional nursing and library bodies and organisations.
- *IFM Healthcare (*IFM*)*: Its members include librarians and intelligence officers working in the *National Health Service* (*NHS*) to serve the information needs of managers. Its objectives is to facilitate the flow of relevant, timely and accurate in-formation between providers and users in the management of health care. It publishes the quarterly IFM healthcare newsletter.
- *Community Care Network* (*CCN*): It focuses on the needs of librarians working in the community care sector.

HLG has a varied programme of meetings and study days. The main event is the annual weekend study conference held annually in different location. Communication with members is maintained through a newsletter, which is also issued as part of HLG journal: Health libraries review published by Blackwell Scientific Publications.

Aslib: The Association for Information Management

It promotes better management of information as a resource. It has a corporate, rather than individual, membership. However, its special interest groups are open to individuals members with an interest in the subject. There is an *Aslib Biosciences Group* (ABG) which promotes the ex-change of information in the fields of agriculture, biology, medicine and environment. Aslib organises conferences, seminars and meetings for individuals, and supports 12 special interest groups. It publishes a comprehensive range of books and eleven journals and reference sources covering many aspects of information management.

The Institute of Information Scientists (IIS)

It has more than 2000 members from UK and other countries. It has branches and special interest groups, but none are specific to health. It publishes the Journal of information science quarterly, and a bimonthly newsletter, Inform. The IIS is now in the process of being united with the Library Association.

The Association of Information Officers in the Pharmaceutical Industry (AIOPI)

It is open to all those engaged in medical, scientific or technical information work in the pharmaceutical sector, and opens its meeting to non-AIOPI members. It runs a one year training course for members on all aspects of medical and research information.

Medical Information Working Party (MIWP)

It is a group set up by HLG, the Publishers' Association and the Association of Subscription Agents in the UK, for the exchange ideas.

This group publishes:

- Forrest;
- Maureen and Prior;
- Albert.

The core collection of medical books and journals, which is designed to be an acquisition guide for small or medium-sized libraries in hospitals, postgraduate teaching centres or medical institutions.

INTERNATIONAL ORGANISATIONS

WORLD HEALTH ORGANISATION (WHO)

WHO is one of the UN specialized agencies. Its principal work is directing and coordinating international health activities and supplying technical assistance to countries. It develops norms and standards, disseminates health information, promotes research, provides training in international health, collects and analyses epidemiologic data and develops systems for monitoring and evaluating health programmes.

It operates through its headquarter, its six regional field offices and WHO representatives in individual countries. The WHO library is on the website named WHO *Library and Information Networks for Knowledge* (LINK). All forms of the library's collections are referenced in the electronic database, available to the world through WWW.

The Library maintains the following:

- *WHOLIS*: WHOLIS indexes all WHO publications from 1948 onwards and articles from WHO-produced journals and technical documents from 1985 to the present.
- Full text and bibliographic databases.
- *Current Awareness Services*: Available to WHO staff: WHO in the scientific press, SDI service, table of contents services, providing Internet access to table of contents and abstracts of over 20,000 journal titles, and Interlibrary loan services.
- *Historical Collection:* Blue Trunk Libraries. A WHO Library project aimed at assisting district health teams obtain medical and health information that they need through the establishment of 'ready-to-use' mini libraries contained in portable blue metal trunks.
- *WHO Library Publications*: These include WHODOC, Liaison, WHO Library Digest of Africa, List of newsletters issued by WHO and numerous essential Lists on current topics of interest.
- *International Health Literature Exchange*: The membership list of exchange includes medical libraries

in the developing countries that are in need of items that another library may be considering discarding.

- *Borrowing and Copying Facilities*: Available for WHO staff only.

Information sources and resources of WHO may be summarized as follows:

- *Basic Documents*: Documents about WHO policies.
- Bulletin of the World Health Organisation Disease outbreak news.
- Evidence for health policy.
- Executive Board documentation.
- WHOLINK.
- Press material.
- Publications.
- Terminology services.
- WHOSIS-WHO Statistical Information System.
- World Health Assembly documentation.
- World Health reports.

WHO provides other information services through its six regional field offices. Among these regional offices is East Mediterranean Regional Office (EMRO).

The major information ser-vices of EMRO are:

- *Health Literature Services* (HLT): It is responsible for all library services in the Regional Office, WHO Representatives' Office and Country Programme supported by WHO. It has a dual basic role:
  - — To provide library services to WHO staff members in sup-port of WHO programmes; and
  - — To cooperate with member states to improve health sciences libraries, documentation centres and literature services at country level.
- Development of EMRO Intranet.
- Development of EMRO Home page on the Internet
- Development of EMLIBNET to make available and/or accessible the widest range of health and bio-medical literature to potential users in a cost-effective way in the Region.
- *Document Delivery Services*: Provision of health and

biomedical databases on CD-ROM has been as follows: 63 subscriptions to MEDLINE, 17 subscriptions to Extra MED, and 95 subscriptions to other databases, for 19 countries.

- National Training Activities and Fellowships.
- EMR Index Medicus. This index was started in 1987 by indexing the health and biomedical journals of the Region published in 1984. In 1998 the index has become a quarterly current content bulletin. It is now available in print version, on EMRO website and on CD-ROM. It covers 138 titles.
- Introduction of the Blue Trunk Library.
- The Unified Medical Dictionary. This dictionary includes 150,000 entries and is available on the Internet and on CD-ROM. It will be later available in print version. It has also published " List of basic sources in English for medical library faculty. 8th ed. 1999 " which includes 1568 items. It has also translated MeSH into Arabic.

The other regional office to be mentioned here is the Latin American Region. This Office is responsible for REPIDISCA which was created in 1982. REPIDISCA selects and analyses bibliographic materials, with special emphasis on documents produced in Latin America and Caribbean. It closely cooperates with BI-REME of the *Pan American Health Organisation (PAHO)* which will be described later.

Moreover, WHO has joint projects with other UN agencies. The following two examples may be mentioned here:

- *UNAIDS*: This is a joint United Nations Programme on HIV/AIDS. It is cosponsored by UNICEF, UNDP, UNFPA, UNDCP, UNESCO, WHO and World Bank.
- The WHO Reproductive Health Library. This is an electronic review journal focusing on evidence-based solutions to reproductive health problems in developing countries. Presently it is produced on diskettes as a Microsoft Windows programme. The second Issue, 1999, is on two diskettes and contains 40 Cochrane reviews selected from the Cochrane Library. It is jointly sponsored by UNDP, UNFPA, WHO and the World Bank.

OTHER UN AGENCIES

Many of the UN agencies are involved in health and information. The following are examples of such agencies and/or departments:

- UNICEF
- United Nations Population Fund
- UNDP
- *United Nations Environment Programme* (*UNEP*)
- *United Nations Institute for Training and Research* (*UNITAR*)
- FAO
- *International Atomic Energy Agency* (*IAEA*)
- World Bank
- UNESCO

NON-UN INTERNATIONAL ORGANISATIONS

There are many international organisations representing specific large geographic regions such as Europe, the Americas, Arab countries. Most of them deal with the health sector at different levels. An outstanding ex-ample of these organisations is *Pan American Health Organisation* (*PAHO*). Its essential mission is to strengthen national and local health system and improve the health of the people of the Americas, in collaboration with ministries of health, other government and international agencies, nongovernmental organisations, universities, social security agencies, community groups and many others.

PAHO members states include all 35 countries in the Americas; Puerto Rico is an associate member; France, the Netherlands and UK are participating states, and Portugal and Spain are observer states. PAHO disseminates scientific and technical in-formation through its publication programme, its Internet site and a net-work of academic libraries, documentation centres and local health care libraries.

10

Management and Marketing

Leadership and management are two terms that are often used interchangeably. In fact, they describe entirely different concepts, as leadership is more than a component of the functions of management. Management is the process of administering and coordinating resources to ensure than an organisation accomplishes its mission and goals. *Library and information science* (*LIS*) has a managerial focus; librarians manage the infrastructure of a library: its collections, staff, technology, and facilities. For this reason, the interconnection between management and leadership is the domain of LIS theory and practice.

The purpose of leadership is to challenge the status quo as libraries undergo a transition in organisational culture, the services they offer, and workforce restructuring as they try to better fulfill the organisational and broader institutional mission. Management, on the other hand, prepares the infrastructure for that transition. As early as 1950s, the term *managerial leadership* was coined, but its definition was imprecise. "No definition of the phrase 'managerial leadership' has gained general acceptance. In fact, it is often referred to but left undefined" or merely equated to particular leadership theories and styles.

The term recognizes that leadership is not exclusively a top-down process between the *boss* as a leader and subordinates. This paper, which aligns with the programme in managerial leadership in the information professions at Simmons College, views managerial leadership as encompassing an examination of leaders, followers, the interaction between the two groups, and, in this context, leadership becomes a process whereby people influence others to develop, accept, and carry out a shared vision that guides future actions of the organisation.

As a result, that process is longitudinal and involves events. Because leadership is not always effective or positive, it should not automatically be assumed that goals and events are always successfully met or that staff members are sufficiently motivated or inspired to challenge themselves and others. The purpose of this paper is to build on the international research agenda that Candy Schwartz and I presented in 2008 and that illustrates that LIS research needs to go beyond a preoccupation with understanding the style, personality, traits, and other characteristics of the boss and that person's influence on organisational dynamics and performance.

LEADERSHIP

In addition to focusing on a shared vision, leadership is about giving people confidence to meet organisational expectations and to serve as change agents. It also encourages them to seek, be given, and benefit from team coaching and mentoring aimed at enhancing their knowledge, skills, abilities, effectiveness, and commitment to the transformation process. A library's staff might consist of both followers and leaders who are willing to collaborate with other institutional partners.

As well, the director, if that person is truly a leader, might be more so within the organisation than in representing the library to other stakeholders. With so many libraries organised into teams or small groups and involved in managing change; with new staff members expected to work together to plan, implement, administer, and evaluate services; and with libraries forging new partnerships at the institutional, local, and other levels, more librarians are becoming increasingly interested in knowing about and applying leadership theories, styles, traits, and roles.

They are also trying to develop their leadership potential. Within this context, there is much interest in transformational leadership and emotional intelligence, which helps leaders move beyond basic 'people skills' to understanding how one's own reactions and feelings impact how one is perceived by others.

Leaders and managers need to understand their own emotions and recognize and understand the feelings of those around them. Leaders are more successful when they pay attention to their social interactions with others in the workplace and the impact they as leaders have on those around them. It is also important for leaders to understand the impact that others' emotions have on them. When leaders are aware of the emotional side of the workplace, they are better able to create a working environment that encourages excellence.

As librarians gain an understanding of such theories, it is important to remember that, as Peter Northouse points out, leadership has 'many different meanings;' this is evident when people "finish the sentence 'Leadership is....'" Their responses might ignore social influence, add new elements, or confuse leadership with someone holding a managerial position. They might also fail to recognize that there are also spiritual, legacy, moral, ethical, charismatic, and other types of leadership. Each of these areas actually produces separate leadership theories that have been long investigated but rarely connected to LIS.

CONTEXT

Even though this paper focuses on topical areas for future research and selected methodologies, it is important to remember that methodologies do not frame a research study. Research, which engages in problem-solving, is shaped by a reflective enquiry. These components, as well as the study procedures and data quality, comprise a framework in which each component should be bonded to the others through, what David R. Krathwohl calls, a 'chain-of-reasoning.' That 'chain,' he points out, 'is only as strong as its weakest link' and 'all links...should be built to about the same strength.' He further explains that, "as the work load is picked up by the first link and passed to successive links, the work load—and therefore the nature of each link—is determined by the previous links."

Furthermore, "where several links together join those above and below them, there may be trade-offs to compensate for weaknesses. It is beyond the scope of this paper, however, to present and relate the entire chain-of-reasoning. Still, I would be remiss if I did not underscore the importance of the theoretical framework. Vincent A. Anfara, Jr. and Norma T. Mertz provide an excellent overview of theatrical frameworks and the impact of 'good and useful' theory on the chain-of-reasoning. In the case of managerial leadership, like other areas within LIS, there are numerous theories, some of which fit a given problem statement and set of objectives better than others.

One such theory might be constructive-development theory, which relates directly to leadership and which offers a way to view the complex problems that organisations face from multiple perspectives. This theory describes "how adults develop more complex and comprehensive ways of making sense of themselves and their experience." Another concept relates to trust, which is an essential component in motivating or inspiring others and which is more than a trait.

RESEARCH DESIGNS

As a prelude to methodologies, research designs for leadership research might call for a longitudinal study and a comparison of several organisations. Widely used research designs centre on either a case study or the application of grounded theory. A case study is a means "for learning about a complex instance, based on a comprehensive understanding of that instance obtained by extensive description and analysis of that instance taken as a whole and in its context."

Grounded theory, on the other hand, "is a method for discovering theories, concepts, hypotheses, and propositions directly from data, rather than from a priori assumptions, other research, or existing theoretical frameworks." Theory emerges from, and is grounded in, the data themselves.

DATA-GATHERING TECHNIQUES

This part focuses on some of the most prevalent methodologies used in leadership research, especially within LIS. As such, it builds from Karin Klenke's work on leadership research. It is increasingly common for researchers to apply qualitative methods. The accompanying table offers examples of some methodologies applicable to the study of leadership in LIS that will not be discussed in the body of this paper. The sources in that table came from an extensive review of the vast literature on leadership produced outside LIS.

The largest number of research studies related to leadership involves the distribution of a self-report survey or questionnaire. Such surveys are often in paper-and-pencil format, although more recently Web-based surveys have appeared with increasing frequency. The survey might involve the use of a predeveloped, behaviour-based leadership assessment tool that is distributed to those heading the organisation or to subordinates who are asked to evaluate the director or boss as a leader or their immediate supervisor.

As an alternative, surveys might probe respondent preference for a particular leadership theory or style and ask them to rate themselves or identify the most important attributes for individuals in their position. Complementary to a questionnaire that is mailed or otherwise distributed, investigators might use personal or focus groups interviews. Responses to open-ended questions might be subjected to content analysis, which "is a set of procedures for transforming nonstructured information into a format that allows analysis." On occasion, biographies of people identified as leaders have been developed and their content subjected to analysis for discussions of leadership.

Available historical records, however, might focus more on their accomplishments than the story behind those accomplishments: how did the individual co-opt and navigate different stakeholders and the staff to bring about that change? If a shared vision emerged, how was it developed? Some other means of data collection include an analysis of citation patterns of a body of works on leadership and a characterization of the most cited works and authors, as well as the age of the cited material. Additional insights might be gained from a consideration of the journal's impact factor and the number of copies of a work that libraries hold.

Assuming the availability of a body of independent studies focused on the same aspect of leadership and that describes the research design, the methodologies and data-collection instruments used, information about the population and sample, and so on, meta-analysis might be appropriate. Such analysis refers to a set of statistical procedures used to summarize and integrate those studies. It reveals sources of bias and is helpful for posing research questions for future study.

Among other things, it cannot exceed the limits of what the researchers report. Another method, known as the Delphi study or technique, is a procedure relies on the use of sequential questio-nnaires in which experts share their perspectives on issues. The Delphi technique is not necessarily designed to generate consensus, but it does involve a systematic refinement of prior responses. It has been applied to seeing which leadership attributes are most critical for future managerial leaders.

Concept Mapping

Concept mapping is both a process for representing data in the form of pictures or maps and a structured methodology for organising the ideas of a group or organisation. The goal is to bring together groups of multiple "stakeholders ... and help them rapidly form a common framework that can be used for planning, evaluation, or both." The maps represent the groups' thinking about a topic, show how their ideas are related to each other, and, in general, indicate "which ideas are more relevant, important, or appropriate."

Interviews and other techniques might produce datasets that might be examined by the use of concept maps. These maps provide a graphic illustration of patterns among the findings. Jan Schilling, for instance, takes interview data about negative leadership and produced maps that show the antecedents of such leadership, negative leadership behaviours, and the consequences of negative leadership.

Simulation and Scenarios

A simulation study, as G. Yukl explains, involves a realistic task that continues for several periods of time and asks participants to assume the role of top executives in an organisation and to engage in team and organisational learning. Simulation "is also relevant for understanding how collective learning occurs among people whose decisions and actions affect organisational processes and performance." Instead of doing a simulation exercise, researchers might develop scenarios that make projections for the next fifteen years; forecaster Joseph P. Martino indicates that the accuracy in predicting what will likely occur declines dramatically with a longer time frame.

Scenarios, as a prime technique of future studies, have long been used by government planners, corporate managers and military analysts as powerful tools to aid in decision making in the face of uncertainty. The idea behind them is to establish thinking about possible futures which can minimi[z]e surprises and broaden the span of managers' thinking about different possibilities.

They recommend that the number of scenarios not exceed four and that any scenario should meet criteria such as:

- *Plausibility* (each is capable of happening),
- *Differentiation* (each differs from the others and together they offer multiple futures),
- *Decision-making utility* (each offers insights into the future that help in planning and decision-making), and
- *Challenging* (each challenges conventional wisdom about the future).

RESEARCH AGENDA

The accompanying figure, which updates the depiction that Schwartz and I created, centres on three broad areas that relate to planning:

- Accomplishments (translating vision into effective organisational performance);
- People (creating an organisational climate that values staff and inspires them); and
- Transformation abilities (focusing on the change process that brings people together to accomplish the organisation's mission and goals—preparing the organisation of the future).

These areas match those that guide the doctoral programme in managerial leadership in the information professions (Simmons), which the Institute of Museum and Library Services has funded since 2005 with two multi-year grants. Those areas, originally modeled by the National Centre for Healthcare Leadership, cover twenty-five distinct leadership competencies. Under each of the broad areas, numerous topic areas emerge.

At the same time, relationships among the areas might be probed. As directors or other members of the senior management team retire or depart, their replacement might be someone who serves on an interim basis. Are such people leaders or caretakers? The answer might take into account the library but also engagement beyond the library, transformation abilities, mentoring, and talent management. Focusing solely on talent management, many businesses engage in succession management or planning, but do libraries?

Succession planning and management are not synonymous with mentoring. In some countries, if there is leadership, it might be characterized as autocratic. Such leadership merits analysis. Finally, various aspects of the figure might be probed in the present recession as libraries make significant decisions about collections and staff that will likely have a long-term impact. Turning to other topics, James G. Neal discusses 'feral library professionals,' which refers to the hiring of more people into traditional and nontraditional library positions who do not have the credentialed degree from an accredited library school programme.

Comparative case studies might analyse the emergence of leadership in organisations that employ both feral and non-feral professionals and that include staff who represent different generations. How cohesive are staff within and across departments? Do they share a common vision—do they need to share one? Studies might probe LIS educational programmes and see whether they incorporate leadership as a student learning outcome, one that reflects what students have learned throughout their programme of study and demonstrates what they can apply upon graduation.

Some other possible topics include the role of power in effective leadership, the major trends in making leadership effective, the communication networks of leaders, transformational leadership and its relationship, for instance, to

- Emotional intelligence, which deals with one's ability to manage emotions and relationships and to use this ability to advance the organisation's mission and goals. Emotional intelligence presumably requires *sense-giving* or shaping how people understand themselves, their work, and others engaged in that work.

- Resonant leadership, which focuses on self-awareness and self-renewal, and which enables individuals to recognize and cope with work stress.
- Distributed or shared leadership, which views leadership as more than a top-down approach. Leadership moves up the organisation as well and is distributed among a number of people working in teams and groups.
- Servant leadership, which recognizes that leadership is not confined to those in formal managerial positions and who lead as a way to extend service to others. The servant leader focuses on the needs and the development of followers.

Recognizing that libraries serve multicultural communities, employ a diverse staff, and deal with myriad stakeholders, it is critical to assess different leadership theories, recognizing the strengths and weaknesses of each. Many of the prevailing theorists have not considered how multiculturalism influences what they propose. Perhaps the best illustration of this comes from Linda Sue Warner and Keith Grint, who adopt a historical perspective and compare American Indian and western approaches and perspectives on leadership. There are differences between the practice of leadership in a tribal setting and in other organisational settings.

EXAMPLE

Although library directors cannot be equated with the president of the United States and other heads of government, political commentators have identified areas in which the leadership of those aspiring to be president might be probed. Prompted by the lack of penetrating questions raised in presidential debate and the quality of the responses, David Gergen and Andy Zelleke identify a series of important questions that deal with leadership and that require answers of more than a number or brief response. Their categories and questions have been reorganised and combined with the categories that Jack and Suzy Welch would like considered.

The revamped questionnaire was pre-tested with one university library director and one library consultant. Based on their comments the questionnaire was revised. As of this time, the author of this paper is conducting a study to fine-tune the instrument and to gauge the responses of some library leaders. Instead of presenting preliminary data, this part probes relevant methodologies that might be used to address the open-ended questions and determine the relative rating of the categories. The methodology part of a hypothetical study might be based on a survey that is most likely administered in the form of an interview, either in-person or by telephone.

Directors might be unwilling to devote the time necessary to complete a paper-and-pencil survey or be unwilling to write detailed responses to each question. It might be difficult to find a time when five to ten directors could meet and participate in a focus group interview. For additional data collection, the investigator might ask for historical documentation or visit the institutional repositories of selected institutions to gather data for event history analysis, assuming such information has been gathered and is publicly available.

Interview results might be analysed in terms of grounded theory and content analysis. The rating of the categories on a seven-point scale might be visualized in terms of concept mapping, and such mapping might also apply to the responses to the various questions within a category, especially if responses can be gathered from the same scale. A follow-up study might concentrate on selected categories and probe responses more deeply.

For instance, under 'Coalition Building/Advocacy,' participants might meet and be asked for an example of when they became a catalyst who brought groups with polarized opinions together so that all voices were at the table. The examples generated might be cast in terms of a concept map, or the investigator could make the topics recurring most frequently and pursue them more with the Delphi technique. A different study might recast question responses to the initial study or one focusing on selected categories as scenarios or as simulation exercises.

It is also possible to take selected responses from the first study and select particular sites for in-depth case study analysis. That instrument, however, is framed in such a way that the research focuses on leadership as events and assorted methodologies are applicable. Leadership, after all, "is a process, a series of activities and exchanges engaged in over time and under varied circumstances." As such, accomplishments might be viewed as events in that leadership is an ongoing, never-ending process.

To gain a more complete understanding of the phenomena under investigation, it is common for studies on leadership, like other topical areas, to incorporate more than one method of data collection. Mixed methods, which are most prevalent with case studies, integrate quantitative and qualitative methods into one study and therefore strengthen the chain-of-reasoning presented in study findings. While it is important to expand the methodological tool-chest that researchers within LIS use, it is also important to shift from studying leaders to investigating leadership events.

Many aspects of leadership presented in the figure have not been addressed, and a need emerges for a fuller body of evidence-based research relevant to change management within libraries and similar complex organisations on a global basis. It is also important that those within LIS contribute to the broader literature on leadership and that their works be recognized by those in other disciplines.

LEADERSHIP AND SERVICE PROVISION IN PUBLIC LIBRARIES

In USA and Western Europe, we do witness the same types of developments in public libraries and we see very similar themes of discourses independent of the national and local culture in which these libraries operate. Some of the themes concern the management structure and organisation bur more important is probably the current think about service delivery in a broad sense. Service delivery concerns the activities. It is areas like collection and collection management, the allocation of resources to the different part of the collection, the interplay and relationship between national internet-based delivery and the local service.

Another important theme is the effort concerning the public library and its integration into the community taking up different forms of citizen services, cooperation and partnership with the local community, but also a focus on playing a new and more active role in the cultural scene by for example emphasising learning activities, lifelong learning, internet courses and different forms for events and exhibitions. The ambition is to become a local meeting place, a third room; a common intended to generate social capital.

This discourse and many of the activities resulting from it like 23 thinks, the libraries in the second world and experiments with various forms of social technology appear to have great appeal in the library profession. However, both library statistics and numerous studies of users and their preferences give a more differentiated picture. In most countries, the public libraries face economic hardship. They witness stagnating or decreasing numbers of visitors and the issues of traditional materials also tend to decrease. The public appear to value especially the services and products that suffer due to economic pressures and the internal priority setting in libraries.

Overall, it appears—at least at the surface–that users do have a rather traditional view of the public library and their stated preferences also seems to be very traditional as they are oriented towards books and information and to a lesser degree towards new services and delivery forms. It is of course of paramount interest to investigate possible discrepancies between the discourse and the practices in the professions and the users' preferences, priorities and level of satisfaction.

There is probably no right solution to the problem, but it is of both a practical and theoretical significance to investigate which factors influence the development of the discourse and the activities in the professions and in the public libraries and is also important to be able to measure users perception of the significance and importance of the service delivery and to which degree this is connected with measures of satisfaction. The paper further discusses the factors behind the profession's discourse and practices.

The concept of an organisational recipe is introduced in relation to organisational culture as two factors that have influence on the way libraries tend to adopt different forms of innovations. Of course, leadership plays an important role and the keynote also introduces measures of the personality traits of library directors and discusses this in relation to the innovation and development process but also in relation to the 'sense' or construction the profession is creating of the user.

This paper departs from 2 different theoretical perspectives of pertinent interest for management of institutions. One of the perspectives is concerned with the question about how management information and management recipes are adopted and interpreted in organisations like libraries. The other perspective concerns the role of the directors' personality in this context especially how they acquire management information and how they value and use management information in relation to organisational change processes. This paper is built on several studies into leadership in libraries in Denmark and United Kingdom. The paper also builds on several user studies.

LEADERSHIP AND PERSONALITY

During the last couple of years, the interest in leadership and management topics has increased very much. This is also the case in library and information science. It is due to the very fundamental changes that takes place overall in the public sector. Many of these changes are connected to requirements concerning accountability, user orientation, outsourcing, quality, information technology and staff-related issues. It is a widespread notion that the requirements in relation to leadership and management have become much more complex.

The complexity is connected to environmental turbulence, change processes and to the amount of vast information that leaders need to deal with. Information in the form of management tools or recipes is one way to confront the organisational problems arising from the changes. Leadership is an important element in the configuration of organisational culture and both leadership styles and the leaders approach to innovation, change, and competency development are of importance in relation to the directions of the organisation. Leaders are both part of an organisational culture but they also have the possibility to be change agents in relation to the culture. The relationship between leadership priorities and organisational culture are important.

One can argue an interesting relationship between the directors' personality and preferences and the direction and change processes in libraries and this is exactly the focus for this paper. The Revised NEO Personality Inventory is one of the most widespread personality tests based on the Five-Factor model and it was employed in this investigation. Besides allowing for both a general and detailed description of personality, the test is also build up in such a way that it takes into consideration the characteristics of the specific test-person in focus. Specific norms for groups of people and profiles have been developed from research to help validate the testresult.

The NEO-PI-R measures five broad personality factors. Each of these is a summary and an average of six facets. Each of the five factors and their associated 6 facets is measured through 48 statements, implying that all 30 facets are measured through 240 statements. The result of the 240 statements is distributed into low and high scores on the 5 factors and the 30 facets, hence demonstrating a personality profile. As suggested, now turn to a short profiling of the 8 library directors.

The profiles of the directors as a whole are very congruent with modern expectations of leaders and managers. They tend to possess emotional stability. They are extroverted and open to change. They all score high on the facet assertiveness. They score high on conscientiousness. Overall, the profiles of the library directors appear to be very far away from the traditional stereotypes of librarians as shy, introverted, a bit oldfashioned, nervous and timid.

The factor named openness is often considered as an important factor in relation to chance processes and it is clear that all directors except one scores high on this factor. One director is distinct from the others, scoring rather low. It is director B that scores low on 3 of the 6 facets. What is more interesting is probably that all directors score high on some of the more important facets related to get things done. All score from middle to very high on actions, ideas and values indicating openness to new ideas.

Common for all the directors have been the fact that they have been involved in change processes. These change processes have focused on both the provision of services and on organisational development implementing more flexible and democratic structures. They have all succeeded to change the libraries both internally and in relation to the users. One of the reasons that change processes have been successful overall can possibly be attributed to the assertiveness of the directors, their overall openness to experience and change and their general high degree of conscientiousness.

The organisational culture is a very important mediating factor both in relation to how information in the form of recipes are adopted and translated both also in relation to the actual possibilities the director possess for implementing change. But the style of change management varies. This can be partly explained by situational factors like the local political climate, restrictions due to the building and economy, the organisational culture and other important factors.

The relevant facets or traits that relates to interpretation and adoption of new standards are some of the traits that relate to the factors named openness and conscientiousness. The facets under openness can possibly give an indication of how willing the director is to seek and implement new recipes in the organisation and the facets related to conscientiousness can indicate how through the process of implementation is conducted. These facets will also relate to the directors' sense of the usefulness of own participating in leadership courses and development.

We emphasise that it is broad hypotheses. Another more general aspect is how the directors value innovations or changes. A comparison of D with H indicates the usefulness of analysing behaviour using all the facets and not only the factors. It is evident that the profile of H indicates a person oriented towards actions and change. H also possesses a high degree of impulsiveness and a middle orientation towards ideas. H is more of a doer than a thinker and this is also the way H comes forward in the interview and in interviews with the staff.

Things must happen and failures—both own and staff failures—are accepted as inevitable. Some of the change processes are conducted nearly on the spot and many traditional activities are set in motion. In some ways, the change processes runs in a very goal directed manner but there is a high degree of acceptance of a chaotic nature of some of these processes that involves staff very much because the director delegates much based on both trust and on a disposition to take up new challenges.

The change processes that have taken place in D's library are conducted in a very different way. They are just as goal directed and strategic but they are much slower and much more deliberated and it is evident that the D places a very high value on bringing the staff along. The disposition for activity seeking is much less here than in relation to H. It results in a 'flavour' of the library as a bit more old-fashioned and a bit slower or a bit more cautious in change processes.

The implicit formulated hypotheses about the relationship between personality traits and profiles indicated that the director's openness to especially intellectual experiences or practical innovations and changes influenced the process of implementation of both structures and processes of competences. It also influenced the way the recipes and standards were conceptualised in the organisation. The integration of the recipes was influenced by the perseverance of the director with cultural factors as a mediating factor.

DISCOURSES AND ORGANISATIONAL RECIPES

These figures contrast to a certain degree to the dominant discourses in the public library profession. The dominant discourses are concerned with modern topics and issues like library as a place and libraries as generators of social capital and societal trust on a more general level. In relation to services the emphasis in the discourses are on issues like lifelong learning, information literacies and integration of the physical library into the digital services. The discourse also contains strong elements of the need for permanent change for example in relation to continuing professional development.

There is also much debate on phenomena like 23 things, facebook and other digital services. A discourse is characterised by dominant themes but is also delimited by themes that do not occur and these absent themes signifies the themes in the discourse. In the 80'ies and 90'ies, the library profession had focus on collections and collection management and especially the concept of immediate availability was a central topic.

Today, these themes of discussion are missing from the professional debate. There existed also a rather interesting debate or discourse concerning the proper relationship between supply and demand in relation to the collection. It is interesting that these topics seldom are covered in the present discussion because the different digital possibilities emphasise new turns of these central concepts. Just to give a few hopefully illuminating examples one can ask questions about the links on libraries' websites and enquire if a link is part of the collection or not.

The answer to that question is interesting because if the answer is yes it follows that the libraries have the responsibility for dead links and for the misinformation contained in some of the links. Another interesting question is the transformation of topical needs into specific needs due to the way people search the digital databases. Librarians are not discussing the increase in the selling of books and the reasons behind this interesting fact. Is it because of an increasing affluence in society or is it because of a want for instant gratification?

Many of the elements in a given dominant discourse relates to organisational recipes or standards. A recipe or a standard that becomes a trend has the following characteristics: It often originates in an academic setting but very often it is created in cooperation with the professional world—be it libraries or business. It is blueprinted by leading members of the academic and professional communities and it is taken up also by the consultancy industry.

Prestigious firm and companies use it. The recipe incorporates the promise to solve serious problems in the companies and in the institutions they are interesting to work with. They are marketed and they are frameworks for actions but most of all they are interpretable meaning that institutions can adopt them, change them according to the national and organisational culture. They are very often connected to stories of success and the story behind the recipe often takes the form of a drama.

Successful recipes tend to hit a trend in the time and use this as a kind of vehicle for its travel across boundaries and cultures. Some recipes like the balanced scorecard have a rather long life. Other—not as successful like for example business process reengineering—have a shorter lifespan. It does not mean that they are not used. It could mean that they are incorporated in the organisational operations but people have stopped talking about it.

Finally, all recipes have dimensions of both content and symbolic aspects. It is of course extremely interesting which recipes become dominating themes in the discourse of a profession. It is also of huge interest which recipes a given profession does not include in its arsenal of themes in the discourse. There is no doubt that the profession as a whole has a very determined focus on change and the need for change.

The catch phrase that the libraries stand on a burning platform has been brought forward several times in the discourse and this catchphrase has been used as a kind of rationale for changes. This is of course the consequence of a special or peculiar interpretation of the environment. However, there is no doubt that the ideology of change and the need for change is deeply integrated in the professional identity of public librarians and leaders in the public libraries. It is an interesting question if the interpretation of the environment is in accordance with other indicators of changes in the environment.

USERS AND PREFERENCES

One aspect of organisational effectiveness is a system's ability to cope with users and non-users expectations and needs enabling the system to deliver services appropriate to satisfy needs and expectations. Organisational effectiveness has been one of the ultimate goals and objectives for the performance measurements endeavours for many years. Organisational effectiveness is related to processes, products or services and the customer or the user and it is normally seen as an important element in the quality of a service. The importance or significance for the users of the single services is of course a very important element for the libraries' planning process and assessment of how to proceed.

Libqual is a measurement instrument that is often used for this kind of investigation as it specifies the minimal level of service people would like. However, Libqual has not been employed in these surveys. We have simply asked people to attach the significance or importance for themselves on different services. The end result is a kind of ranking that probably is rather robust. The importance or significance is calculated on a scale from 0 to 100 and it forms the basis of the ranking. The ranking of the importance or the perception of the significance of the public libraries' services follows:

Table 10.1 The Users' Perception of the Significance of Different Services in Two Surveys

	High School	Rank	Aarhus	Rank
A kind and polite service	72	1	90	2
Distance to the library	67	2	91	1
Ambience	64	3	84	3
Collection of non-fiction	62	4	66	5
Quite and peaceful place in the library	59	5	65	6
Collection of fiction	55	6	78	4
Places for relaxation	43	7	51	8
Collection of music	41	8	46	10
Wireless network	40	9	21	14
Collection of film	37	10	47	9
Group work facilities	35	11	15	15
Computers	34	12	28	12
The Library's homepage	34	13	63	7
Study places	33	14	21	14
Exhibitions, lessons	28	15	45	11
N	978		243	

Translated into normal text, one can say that the high school students and the 'traditional public library users' prefer a kind and polite service in nice quite rooms in library with ambience not too far away and filled with books. There are differences between the preferences and significance attached to services among the two groups but rank correlation analysis shows a Spearmans Rho of 0,81 which indicate a very high degree of similarity in ranking the services. The ranking between the two groups are more or less similar, but there appears to be differences in the importance attached to the service.

One explanation for this discrepancy is simple and it is, that the group of high schools students consists of students relying heavily on public libraries and groups or segments that rarely, seldom or never use the public library. This composition of the total group tends to decrease the average figures. In comparison, the respondents from the Aarhus group were all public library users. In the 2006 investigation in Furesoe, we also asked questions about preferences and significance, but we employed a measurement tool based on forced pair-wise ranking.

It is impossible to make a direct comparison, but one can look at the trends and compare these with caution. The most striking feature of the answers to this question is the similarity in preferences. The respondents were asked on a forced scale where they had to prioritise alternatives. Overall, the users preferred present openings hours more than longer opening hours with less staff service. The preferred more books in favour of longer opening hours or music.

The preferred more film than more music. They preferred a broader range of literature more than additional copies of the popular books. We did not find any differences in pair-wise preferences in relation fiction versus non–fiction, computers versus more reading places or more reading places versus more places for relaxation or social interaction. The conclusion is that users–even the young age group—want more documents. It is a very clear first priority.

We do see that this priority and preference increase with age, but it is still a very striking result that young people that rely heavily on and use the library's collection of film and music much prioritise books and documents more if they had to choose. The preferences and the prioritising are probably an expression of the perception of what a public library is—and ought to be. It is obvious that the structure of preferences in relation to public libraries is rather traditional. The nationwide study of high school students also showed some interesting features of the significance they attached to the services in relation to different demographic factors.

Table 10.2 The Students' Perceptions of the Importance of Services and Facilities in Relation to Demographics

	Type High School			Gender		Study Year		
	G	B	T	Female	Male	1	2	3
A kind and polite service	77	69	63	76	66			
Distance to the library	74	61	61	72	61			
Ambience	68	61	59	67	60			
Collection of non-fiction	70	54	52	66	56	56	61	68
Quite and peaceful places in the library	63	55	51					
Collection of fiction	61	49	49	63	44			
Places for relaxation						49	44	36
Collection of music						45	36	38
Wireless network						45	40	35
Collection of film Group work facilities						41	35	28
Computers				32	37			
The Library's homepage	37	28	33			28	36	37
Study places						38	30	29
Exhibitions, lessons								

First of all, there appears to be differences in perceptions of significance and importance dependent on the type of high school. There are 3 types of high schools in the country. The general high school is the classic one. In the table it is called G. There is also a high school oriented towards business topics called B and at last a technical high school called T. The general picture is that the high school students from the general school place more significance on most of the library services than students from the other two hig schools do. We also notice marked differences between male and female high school students.

Female high school students tend to value the collection of fiction an non fiction much more than the male students. It is also interesting to note that the students through their study process tend to place less significance to the library as a place to be and work in. However, overall the ranking of the single services is not hugely affected by this segmentation, but the segmentation indicates that the different groups have very different preferences and strength of preferences attached to the single services.

LIBRARIES AND POTENTIAL USERS: METHODOLOGICAL APPROACH, THE CASE OF GREEK LIBRARIES

Libraries in the fast communicative environment they live, implement three spaces of interaction:

- Between librarians who decide the offered services, the resources, the manuals and every necessary equipment for users satisfaction and the exploitation of the service.
- Among users and librarians who are responsible. The communication aims to identify the users' needs and the relevance of the resources to them.
- Between Library and users community as a whole. Users receive modified information that can be used to their work. This is the step that library proves its usefulness and illumine its image.

Libraries are social places, where individuals, teams, social groups interact. Social theories, behaviourism, socio-psychological analyses drive to the recognition of special characteristics of libraries and of every target group they refer. Libraries are also one of the key factors that can impact the development and the prosperity of the social entity they refer. Consequently, we can say that they involve competitiveness and entrepreneurship.

They take into account the following factors before decision making:

- Target focusing;
- Strategic planning;
- Efficiency and effectiveness;
- Resources saving;
- Cost-benefits analysis.

The coupling of these different options, social and business, designates the communication methods and the policies that libraries choose on occasion. The synthesis and the identity of the unity that we call 'library users' is a continuing changed variable, as it strands upon the dynamic of human mobility, potential individual needs, and behavioural rules of societies. Users can turn into non-users, actually without caution, but not without any cause. Equally non-users could turn into new, enthusiastic users.

THE RESEARCH AND THE METHODOLOGIES

The questionnaire consists of items that derived from:

- The subject as come up for discussion in the literature;
- The marketing plans of business;
- The adjustment of them to library context.

Needless to say that the findings analysed by qualitative methods. There is an integrated combination of qualitative and quantitative methods, what is referred as mixing methods. Libraries need to know the synthesis and the characteristics of the population they refer to, in order to successfully appeal them. The major problems on this face the public and the special libraries, which the target groups are fuzzy and random. The social stratification is a matter of research of specialized organisations that collect data on the population structure, family synthesis, economic activities, education, leisure etc. The data is completed by using qualitative methods like interviews of opinion leaders, structured observation, discussions with famous public people. The target is to be ensured that the concept, the structure and the procedures of a service are harmonized to the target group.

MARKETING AND LIBRARIES

Marketing is the wide range of activities involved in making sure that you're continuing to meet the needs of your customers and getting value in return. These activities include market research to find out, for example, what groups of potential customers exist, what their needs, are, which of those needs you can meet, how you should meet them etc. Marketing also includes analysing the competition, positioning your new product or service pricing your products and services, and promoting them through continued advertising, promotions, public relations and sales.

Marketing is connected with library's operation itself. Value added works such as cataloguing and classification corresponds to the product packing, embodied also the concept of the product:

in this case is knowledge, research, information, entertainment. Shelving, Abstracting and Indexing, bibliography compilation correspond to the promotion. Regarding the users training programmes, the location of material in the library correlates with marketing practices, such as study of consumer behaviour, product promotion etc.

The mission and the objectives of libraries are modified according to the conditions; services, procedures, rules and operation follow the change. Consequently the Marketing Mix changes too. To catch the alterations, a marketing plan is necessary in order to define the policies, the promotional practices. On the other hand and because of the 4P balance differs for every target group, it is necessary the research on the groups of population that are the potential clients of the library.

4 Ps of Marketing Mix of libraries:

- Product is the value that librarians add through their knowledge, expertise, and informational, organisational, and retrieval skills. Product is library's services. Collections consists the basis of the 'product', but the main one is an *Idea, an intangible product,* in which the tangible good, the services and the processes are incorporated;
- Place is the space of the library, either physical or virtual. Place is an important factor that can appeal the potential users. Another factor relevant to this is the location of the building, how easily accessible is it. Relevant to this point is the mention that the place nowadays is both place and space, equally physical and virtual;
- The Price of library services or products consists of both the staff time spent in ensuring that resources and services are available and accessible and user's time in finding and using resources efficiently. Libraries do not Price their activities and decisions. However they assess the cost of services, of acquisitions, of operation. The main interest of libraries is the best exploitation of their resources, the advancement of their services, the improvement of their quality, without increasing of their cost;
- The communicative policy of the library is the

Promotion policy and its part of the strategic marketing. Promotion consists every positive action, even the politeness of the staff, but in practice, promotion targets to explain to users and non-users why they need the library in their everyday life.

THE SURVEY AND THE RESULTS

The questionnaire contains questions for collecting quantitative information, questions for seeking behaviours and attitudes scaled to 4 degrees. The third unity contains questions on the organisational level of the library, its resources, its finance and fund raising. The stratification of the sampling of libraries who participated to the survey is analog to the number of libraries that belong to every type. The questions and the analysis follow the structure of a marketing plan.

Mission and Goals of the Library

The diagrams show the weak idea that Greek libraries have on the strategic management:

- More than half of the libraries have a fuzzy idea of their mission;
- Only 37, 5 per cent has written specific explicit mission.
- Only 11,4 per cent writes down the strategic plan, shared to the whole staff; and
- 21,5 per cent of libraries share the plan to employees relevant to the its content.

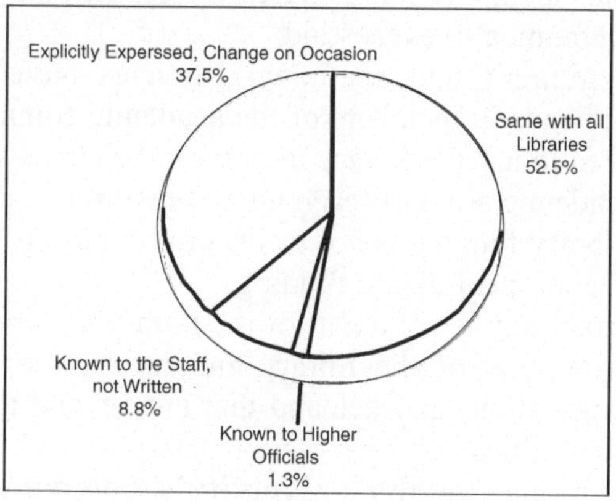

Fig 10.1 Library's Mission

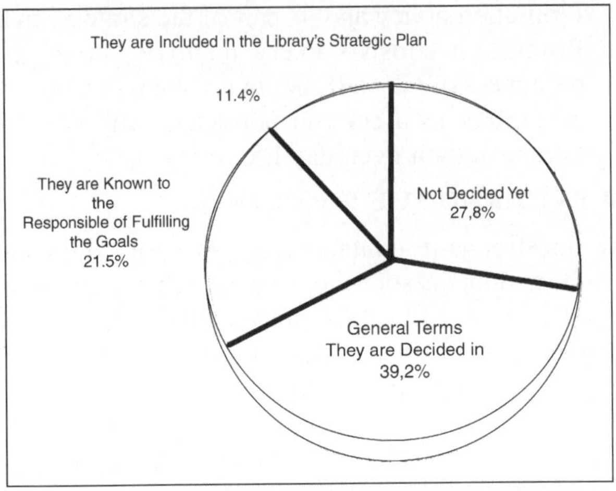

Fig 10.2 Means for Achieving Library's Goals as they are Ordered by its Purpose and Strategy

Furthermore, as usual, the 56 per cent of Libraries deny to set economic goals, but the 57, 5 per cent of libraries set non-economic goals, which they achieve and sometimes they overcome. Needless to say that an economic goal is not a business goal: it could be a cost effective goal, or the better exploitation of the resources or the decrease of operational expenses etc. Libraries are negatively biased on economic and public relations actions.

Marshall mentions some causes for academic libraries that seem to be common to every kind:

- Argument that academic libraries have a captive audience in members of the academic community who need to use the library in order to be successful in their academic areas of teaching and research;
- Library funding is not a concern because it is linked to overall institutional funding;
- Promotion is not a part of the library's purpose;
- Promotion of the library and its services will crate expectations and demand that are beyond the library's capabilities;
- Reliance on the university's communication or

development office to perform a public relations role will suffice.

Product (Life Cycle, New Life Design)

Because of the lack of strategic thought and promotional vision, libraries gave the following answers:

- 69 per cent declare that the strategic planning is unofficial, and
- 54, 5 per cent answer that there are no procedures for the creation of new services.
- Not users but other factors determine the orientation and establishment of new services.
- The questions on the life cycle of the services reveal that libraries mainly operate as traditional organisations and low communicated.

Market (Target–groups)

- Most of the libraries (86, 8%) know their population and their mobility;
- They study the attitude of people; and
- They try to form a special policy for every group.

The kind of libraries that answered explain it:

- 44,3 per cent does not examine the target group, and
- 30 per cent systematically focuses on numerous groups of the population.

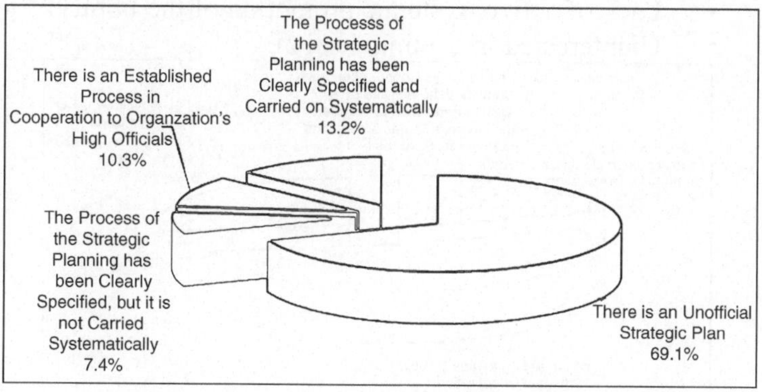

Fig 10.3 Is there Any Strategy for Developing Library Services

The Library's Image and the External Relationships

As it is clear up to now, libraries operation is mainly collection oriented than users-centred. The modernization steps parallel to technology, without harmonizing processes, management, and services. They use technology without innovative processes.

The following answers confirm the lack of a strategy for appealing new groups of population and new users.

- Only 1,4 per cent collects systematically data on users' and groups' behaviour; and
- 7, 8 per cent focuses on the appealing of new target groups.

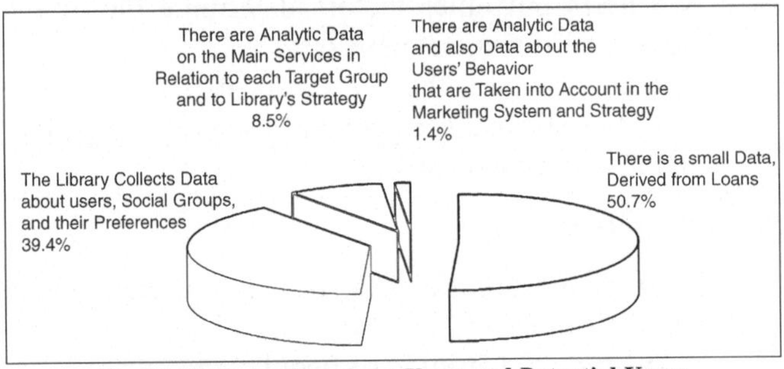

Fig 10.4 Information about Users and Potential Users

External relationships:

- 8,3 per cent agree that strategic alliances increase the users and advertise their services, and
- 52,8 per cent agrees to evaluate cooperation proposals that could cause the increase of the users;
- Lack of active, systemic promotion of the library;
- Uninterested in communication.

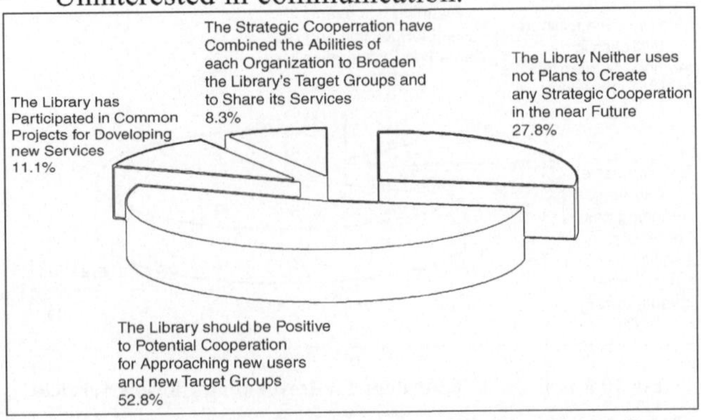

Fig 10.5 Strategic Cooperation for Approaching New Target Groups

Nevertheless, half of the people that participate to library's events use the library, become members. The opposite valid also: the majority of the members are interested in library's events. That means that users' attitude is positive, but how many people use it? That's the crucial question. That's the main problem of libraries: not the whole people who need libraries use them.

THE QUALITY OF INFORMATION AS BASIS OF THE LIBRARY MANAGEMENT QUALITY

A great number of scientific, reference, educational, methodical and practical publications is devoted to the quality of library activity in Russia. One of the most characteristic tendencies is the active interest to management, especially quality management that explains the fact of formation of new management concept in the sphere of library science. Modern management researches show a great significance of rational information processing for achieving strategic and operative aims. The quality of information defines the quality of management because information covers all spheres of management.

Being the most important function of management process, information must meet the following requirements: authenticity, accuracy and completeness, efficiency and regularity, its conformity with management level. Management of documentation as function of management is realised in the conditions of decision making process to achieve the aim. That is why documentation management is closely connected with the problems of management, organisation structures, the problems of design of information systems management, their implementation and operation, with automation of managerial procedures and processes.

Urgency of the problem consists in support of the processes of documentation information management due to more effective technologies of its processing including analytical components and the connection of management functions with documents, their servicing. The development of new management technologies plans systematic approach to the decision making process on the base of flexible information analytical integrated management system.

DOCUMENTS MANAGEMENT

The organisation of work with documents is a very important part of management processes and taking managerial decisions influencing efficiency and management quality. From the point of view of information technologies documentation information management activity and the management activity itself—as a subsystem of an integrated technological system of library. So, the library management is characterised as technological process that supposes regularity of management. In management activity a document is a tool, means or method of management. The whole documentation is closely connected with the concrete management function for which it is created. It allows, in Larin's opinion with the help of systematic analysis to identify the content of managerial documents and to connect it with the definite management function.

Optimal system of internal legal regulation helps to provide successfully and realise substantially the local legal regulation of general principles of activity, some decisions and concrete aspects of library operation. The complex of internal regulated documents, being formed in each library objectively consists of a package of separate interrelated and mutually complementary blocks. The documents, included, reflect legal organisational and technological sides of professional activity, fix aims, order and conditions of library functioning as informational, educational and cultural institution.

Pilko suggests to classify the complex of documents regulating the activity of the library for convenience according to the following functions: organisational—administrative documentation, scientific—methodical documentation, normative documentation and technological documentation. At the present stage in the system of library management the whole range of documents concerning different types and kinds of documentation systems and being a part of documentation support of management.

INFORMATION MANAGEMENT SYSTEM

The use of information technologies in the sphere of management gives opportunities of more effective and rational organisation of information processes, increase of their flexibility and dynamics expansion of the range of analysed factors when making decisions. 'Perfect' information system of management must automate all or the majority of protective kinds of activity in the frames of integrated information space and in interrelation of automated functions.

It is more optimal to use the system which is the part of the architecture of the system of complex library automation that implies the use of joint technologies of management automation and documents circulation. The creation of the system of automated management of documents or service database in the library is a very complicated organisational technical task, administrative office automation being the main, basic platform within information library system. Designing database, one should orient on the use of standard management system of data and technology 'client–server' which allows to combine operative work with archiving documents.

Automated system in the library:

- Provides coordinated work of all departments;
- Simplifies work with documents, increases its effectiveness;
- Increases labour efficiency due to shortening time for creation, documents processing and search;
- Increases efficiency of access to information;
- Allows to delimit the competence of access of workers to information.

The implementation of such system in the library will optimize the activity of the library in whole, to get analytical information for using and taking important managerial decisions. Without any doubts, the system will influence on effectiveness of library activity as well as on increase of professional personnel training, the culture of the use of modern information technologies.

DATABASE OF REGULATING DOCUMENTATION

For solving intersystem tasks of the library one can suggest the module of service database of regulated documentation as foundation of effective library management. Designing technological project of database we relied on methodical basis and regulations considered by Pilko and Voroisky. The main source when forming database is regulated documents of library.

Database supports the main functions of documents processing on-line which include: documents development and custody; search of documents according to different parameters, input, support and custody of any kind of documents; control over implementation of documents; protection and management of separation of rights for access.

Database includes the complex of functional means realised as a programme modules helping to plan work, to get interim and resort valuation of separate operations, to control and, if necessary, to correct the plan or process. The idea of centralised storage of e-documents is also obvious: integrated database in server keeps documents safely, systematizes them and finds necessary information very quickly. Not the least of the features of the system is unification of the most widespread types and kinds of documents in management, development and use of patterns.

Database is corporate storage of regulating documents of the library. In includes the catalogue of organisational efficient, regulatory–methodical and technological documentation, unified forms of documents, documents archive, office documents of departments or separate workers. Through interface of database, installed in all computers, the workers of the library get access to hierarchy of folders and operations concerning design and search of documents. The search of documents is realised through folders navigation.

Creating a new document a database offers users to identify its belonging to concrete theme by classifier and to use standard sheet, pattern. Information, formed by users in the process of selecting data, is displayed as a reference in matrix format, graphic material, fulltext document or pattern. Different functional and practical tasks are solved by the method of contiguous look of database modules and data selection or seriating. The tasks can be operational analysis of technological processes; valuation of resort support of processes; valuation of work content of library production.

Managers of a library, having full access to all documents, can control the process of creating office documents any time. The analysis of report documents formed in database, gives opportunity to correct the library activity, to improve organisational structure, character and content of implemented works, personnel, provision with financial, material and other resources.

11

The Change of Libraries

THE METHODOLOGY OF ACHIEVING ORGANISATIONAL CHANGES

Recent years were for the libraries a period of faster, greater and more dramatic changes than has ever before been experienced. The omnipresence of the new technologies, the ever-increasing cooperation, the globalization as premises of the evolution towards the *Global Information Society,* the emphasis on quality, the diminution of the financial resources are the main agents imposing the change of libraries. Implementing the necessary changes for the academic libraries is no easy job as it requires a differentiation between changes to ensure the coherence of actions within the available resources.

It is also important to use planning and control methods that contribute to reduce the span of the change process and to optimize the use of resources. Finally, it requires suitable structures, staff training and overcoming the resistance to change. All these respects are subjects of change management—a distinct discipline whose key-aspects-in point of increasing the success and the efficiency of organisational changes—we present. The concept of organisational change, as defined by the management theories, is a significant, extended, important change that affects the entire organisation or parts of it.

Such changes do not occur naturally, they are changes whose implementation is the task of the management team. The methodology of achieving these changes is one of the main issues of change management and it is treated in very different ways by management theoreticians. The best known approach is the one proposed by Kurt Lewin and E. H. Schein that identifies three essential stages in the process of organisational changes, stages somewhat similar to chemical processes: unfreezing—the trial to create the reasons for change; moving/implementing change—identifying solutions adequate to circumstance and applying them; freezing—a new equilibrium is crystallizing.

From the point of view of implementing changes in the university library, the methodology presented by Popescu, M. has the advantage of a pragmatic approach that defines two major stages of the process of starting and implementing change: identifying the need of change and achieving change. Identifying the need of change aims to establish the favourable changes that may add value to the organisation.

In the authors' opinion the important changes must be implemented from a strategic point of view; this means that, when establishing the changes that must be done and their order, the mission and the strategic objectives of the organisation are kept in mind. This way one can avoid the risk of starting complex and expensive processes that can not be financially supported or that have little or no effects upon the performances of the organisation. Several studies discussing changes in libraries develop the above idea.

Thus, Troll, A.D. underlines that the evaluation activity usually carried out in libraries is not enough in order to plan changes: without knowing the external and the internal context and the library's strategy, such an evaluation is of no help in understanding what changes are relevant and can assure the accomplishment of the library's mission. It's necessary to define clearly the strategic objectives and the main lines of change that sustain planning changes in the library.

To complete this idea we state that, once the strategy is elaborated it has to be communicated; making public and discussing the mission, the policy and the general objectives of the library are means of communication through which the top management acknowledges everyone concerned its view on the future of the library and obtains their support. Communicating, informing and involving the staff are elements that contribute to overcome the resistance to change which is normal in the case of any major change. The bigger the changes, the greater the resistance to change and ignoring this is the source of many failures as shown in many studies on this topic.

Achieving change, the second stage, is a complex process having clearly stated beginning and ending points and, between, a sequence of three activities:

- The preliminary study or the planning–it's goal is to define change, to evaluate the achieving conditions and the expected results;
- Projecting the change–it refers to defining solutions and including them in specific documents;
- Implementing and checking the results–it is a stage that, paradoxically, often raises difficulties because of the resistance to change.

These three activities are intricately interconnected: change is achieved progressively, but the process is not linear, solutions adopted in one stage are often rectified in a following one. The amount of innovation the solutions bear, the fact that change by definition involves contouring and implementing new solutions—what causes it to seem unique and risky—the important quantity of resources involved, the participation of many specialists and actors from different structures are characteristic elements that render complex and difficult the achieving of organisational changes.

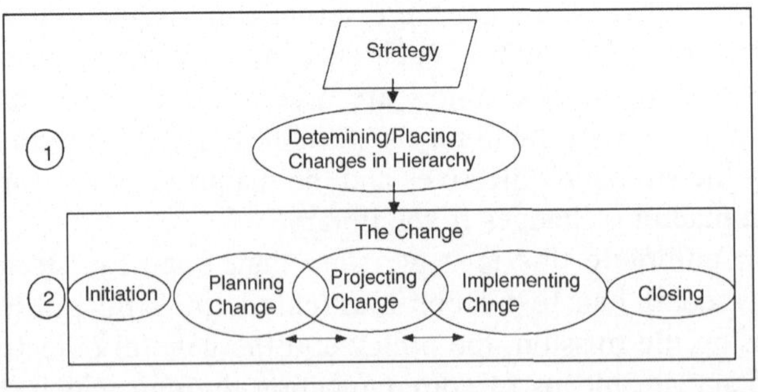

Fig 11.1 Stages of the Process of Achievement Organisational Changes

The solution is to approach them as projects, in the manner proper to project management. The scheme in figure synthesizes the methodology for accomplishing the organisational changes, whose application ensures: on one hand–the coherence of the actions, through relating to the strategy of the organisation, on the other hand, advantages determined by approaching the change as project, by using the project as 'vehicle for the change', which means, implicitly, applying the principles and methods specific to project management.

CASE STUDY: LIBRARY OF TRANSILVANIA UNIVERSITY

The case study realised at the Library of Transilvania University of Brasov sets out to analyse the changes made during the last decade within the university library, from the perspective of the change management, to present the change priorities inscribed in the library strategy along the years to follow and to identify the key factors on whom there depends the success of the change projects. *Transilvania* University of Brasov is an institution of higher education and research, which enjoys high prestige on the local, national and international level.

It is an extended university, with 16 faculties—8 are of technical profile and 8 of university profile, with more than 22.000 students at the university degree, master's degree and doctorate cycles, full time and distance learning. In the context of globalization, of Romania's integration within the EU, the University achieved important changes in all fields of activity and structures, in view of harmonizing with the new requirements and in view of assuring the quality of the services of education and research.

The Library is a structure of *Transilvania* University of Brasov, an entity without its own judicial personality, subordinated to the top management of the university. The mission of the university library is to ensure the documentary and information basis necessary for the education process, to enhance and to communicate them, as well as other services, to the benefit of the information users, facilitating the diversified and rapid access to all categories of sources.

The documentary patrimony of the Library of *Transilvania* University of Brasov includes: books, serial publications, manuscripts, cartographic documents, printed musical documents, audio-visual documents, graphic documents, electronic documents etc. The collections of the Library are constituted and developed through acquisition, transfer, national and international exchange, donations and sponsorship. The endowment is ensured through financing from the university management, as well as through transfers, donations and sponsorship.

The organisation and the functioning of the Library observe the provisions of the specific legislation elaborated on the national level, as well as the internal regulations of the university. The Library has its own strategies and plans of activity whose approval by the Senate of the University ensures the integration in the general strategy of the institution. Like the university it is part of, the library achieved a series of changes in order to improve its performance. The synthetic situation of the important changes within the library, achieved during the last decade is presented in table.

Table 11.1 Organisational Changes from the Library of Transilvania University of Brasov

Objective of the Change	Description of the Change, Period
Concentration of the library activities and improvement the working conditions and the documentary collection storage	The movement of the Library in a new, large building centrally placed, easily accessible to of the users and also to the staff. In 2006 of there was set up the new free access room and in 2007 the central deposit for the loan of publications.
Automation of the processes of document management communication	Provision with computers, linked in network and connected to the Internet; and implementation of the Library integrated software Liberty 3, the fourth in chronological order, used since 2007.
Access to digital information: electronic documents, data-bases, internet resources	The acquisition of electronic documents and the subscription to on-line magazines (since the end of the '90-ies) and databases (after the year 2003).
Improvement of the system activity evaluation	Making up reports with respect to the of publication circulation and to the user

(Contd...)

	frequency at the free access room; Users' statistic evidence and that of the publications made up by the loan service; improvement of the data collection for making up the official statistics required by the local and central authorities. They are realised partly automated, the tendency being of generalizing the automated means of quantitative evaluation.
Development of the human resource in the library	Employment, professional training, life-long education of the staff.
Improvement of the management structure	Redefining the compartments and the posts taking into consideration the new strategy of the library.
Optimization of the processes	Analysis, optimization and description through procedures of the key processes.

Seen from the perspective of the results, the described actions display a series of defaults.

For instance:

- The relocation of the library became a strategic objective during the year 2005 after the finalization of a building with another initial destination. The placement of the Library in this building ensured the concentration of the activities and the amelioration of the working environment, however the adaptation costs were high, without ensuring the perfect compliance with the needs of the library;
- The automation of the processes of document management and communication is likewise questionable under the aspect of the adopted solutions, taking into consideration that the used software requires expensive hardware resources, and the results with respect to the performance of the processes were not up to the expectations;
- The efficacy of the actions undertaken within the library for the access to digital information may be appreciated as reduced, because of the lack of correlation between the equipments in the structure of the informatics

system, as well as of the insufficient training with respect to the users' access to these resources. These resources did not benefit from an adequate promotion among the users who, to a too great extent, ignore their informative value and even their existence;

- The modernization of the evaluation system is slowed down by the lack of an adequate evaluation model and also by the generalized delay of the automated means for collecting and processing the data, and the efficiency of the evaluation is also affected by the persistence of the non-trained and disinterested staff in accomplishing this activity.
- The endowment with sufficient, stable and qualified staff is hindered by the still low number of librarians with specialized studies from the geographical area, by the unattractive level of the wages, by the rooting in certain posts of non-efficient employees, refractory to the new.

The outlined deficiencies are, at least in part, determined by the manner in which change management was implemented in the university library, both as regards planning the changes and settling the solutions, and as regards their implementation. It is to be observed especially the neglecting of the social aspects with respect to the staff's training, the resistance to change etc.—as factors which have negatively influenced the efficacy and the efficiency of the change processes.

The university library will continue the process of the qualitative transformations during the following period, but in different ways. The aim is at using efficiently the strategy, as management instrument and at developing mechanisms that should allow the continuous control and improvement of the library performance through systematic actions. To this purpose, in a first stage there was carried out the diagnostic analysis of the management system of the library, whose conclusions are presented as follows, synthesized in strengths and weaknesses.

STRENGTHS

- There is a strategy of the library, harmonized with that

of the university. The mission of the library and the system of values are published on the site. The objectives are realistic, measurable; the accent is laid on improving the performance, in order to contribute to ensuring the quality of the educational and research services carried out by the university. There was set as priority axis of research the implementation of a system of quality management, through which there is created the framework for the continuous improvement of the quality.

- The university and library management has the capability to professionally approach the changes, evinces competences as regards the ample perspective and its concretization in valid strategies of development, the settling of the plans for further action and the provision with the resources necessary for accom-plishing the change projects, the optimization of the structure, the implementation of modern methods of management.
- Human resources: the library has 52 employees, among which 32 with higher education and 11 with higher education in the field. The staff benefited from training and of mobility exchanges in the country and abroad.

WEAKNESSES

- *Control of the Performance*: The library achieves the assessment of the performance every year; however the criteria and the indicators which are used do not reflect the qualitative aspects of the activity, the effects of the library services upon the educational and scientific research processes. There is no management system that should measure the costs of the services/activities realised by the library.
- *Control of the Processes:* There has begun to be implemented the management through processes, however the action is in an incipient phase of analysis and description of the key processes through procedures.
- *Human Resources*: Staff's evaluation is done in compliance with the law, however the insufficient

resources used in this process make the evaluation not always relevant. The participation of the staff in solving the problems is unequal and the rewarding system is non-stimulating.

- *Organisational Culture:* There is no culture of the quality, there are insufficiently promoted values such as team work, staff's implication, opening towards change.

Taking into account the submitted situation, the priority axes for the development of the capability of the library to continuously improve its performance are the following:

- *People:* The continuation of the process of staff training in quality management, with accent on achieving behavioural changes, on raising the degree of implication in solving the problems and on team work.
- *Users:* Orientation towards the customers, definition of the requirements and evaluation of their satisfaction. This implies in the first place the improvement of the system evaluating the library performance, through the introduction of criteria and indicators that should better reflect the effects upon the quality of the educational and research processes. The control will be also extended upon the costs of the services and of the activities realised by the library.
- *Processes:* Development and implementation of instruments and also of working and control procedures that should ensure the optimization of the processes and their continuous improvement.

The achievement of the change processes will be coordinated by the Management Council of the library. Both the initiation of the projects and their unfolding will be largely promoted in the framework of the library, for obtaining the feedback and for attracting the people in realizing the changes. The financing of the projects will be done from its own funds, but there will be likewise accessed funds from the Operational Programmes.

CONCLUSIONS

The existence during the last decades of the university

libraries has been characterized by ample changes, a process that will continue. The achievement of the changes is an issue of the management library, whose results may be considerably improved through a professional approach, based on the methods of the change management. The case study developed by the authors presents the first sequences of the change programme that will be achieved during the years to follow at the library of *Transilvania* University of Brasov, with reference to the methodology of change elaboration and implementation.

CASE STUDY: 'A SMALL LIBRARY WITH BIG GOALS' THE LIBRARY FOR GERMAN LANGUAGE AND LITERATURE, UNIVERSITY OF TARTU

BRIEF HISTORY OF THE UNIVERSITY OF TARTU

I will start my presentation with a small overview of the University of Tartu as our library is a part of the university and it is not possible to observe them apart. The University of Tartu is the oldest university in Estonia and one of the oldest in the Northern countries. On 30 June 1632, King Gustav II Adolf of Sweden signed the Foundation Decree of *Academia Dorpatensis*, which marks the beginning of our university's history.

We can distinguish five periods when we speak about the history of the University of Tartu:

- The Swedish period 1632-1710
- The Imperial Tartu University 1802-1918
- 1919-1940 Tartu University in the Republic of Estonia
- 1944-1989 Tartu State University
- 1991-Tartu University in the newly independent Republic of Estonia

I only describe three of them as the important ones for my presentation. The first, the so-called 'Swedish period', is important while it turned a small provincial town to the university town. The Town Council was interested in having the university here to restore its former prosperity. Tallinn and Riga were big and important centres and not at all interested in the university and the noisy and hectic young men-students.

Sweden in its turn wanted to:

- Strengthen the Lutheran religion in the former Catholic country;
- Strengthen the presence of the Swedish kingdom.

The students were mostly Swedes and Finns. We are proud that our university is so old but in fact the university, established during the Swedish period, was not one of the best reconized universities in Europe. The university in Tartu functioned with the Faculties of Philosophy, Law, Theology, and Medicine, enjoying the privileges similar to those granted to the University of Uppsala.

The University of Tartu was closed in 1710 after the Swedish army had surrendered to the Russian forces after the defeat in the Northern War. The second period of the history of the university was 1802-1918 'reopening of the university'. This period can be characterized as the prosperity of the university. The Baltic Germans needed the university to educate their children. After the French Revolution studying abroad was not allowed. Russia also needed its own university. So in Tartu the European science and the Russian state met. The Germans wanted to have a small Heidelberg or Göttingen and somehow they succeeded in it.

The official language at the university was German and the religion was Lutheran. The 19th century was the period of prosperity of the university, the scientists K. E. von Baer, J. W. Struve and many others show us the level of scientific research in Tartu at that time. The teaching of Germanic languages also goes back to this period and has long traditions. Already in 1865 the Department for German Language at the University of Tartu was established. The first professor at the department was Leo Meyer, a linguist from Göttingen who stayed in Dorpat for 33 years. The number of students increased every day, Rutiku and Kegelmann.

OVERVIEW OF THE FOUNDATION OF GERMAN LIBRARY

I concentrate my attention on the fifth period which begins in 1991 while at that time our library was established. After the collapse of the Soviet Union the situation in our country was changing. We had to build up new society, a new educational system. The example of our library illustrates the developments in Estonia very well. In many areas we had to start from scratch. When learning foreign languages, it is natural that the dictionaries, lexicons and scientific literature are at students' disposal, but in Tartu it was not so.

The first German DAAD—Professor in Tartu—Claus Sommer-hage—started establishing a library. Among the many names the DAAD-Lecturer Claus Sommerhage should be emphasized. In 1992-1997 Dr. Claus Sommerhage was Guest Professor at the Department for German Language and Literature, 1997-1999 Extraordinary Professor. He innovated new curricula in teaching German literature, especially Modern German Literature.

Since his coming only the overview courses had been taught. He started with analytical literature seminars, Rutiku and Kegelmann. The most important thing he did for the department was establishing our library. He knew that without a library teaching literature was impossible. As Sommerhage had said we had a couple of copies of the novel Aula by Hermann Kant on our shelves. He was right. He started looking for funds in Germany and Switzerland, he used his own connections and personal charm. Without intensive support of the German and Swiss funds our library would not exist today.

FINANCING, PROGRAMMES, FUNDS

Our library is unique because until 2003 there was no budget for it. Nevertheless, it was increasing with every day. At the beginning many books were donated to our library. Tartu is an old university town and professors and lecturers had their own very good libraries. Many professors and lecturers decided to give their German books to our library. The theatre 'Vanemuine' liquidated its library in 1999 and we received all their books in the German language. From there we have our 23-volume complete works of Dostoevsky from 1922 which is considered to be the best Dostoevsky translation since then.

The oldest book in our library dates back to 1780. We also received books from our German friends. More than 15 years

Professor Norbert Nail from the University of Marburg equipped us with every kind of books and journals about the German language and linguistics. Since 2001 our library is in the project of Gebert Rüf Fund-the Swiss Baltic Net for the Swiss Libraries and Swiss Literature in the Baltic States. We can order German Swiss literature every year for 1000 ChFr. The sum is not big but very valuable for our library. The project also coordinates the work of Schweizer Lesezimmer in the Baltic States.

We meet every year in Lithuania, Latvia or Estonia to present our annual work and discuss our problems. These meetings are always useful and interesting. This time the meeting takes place in Vilnius In 2005-2007 our library was involved in the programme 'Menschen und Bücher', an initiative of the Goethe Institute for Central and Eastern Europe.

For our library it was a great privilege to be involved in the programme because our financial resources have always been limited. This time we could order books necessary for us and all our lecturers were involved in the ordering process. So we could efficiently enrich our library and every lecturer could order books for his or her course. The budget was 15,000 EUR and we could also invite a German author to Tartu.

DEPARTMENT LIBRARIES AT THE UNIVERSITY OF TARTU

Since 2003 the University Library has pursued the policy of supporting department libraries. Until then the status of a small department library was obscure. At the Department for German Language and Literature the library policy was always clear. We needed a well equipped library for students and lecturers, we were for the open access. Since 2002 our books are in the library system INNOPAC, which makes every process with books very easy and transparent. Sometimes the department libraries are in a bad state, the books are available for very few readers but our policy was different from the very beginning. When we do have a book, people must know about it, they must have access to it.

IMPORTANCE TO THE STUDENTS AND LECTURERS

One of the priorities of our library is its closeness to students and lecturers. We are informed of every need very quickly and for the students it is comfortable that everything about one subject is concentrated at one place. Since 1999 the Department for German Language and Literature has its own rooms in the former printing-house in the centre of the town, opposite the university main building. The renovation of the building had been contributed by different foreign embassies. It houses Departments for German, French, Spanish and Scandinavian Languages and is called 'Paabel'.

For our library it gave a possibility to expose all the books better, to create a real library system, to create a room where people like to work. The rooms for the German library in this new building are next to the seminar rooms. The students can use library early in the morning and between the lectures and seminars during the day. Our users are the students of the Department for German Language and Literature, the students of the Language Centre of the University, the Master's course students who study translation and interpretation. Every reader who possesses the university library card is welcome in our library. Closeness also means that we always consider the requests of the students.

In the last years when we received our budget, we have ordered books for the students who need them for writing their Bachelor's or Master's theses. The priority of our library is to be of high scientific quality. This is the direction Claus Sommerhage gave to our library and we still hold on to it. It is sometimes difficult because of our insufficient financing, but we always choose books carefully, ask advice from our German patrons and friends, try to be informed of the newest scientific literature. So we can affirm that our library has been created by professionals and it fulfils its tasks.

One of our main tasks is to support the study process. At the Department for German Language and Literature the main research areas are linguistics, sociolinguistics, contact and text linguistics as well the Swiss literature and the German literature by women writers and the Baltic-German literature. Some subject areas in our library are very well presented, for example German linguistics, literary science, German history, German language history. In the last years the collection of our dictionaries and lexicons is almost ideal.

As translation and interpretation are taught at our university, the collection of these books is almost excellent. We also have a good collection of German language textbooks. We have a sufficient number of copies thanks to 'LUKKA'—EU supporting programme. At our department teaching of modern Swiss literature has long traditions. Associated Professor Eve Pormeister has taught it already for 20 years and even wrote her Doctoral thesis on this subject. She has connections with the Embassy of Switzerland, Swiss Funds, Pro Helvetia. Her special interest is the reason why Swiss literature is so well presented in our library.

PLEASANT MEETING PLACE, NICE INTERIOR

Last but not least, in a small department library, the milieu plays a big role. There are people who never go to the main library of the university. They do not like too big bleak rooms without cosy corners, with too many strange people. Our library is a kind of a social gathering place for the students who study the same subject, have the same problems and pleasures. The nice and comfortable interior plays an important role here.

As our rooms have interesting architecture, it is possible to establish exhibitions and that is what we regularly do. The last exhibition is from our student who studies art as her minor. She was happy to have an opportunity to show her paintings to her friends and fellow-students. We all can enjoy her colourful and interesting works.

Bibliography

Abdullahi, A.: *Library Organization and Its Development in India*, Philadelphia, PA: University of Pennsylvania Press, 1998.

Adrienne, Stone: *Integration in the Library Organization,* New York: Oxford University Press, 2003.

Agosin, Marjorie: *Emerging Trends in Library Organization*, New Brunswick, NJ: Rutgers University Press, 2001.

Allen, Robin: *Public Libraries: Their Development and Future Organization*, New York: Oxford University Press, 2002.

Alston: *Handbook of Library Organization*, New York: Oxford University Press, 2003.

Anaya, S.: *Knowledge Organization in Digital Environment in Libraries*, New York: Oxford University Press, 2001.

Andreassen: *Manual of Library Organization*, London: Harvard University Press, 2006.

Baderin: *The Dynamic Library Organizations in a Changing Environment*, New York: Oxford University Press, 2003.

Bailey, Sydney D.: *Public Library Organization and Structure*, New York: St. Martin's Press, 2003.

Banda, Fareda: *Library Organization and Library Administration,* UK: Oxford, 2005.

Bard, A.: *Policy and Organization of Computing, Communications and Libraries*, London: Harvard University Press, 2006.

Bartlett, Peter: *Manual of Techniques in Library Organization,* Leiden: E. J. Brill, 2006.

Bayefsky, Anne F.: *An Introduction to Public Library Organization*, New York: Transnational Publication, 2001.

Chatterjee, S.: *Teaching Aids Library: Organization of Materials*, UK: Cambridge University Press, 2003.

Chesterman: *Problems in Library Organization and Administration*, New York: Oxford University Press, 2001.

Clapham, Andrew: *Fundamentals of Library Supervision*, New York: Oxford University Press, 2005.

Clapham, Andrew: *Step-by-Step Library Organization:*, New York: Oxford University Press, 2006.

Donnelly, Jack: *Library Work*, Boulder, CO: Westview Press, 2006.

Drzemczewski: *Library Transition Design Phase Organization*, New York: Oxford University Press, 2000.

Dunne: *Organization as a Management Variable*, UK: Cambridge University Press, 1999.

Eldridge, Phil.: *Knowledge Organization for Digital Library Education,* London: Routledge, 2002.

Elisabeth Burgi: *Document Layout*, New York: Oxford University Press, 2005.

Emberland, Marius: *Library Organization and Containers*, New York: Oxford University Press, 2006.

Franklin, Bob: *Proposed Library Organization Chart*, London: Routledge, 2002.

Frost, Mervyn: *Virtual Organization in Libraries*, London: Routledge, 2002.

Gearty, Conor: *Principles of Library Organization*, New York: Oxford University Press, 2004.

George, J.: *Regional Library Organization and Development in India*, New Delhi: Oxford University Press, 2005.

Gewirth, Alan: *Library Organization: Positions and Relationships,* Chicago: University of Chicago Press, 2002.

Henkin, Louis: *Public Library Organization in India,* New York: Columbia University Press, 2005.

Ignatieff, Michael: *Library Automation and Library Organization*, Princeton, NJ: Princeton University Press, 2001.

Janis: *Managing Library Volunteers,* New York: Oxford University Press, 2001.

Klein, B.: *The Library and Its Organization*, New York: Transnational Publication, 2002.

Korey, William: *Suggestions for the Organization of Libraries in India,* New York: St. Martin's Press, 2003.

Lillich, Richard B.: *Library Management,* New York: Aspen, 2006.

Index

I

M

N

P

R

S

T

V